*Planning and Managing
Housing for the Elderly*

Planning and Managing Housing for the Elderly

M. POWELL LAWTON

Philadelphia Geriatric Center

A Wiley-Interscience Publication

JOHN WILEY & SONS

NEW YORK • LONDON • SYDNEY • TORONTO

Copyright © 1975, by John Wiley & Sons, Inc.

All rights reserved. Published simultaneously in Canada.

Reproduction or translation of any part of this work beyond
that permitted by Sections 107 or 108 of the 1976 United States
Copyright Act without the permission of the copyright owner
is unlawful. Requests for permission or further information
should be addressed to the Permissions Department, John
Wiley & Sons, Inc.

Library of Congress Cataloging in Publication Data

Lawton, Mortimer Powell.
  Planning and managing housing for the elderly.

  "A Wiley-Interscience publication."
  Bibliography: p.
  1. Aged—Dwellings. I. Title.

HD7287.9.L38   301.5′4   74-28099
ISBN 0-471-51894-8

Printed in the United States of America

10 9 8 7 6 5 4

This book is dedicated to three people who have been responsible for many of the creative ideas that have made a success story out of housing for the elderly: Arthur Waldman, Marie McGuire Thompson, and Ollie Randall.

Preface

Housing is big business, and in the past 15 years housing for the elderly has assumed a slowly growing importance on the national housing scene. Many of the photographs shown in this volume portray apparently attractive and socially positive environments for older people. Pleasant modern designs, attractive sites, self-realizing social programs, and happy older people abound in these settings. Naturally, the total range of environments varies from poor to excellent. Although the examples shown here are not necessarily typical, they do give a picture of what housing at its best can be.

This book is designed for both planners and administrators. It is written from the viewpoint of a behavioral scientist attempting to apply scientific knowledge to the "real world" of interacting individuals. Its bias is toward the social and psychological aspects of housing environments, reflecting the author's psychological training. Even more, it reflects the conviction that behavior never occurs in isolated form, but always in a physical and social context. Thus, behavior is seen as the result of an individual's interaction with his physical environment, the other individuals in the environment, and the man-made institutions that impede or facilitate his strivings for self-fulfillment. In short, an ecological, rather than either a psychological or an environmental view of behavior underlies this approach.

In order to enhance the book's readability, references to theory and the methods that preoccupy researchers have been minimized. In general, findings based on hard research will usually be identified, but much of what must be relied upon to guide the evolution of a successful housing environment is necessarily based upon informal, rather than research-based, observation.

This book has its limitations, which must be recognized. Another book still needs to be written to provide the planner and the administrator with information relating to the extremely important area of finances and the business management of housing. It is unfortunate that it has to be this way, because the separation of the financial and social aspects of housing may give the impression that the two aspects are incompatible with one another. The author hopes sincerely that a nuts-and-bolts guide to site selection, design, financing, business management, and personnel problems will be written within the context of social and psychological sophistication. There is, to be sure, natural tension between the wish to serve people and the cost-accounting approach. The conflict may be handled constructively, however. A financially viable operation should be totally possible within the framework of serving older people.

In brief, then, what follows is meant to provide assistance to both laymen and professionals who are at various stages in the conception, planning, and management of housing environments for older people. The book is written in the hope that it will be used in the very earliest stages of planning, when the scope of the effort is being defined, and the factors to be considered in selecting a site are first being specified. Hopefully, the citizen board member of a housing authority or nonprofit organization will be able to view his organization's undertakings more knowledgably with exposure to the material in this book.

Staff members of these kinds of organizations rarely have specific training in the science of adult development and aging; the point of view of this book is strongly conditioned by knowledge from this field.

Architects, physical planners, and designers in particular have only the most elementary (frequently self-generated!) knowledge of the needs and capabilities of older people. Their engineering-oriented training may leave them with a point of view that does not easily consider the implications of a physical structure for social behavior or for the ability of an older person to perform a task for himself rather than being helped by someone else. Although almost half of the book is devoted to management, the author can guarantee that the designer will produce a better building if he is familiar with some of the typical problems of tenants and management.

Much of the social planning for senior-citizen housing is still being done by groups whose expertise is minimal. Health and welfare councils, local governmental officials, city planning agencies, and governmental bureaucrats are hard put to find relevant literature on the design of living environments.

Finally, the administrator himself, at this point in history, has usually come to his job from some earlier occupation. As will be seen later in some detail, he rarely has had professional training that includes either housing management or human relations techniques, yet he strongly wishes to increase his competence in these areas. Since he is in the position of directing a housing environment whose siting and basic structure are already determined, some of the earlier material may appear to be less relevant to him. However, an effort has been made to deal whenever possible with ways in which administration and staff can modify the behavior that occurs in existing physical structures; sometimes actual physical modifications can be made to enhance the social value of an existing design. In addition, it is probable that many people who are now beginning as housing administrators may move on to positions where their knowledge may be utilized in planning new housing.

Thus, it is hoped that the material in this book may be useful to a wide variety of people involved in the total scene of housing for the elderly. A reference list has been added as an appendix, rather than specifically referencing each allusion in the text.

Most of the research leading to the writing of this book was supported by the National Institute of Mental Health and the Administration on Aging of the U.S. Department of Health, Education and Welfare. Thomas Anderson of the NIMH and Jessie Gertman of the AOA have been of inestimable help in the conduct of the research. Two successive Executive Vice-Presidents of the Philadelphia Geriatric Center, Arthur Waldman and Bernard Liebowitz, as well as Maurice Greenbaum, Administrator of the York Houses, and Elaine Brody, Director of Social Work at the Philadelphia Geriatric Center, have been lavish with creative ideas, moral support, and constructive criticism throughout the research and the writing of this volume. Major contributors to the research itself have been the late Ira deA. Reid, Lucille Nahemow, George Nash, Patricia Nash, Bonnie Simon, Silvia Yaffe, Joseph Teaff, Miriam Grimes, Eleanor Maxwell, Diane Carlson, Carlota Salter,

Jacob Cohen, and Eugene Ericksen. Many others who have left their
marks on the history of housing for the elderly have had plenty of
energy left over to enrich the work of the Philadelphia Geriatric
Center: Marie McGuire Thompson, Wilma Donahue, Ollie Randall,
Morton Leeds, William Hughes, Frances Carp, Louis Gelwicks,
Kermit Schooler, and Ruth Bennett. Thanks are also due to the
U.S. Department of Housing and Urban Development for permission to reproduce the photographs taken by Richard Mowrey.
The greatest debt of all is to the more than one thousand housing
sites who gave so much of their precious time in the hope that succeeding generations of older people might live better. These included
housing authority personnel, sponsors, administrators, supportive
staff, and more than five thousand tenants, whose names might be
difficult to fit into a single volume.

M. POWELL LAWTON

Philadelphia, Pennsylvania
September 1974

Contents

*Planning and Managing
Housing for the Elderly*

PART ONE

Background

chapter 1

The older person:
social and
psychological aspects

Within the very brief space of one chapter, the highlights of current information regarding the social and psychological status of older people will be sketched. This brief profile can, of course, in no way substitute for the richness of knowledge that comes from knowing many old people. However, many who become involved in housing may be faced suddenly with the demand to "do something to help old people" without having had a proper opportunity either to know very many of them personally or to study gerontology. Thus, this chapter is meant both to provide a brief resume of scientific knowledge about the elderly and to highlight some social and psychological factors that may be particularly relevant to housing.

A central emphasis will be placed on identifying and distinguishing among (a) characteristics that are intrinsic concomitants of old age, (b) those that are secondary to the older person's state of health, and (c) those that are partially or wholly attributable to the social and environmental context in which the elderly live. To anticipate our conclusion, we shall see that relatively few traits typically attributed to the elderly are the inevitable result of chronological aging. To the extent that a negative characteristic is the result of poor health or a social condition, we can hope to change it by remedial procedures directed either toward the individual or toward the environment. Unfortunately, everywhere one goes one sees evidence not only of negative thinking about the elderly, but also of a tendency to ascribe these negative characteristics to the inevitable process of aging that will eventually get us all.

3

The terms "a cranky old woman" or an "old crock" voice stereotypes not terribly different from those the psychiatrist uses when he writes in his mental status examination "His memory is relatively good, considering his age." Let us look at some of the important facts concerning the health, and mental acuity, the personality, and the social status of older people.

THE WELL-BEING OF THE ELDERLY REVOLVES AROUND HEALTH

Despite the stereotype that many people have of the sick, feeble old person, the majority of older people are able to function quite independently. Only about 5 percent of our 20 million elderly live in institutions. Another 8 percent live in the community but are homebound, sometimes confined to bed permanently. While these people

Fig. 1. The stereotype of old people as sick or disabled is false. (Photo by Richard Mowrey.)

have special problems and deserve the special attention of society, in numbers the relatively independent are far ahead: they number about 17.5 million. This is not to say that the 17.5 million are all "healthy." The National Health Survey has estimated that more than 40 percent of older Americans have some limitation of activity due to chronic disease conditions. The glib term "chronic disease" masks the individuality of the sufferer. Most people afflicted with a chronic disease continue to manage in spite of their illness, but they go about their business with such burdens as aching joints, a tired feeling, shortness of breath, worry over a cardiac condition, and almost universal anxiety over their futures should the time come when their strivings toward independence are no longer successful. For some, behaving as if not ill becomes an obsession, and their independence is maintained at the expense of further depletion of their energy. For all who suffer from a chronic disease, everyday tasks require a greater proportion of total energy investment than they do for the healthy.

Most research studies of older people include some measurement of health status, whether obtained from a physician, from direct observation of the person going about his daily affairs, or from the person himself. Invariably, his state of health is found to be closely related to how well he performs in other areas. As one would expect, the physically healthy tend to have the most positive views of the world, of their ability to live a fulfilling life during old age, and of themselves as people. They are apt to be happier, to have more friends, to maintain activities, and to be mentally alert. Conversely, physical illness is more likely to be accompanied by depression, isolation, inactivity, and mental impairment.

Although it is a truism that physical health leads to a generally more fulfilled life, it is very important to realize that it is within our grasp to elevate significantly the degree of fulfillment of older people simply by connecting those with illnesses with existing means of treating them. That is, a gap now exists that is a function of the right treatment's not getting to those who need it. The gap has many causes, including lack of information about the availability of treatment, social isolation, limited mobility in getting to treatment centers, poverty, unequal distribution of medical resources, and so on. Theoretically, each of these might be improved through better social planning. Thus, there is hope for a significant degree of improvement even before the underlying causes and cures for the major chronic illnesses are found.

INTELLECTUAL ABILITY AND OLD AGE

If we look at intelligence as it develops over the entire span of life, it is clear that it grows in giant leaps during the early years of life. Growth in skill is apparent as each month of early childhood passes, and even during adolescence one can observe the capacity for abstract thinking continuing to grow. Both the poet and the common man have asserted that the cycle reverses itself during old age, that there is a gradual decline in mental acuity—forgetfulness, rigidity, and inability to learn new ways characterize the elderly. To what extent is this common view supported by scientific studies of the aging process?

A first look at a typical research finding appears to support the stereotype. The graph in Fig. 2 shows how people of different ages perform on the most commonly used intelligence test, the Wechsler Adult Intelligence Scale (abbreviated WAIS). This test contains 11 different types of subtests that are divided between "verbal" and

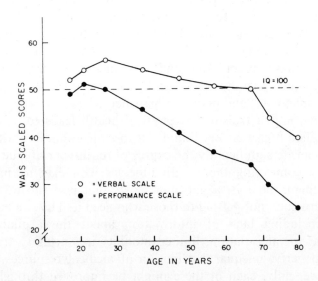

Fig. 2. Wechsler Adult Intelligence Scale scores as a function of age.

"performance" tasks. That is, about half of them require the subject to respond to objects or pictures by actually or implicity manipulating them, rather than by giving a verbal response to a verbal question. It is clear from the graph that as the child matures his functioning rises to reach a peak around age 22, remains near this level during much of his adult life, and then begins to decline, particularly from age 65 onward. While these results are from one research study, similar results have been obtained by many scientists using a variety of different tests. The evidence thus looks pretty ominous: intelligence declines as we age; "second childhood" is a psychological reality.

However, let us take into account important facts:

1. Many research subjects have been recruited from easily available groups, such as institutionalized older people. Are they to be considered representative of the normal aged?

2. Even where subjects appeared to be healthy, thorough medical screening was frequently not done.

3. Despite psychologists' attempts to construct tests that depend less on school learning than on "native ability," the amount and type of a person's education continue to affect his performance on any kind of test.

4. Even the situation of being tested is more familiar to young people than to old. For the past 30 years or so, testing has been a familiar part of school life. But to those who are older, the basic tasks of attending to instructions, using a pencil, realizing that time limits are a factor, and adopting a properly motivated test-taking attitude are unfamiliar. The tests and the tester are apt to be interpreted quite differently by old people. A graduate student's need to please his instructor by being a "good subject" is a far different orientation to the situation than that of the older person recruited by an experimenter who has no intrinsic connection with him.

5. Daily practice in intellectual pursuits is likely to be better maintained by younger people under the demands of jobs, leisure-time intellectual pursuits, helping children with homework, and so on.

6. Older people are themselves very aware of social stereotypes regarding their intellectual prowess and feel under greater strain while being tested; their performances suffer accordingly.

Each of these factors may act as a handicap to the older person as he does his best to comply with the instructions. In recent years psychologists have pursued these issues further, and in general, have found that the apparent "age decline" is less clear as the experimenter is able to remove each artificially imposed handicap. Let us take education as an example. Figure 3 shows the educational attainments of people 65 and over for 1940, 1950, 1960, and projected until 1985. The standardization data for the Wechsler intelligence test were gathered in 1953. It is clear that the people who were 75 and over at that time had had less education than those who are that age today, and the difference will be even greater by 1985. Since amount of education is highly related to test performance, younger people have a strong advantage. When the Wechsler scores of people of different ages who have had equal amounts of education are compared, the apparent age decline dramatically decreases.

The effect of health is dramatically illustrated by a study done at the National Institute of Mental Health. These scientists set out to study the daily functioning of older people, controlling for the effect of physical health. They selected a group of older men whose health was deemed exceptionally good by their physicians. Once these extremely healthy people were subjected to intensive study at the NIMH Clinical Center in Bethesda, Maryland, minor defects in health were discovered in some but not in others. The defects were truly mild in relation to the variation in health found in an unselected population of older people, yet even these *minor* defects

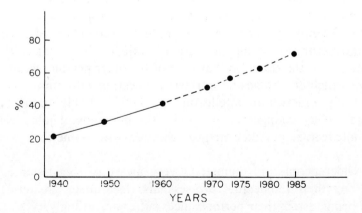

Fig. 3.   Change over time in average educational experience of older people.

were associated with a measurably lower capacity in a number of intellectual and behavioral tasks. If such minor defects can lower performance, the ordinary run of chronic illness in people on whom the Wechsler was standardized must surely have reduced their scores even more.

The Philadelphia Geriatric Center studied the survivors among these same people 12 years later. This method is referred to as "longitudinal" (the same person tested after a span of time) as contrasted to the "cross-sectional" method (people of different ages tested at the same point in time). Clearly, when the same person is followed over time, some of the confounding factors in intellectual performance, such as education, are eliminated. In our study, as in a number of other longitudinal studies, much less decline with age than had been presumed on the basis of cross-sectional studies was noted.

The interesting aspect of much of this research is that all intellectual abilities do not behave the same way as age increases. One obvious illustration of this fact may be seen in Fig. 2, which shows that the Verbal scores seem to decline less than Performance scores. To summarize very briefly a great deal of research in this area, there is general acceptance of the fact that decline due to chronological age in and of itself is not demonstrable in skills depending primarily on past learning. The "decline" that has been demonstrated in many areas has frequently been demonstrated to consist at least partly of socially imposed handicaps, rather than being an intrinsic feature of the aging process. Thus, when the sense of pressure while being tested is reduced, when time is allowed for the older person to familiarize himself with the task, when he controls his own decision-making and response time, the differences between young and old shrink. On the other hand, aging does seem to be associated with poorer muscular dexterity, slower speed of registration and assimilation of information from the outside world, and slower speed of response.

In summary, the aged have had a very bad press. Where they do respond in a less efficient way than do younger people, the cause is frequently ascribable to social factors, and therefore the defect is partly remediable: better adult education, less social isolation, and improved health delivery systems will all help reduce the gap between capability and performance.

The term "senility" has sometimes been used to describe old age as a stage of life, sometimes referring to the occasional forgetfulness assumed to be an inevitable concomitant of aging, and sometimes to the pathological loss of intellectual efficiency that is secondary to the organic brain diseases of old age. The term should be strictly reserved to refer to the latter pathological phenomena.

However, there may be mild "senile" conditions that account for some of the defects that are often ascribed to old age. How prevalent true senility is in the population is not entirely clear. Some investigators, using a very broad definition of senility, have estimated that 40 percent of the noninstitutionalized population suffers from mild to severe degrees of this type of mental impairment. Others, using the more restricted definition of certifiability to a mental hospital, have found a rate of about 8 percent among community residents. Half or more of the residents of nursing homes have been reported to be mentally confused some or all the time.

The point to be made is that true senility characterizes a minority of the population of older people. It is far from being an inevitable stage in the process of aging. Most people live into advanced age without ever suffering major loss of memory, confusion as to who they are or where they are, and without antisocial or self-risking behavior. Many people who do experience mild disturbance in intellectual functioning take compensatory measures that minimize the actual effect of the condition on behavior. As an example, many older people adopt the habit of writing down things they wish to remember. More usually, this is a practice that begins in middle age, when the demands of the external world are at their peak and strain the capacity of the normal person to remember what to pick up at the store, what each of his children has requested, when he must take care of each item of business, and so on. For these people list making during old age is simply a continuation of what they have already learned is an effective way of organizing one's life.

PERFORMING THE TASKS OF EVERYDAY LIFE

Some views of human behavior have emphasized *role* as an integrating concept for the study of personality. A role is the behavior in which the individual engages so as to fulfill the expectations of others as well as the expectations within himself that are historically derived from his relationships with other people. The net resultant of all the different roles that an individual plays is seen as his personality. One of the major theorists in aging, Robert Havighurst, has described the social roles of older people in terms of their behaviors as worker, parent, spouse, homemaker, citizen, user of leisure time, church member, club member, and friend. Research on older peoples' performance of each of these roles has resulted in a substantial literature, which cannot, of course, be summarized adequately here. However, it may be useful to look at the "average" older person as he performs these roles, insofar as the available data allow.

The Worker　For the male and increasingly for the female, the role of worker-wage earner is a central aspect of the self during the greater part of his lifetime. As everyone knows, mandatory retirement has steadily increased, though a substantial proportion of elderly people still choose their own time of retirement. By age 65, however, the proportion of men actively employed goes down below 50 percent, and by age 70 and over, only 18 percent of men and 6 percent of women are employed. Looked at in another way, less than one-third of the income of people age 65 or over was derived from employment earnings. There are some interesting facts beginning to emerge from studies of the retirement process, however. One fact is that a surprisingly high proportion of workers will choose to retire early when given the chance. Another is that as yet there is no compelling evidence of a general decline that can be ascribed to retirement, exclusive of health-related retirement. There are, to be sure, plenty of individuals for whom retirement is a traumatic event, but there appear to be at least as many whose general level of well-being either does not change, or moves upward.

　　Retirement brings with it a radical shift in role, including a sudden demand on the individual to reallocate his time. He usually finds himself with a surplus of time. Other role behavior fills some of the gaps, though for too many, the gap is "filled" with non-role non-behavior—that is inactivity.

The Parent Role　Another major change occurs when the last child leaves the household. Indeed, the entire period of development from childhood through adolescence, adulthood, and the establishment of a separate household constitutes an extended process of detachment of child from parent. What the parent does in his "parenting" role also changes, despite the continuity that is emphasized in "monism" or the "Jewish mother syndrome." It is frequently asserted that older people are isolated from their children during these later years. "Isolation" must be defined relative to some standard, however. If we think of contact between an aged person and a living

Fig. 4.   The grandparent role is alive and healthy. (Photo by Richard Mowrey.)

child as high when they are in touch twice a week or more, then a majority of those with children appear to be in close touch: 65 percent of a national sample of older people saw a child within 24 hours before the time interview and 84 percent did so within the previous week. Only 16 percent of those with living children live further than day-visit distance from a child and about one-third of them live in the same household with a child, while 22 percent have no living children.

The quality of parental relationship is less well researched than its quantity, of course. However, the least that can be said is that there is no evidence in favor of mass alienation. In short, the parent role appears to have great continuity, in contrast to the worker role. In fact, with the average lifespan greatly increasing and the maximum lifespan edging upward somewhat, an increasing number of people are living long enough to be the parents of retired or over-65 "children." The grandparent role is one that appears to have diminished in scope and intensity as household size has decreased. The relatively small amount of information we have on the subject suggests that being a grandparent is most satisfying in small doses, and that the grandmother role is better defined than the grandfather role.

The Spouse Role   As everyone knows, the higher death rate among males that begins at birth and increases throughout the lifespan is responsible for one of the major social phenomena affecting the behavior of the aged population: the large number of widows and the consequent overbalancing of most social groups in the female direction. Among those over 65, 65 percent of males and 35 percent of females are married and living with spouses. This proportion becomes even more lopsided after age 75 or so. Thus, substantial numbers of older people experience sudden loss of the spouse role, which has major and direct consequences for their performance of other roles. Research has demonstrated the radical shrinking of the widowed person's social world and total activity space.

Among those who remain as couples, the spouse role remains the most salient in terms of the dependence of much other behavior on that of husband and wife in relation to each other. Thus, much visiting and leisure-time activity is performed as a couple. Following retirement there is often a redistribution of household roles and a

Fig. 5. While two thirds of all elderly men live with their spouses, planned housing for the elderly serves many more single women. (Photo by Richard Mowrey.)

period of tension as the usual solitary routine of the housewife and the social-instrumental routine of the wage-earner are disturbed. Relatively little is known of the more intimate aspects of the marriage relationship during old age, though occasionally a researcher "discovers" that sexual activity still takes place, or that depression follows the loss of a spouse.

The Homemaker Role   Although the term "homemaker" may describe the overall role of a housewife not in the labor force during adult life, it is inadequate to describe the wide variety of self-maintaining tasks that occupy both men and women during old age. These tasks have been called *physical self-maintenance* tasks and *instrumental activities of daily living,* and are to a greater or lesser extent applicable to either sex. Physical self-maintenance includes the tasks most basic to the maintenance of life and minimum standards of order: toileting, bathing, dressing, walking, eating and grooming. The great majority of older people perform these tasks adequately; defects in their performance come only with gross impairment in physical or mental state. Instrumental activities of daily living require more complex skills than do the basic physical tasks: shopping, cooking, housecleaning, financial management, telephoning, transportation use, medical care, and laundering. Few people habitually perform all of these tasks completely unaided. Society has made it quite appropriate under some conditions for one

Fig. 6. A kitchen is vitally necessary to encourage the maintenance of the home-making skills of a lifetime. (Photo by Richard Mowrey.)

person to depend on another for one or more of these tasks such as in the division of labor between husband and wife during earlier life. Some older people, when faced with more unmandated time than they were accustomed to having before, stretch these tasks out to fill the void. Shopping becomes more leisurely, and perhaps more frequent where health and environmental conditions permit. House-cleaning tasks may be performed at greater length simply to fill time, or in response to a physical slowing-down.

In some instances, the sex-typed division of labor becomes less strict and husband and wife may share many of these tasks. It is clear that engaging in these everyday jobs provides a very meaningful occupation for most older people. These instrumental tasks are most akin to "work" and may satisfy the compulsion of many elderly people to avoid frivolous "play." For anyone, the satisfactory completion of daily chores provides constant feedback indicating that one is still competent; failing to do so will be a very anxious experience for anyone. These tasks for many people form the basic core of existence, in the way that one's occupation did in earlier life.

Citizen Role   The citizen role even during the earlier adult years is frequently relatively little-developed. Volunteer work, community betterment activity, and political participation are roles performed by a relatively small proportion of any population. It is thus not surprising that the elderly appear to be inactive in this role. In one area of citizen role performance, however, the elderly are more active than other age groups: they vote more frequently. Voting during the seventh decade is almost as frequent as in any age range, and even in the seventies it is higher than among youth.

Looked at in one way, performance of these roles may be partly contingent on one's social or financial status. Time for volunteer work, or the base from which to wield political power are selectively available to the more privileged. Today's elderly had relatively little opportunity to practice these roles in earlier life. However, there is every reason to think that succeeding generations of older people will increasingly view this kind of activity as a normal part of life, and continue, or even increase its level during later life.

The Foster Grandparent Program, a federally sponsored effort to recruit older people to work limited amounts of time helping under-

Fig. 7. The Foster Grandparent program gives a role to the older person and enrichment to the lives of the young. (Photo by Richard Mowrey.)

privileged or otherwise deprived children, depends partly on the idea that helping the less fortunate may be seen by the elderly as a meaningful role. A second very important aspect of the program is that it offers the incentive to pay. There is undoubtedly much room for the development of combination service-plus-pay citizen roles for the elderly in other areas. Another program that is based totally on volunteer work is the federally-supported Retired Senior Volunteer Program (RSVP).

Leisure-Time User   The comments made above about the lack of a tradition of citizen-role participation during the earlier lives of today's elderly is even more applicable to leisure-time use. To a generation that grew up with the 12-hour day and the 6-day week, the very concept of leisure time, or recreation, may be meaningless. While we do not yet have good research data on how the use of non-work or non-household duty time changes in the same people over a lifetime, it is pretty clear that the sudden availability of time does not cause a rush even to free activities such as library, museums, or recreation centers.

Most of us who work with the elderly get to this work by way of a middle-class background; our age is such that we either saw the country and our families come out of the depression of the 1930s or if we are younger we never knew gross economic deprivation at all. Thus, we are particularly prone to view the time use of older people

Fig. 8. (*a*) and (*b*) For some fortunate older people, earlier-life practice in the use of leisure time makes retirement a time to indulge the new opportunity for creative pursuits. (Photo by Richard Mowrey.)

Fig. 8   (Continued)

from our own very different frames of reference. We attribute a strongly positive value to hobbies, reading, and group activity. Where these are consistent with the values of the older person, such continued role performance is likely to be most fulfilling. There are relatively few Grandmas Moses, however; one frequently gets the feeling that the professional has too high an expectation regarding the number of people who can be recruited into the middle-class type of activities.

According to the data at hand, television is far and away the winner in terms of leisure-time use of the average older person. In addition to its value as entertainment it may actually help the older person keep his own behavior more in line with the social expectations of the world. The possibilities are great for the formal use of television as a teaching device for the elderly. Continued education programs designed for older people could enlarge their horizons greatly, while other programs designed to teach them how to keep up with Social Security, tax benefits, Medicare, and other confusing products of our bureaucracy could enhance their instrumental skills.

Voluntary Association Participant Havighurst's church member and club member roles are included in this category. Many of the comments made about the citizen and the leisure-time user roles apply to membership and participation in the activities of formal organizations. Membership in such groups during old age does seem to decline. Although pure economics are enough to reduce the participation of older people in some activities, the subtle social processes that signify that one is a has-been undoubtedly promote the relinquishing of such ties. Church attendance is an exception, however. Frequency of participation seems not to decline appreciably with age except when health or other extraneous factors interfere.

Friend Role Friendships during old age have been studied extensively, though not in depth-psychological terms. The most general conclusion is that relationships among unrelated people, especially between people of the same age, are exceedingly important to the older person. It is possible that the quality of friendship may change during the very late years. There is some evidence, for instance, that less intimacy may characterize relationships during this period. The dependence of a friendship upon the relative proximity of the two people is most outstanding. Irving Rosow, a sociologist, has studied this phenomenon and found that people with a middle-class background seem better able to keep up friendships with old friends not living in their vicinity than do people from lower-class backgrounds. Some of this effect may be simply the lesser ability of the poor to pay for transportation. However, all people, especially those from working-class backgrounds, seem more oriented to the close neighbor as friend than younger people are. Old people are similarly very likely to seek help from close neighbors in time of poor health, though a family member is turned to first if he lives nearby.

Cross-generational friendships certainly exist, but are much less frequent than are friendships among older people. Single people's friends are usually of the same sex, but members of a couple tend to have the same friends, often other couples.

A feeling of social isolation is a frequent complaint of older people. It is probable that if one had intimate friends during earlier

Fig. 9. New friends are easy to make in housing where people have lived through a lifetime of common historical experiences. (Photo by Richard Mowrey.)

life and they continued to live nearby during later life, the intimacy would continue. However, one's attitude cannot help but change as old friends die or move away. The structuring of new friendships on a more casual basis may well be appropriate, considering the tenuousness of life and the desires of both the subject and friend to decrease their vulnerability to the possible loss of the other.

Not all desire friendships, however. Most researchers have concluded that there is a minority of people whose adaptive style throughout life had depended on relative isolation from others. Another minority have been socially involved at one time, but choose voluntarily to withdraw from active social participation. Although these somewhat withdrawn people's lives may appear to most of us to be missing a dimension, many of them find it possible to maintain a positve inner psychological state.

Marjorie Fiske Lowenthal's research has underlined the importance of an older person's having someone with whom he feels comfortable talking about personal matters—a confidante. The confidante may be either a friend or a relative. He appears to act as a buffer in assisting the individual to live with a negative outlook on life (low morale), without this outlook's being converted into a mental breakdown.

Thus, not only are social relations one of the most important of the older person's roles, but it matters a great deal whom he has to socialize with, and how close his potential friends live.

The discussion thus far has suggested that if we know how a person performs these social roles we know a lot about him. Let me describe a very real older man in behavioral terms:

Mr. Z. worked a lifetime as a tailor, operating a small shop with the aid of his wife and occasional extra help. He would work from daybreak until well into the night whenever the business would come. He did handwork in dry cleaning and pressing in between the orders for suits. Well beyond the normal retirement age, he developed arthritic pain which eventually made it impossible for him to cut, sew, or press. He gave up the shop, after much urging by his only child, a son who lived in the same city. It was not easy for him or his wife to adjust to his being in the home most of the time. His wife had her own busy routine at that point, and did not appreciate Mr. Z.'s efforts to develop domestic skills. He was alternately short-tempered and blustering on the one hand, passive and idle on the other. The day consisted of one long television show. While both Mr. and Mrs. Z. were still working out their new roles, Mrs. Z. died suddenly. Following her death, Mr. Z. found it even more difficult than before to go about his daily business. His motivation to do the household chores diminished, and he lost the desire to visit any of the couples he and his wife had been friendly with before. Through a friend of his son's, he was referred to the Geriatric Center, where he was judged to be competent enough to live in a semiboarding house operated by the Center; he was also thought likely to be helped by the social contact that was an essential aspect of this living arrangement. He did make several friends in the new community and resumed going to his son's home on Saturday, which he had not felt like doing after his wife's death. However, most of his time was idle. The Golden Age Club did not appeal to him, nor did pottery, weaving, painting, or any other "happy-making" activity. He was asked one day to take some mail from the main office to another building on the grounds. Several employees got the idea and before long Mr. Z. was a regular messenger. The pace of the work was not fast, and he developed several regular stops along his route, complete with conversation and coffee. His day is thus a predictable round of grooming, eating, work, casual social interaction (primarily with employees), and television. Recently a tragedy which one of his grandsons experienced disturbed him greatly, but his actual daily routine changed very little.

Mr. Z. is thus clearly an individual who fills his day with behavior that is relatively adaptive. Is what I have described the "real" Mr. Z.? I suggest that the description is really incomplete. Beyond the objective description of his behavior, he can be called "proud," with high personal standards, perhaps somewhat rigid, not easily tolerating the ambiguity of an uncertain role. He is quietly affectionate, yet uncomfortable when his or other people's feelings become too overt. He is capable of becoming depressed at a time of maximal stress, yet he is resilient and energetic the great majority of the time. These terms refer primarily to the inner self, as opposed to the role behavior described initially. The psychologist would argue that the sum total of a person's social roles can never describe the richness of the individual—his dreams, loves, hates, attitudes, and so on. The "inner personality" is most difficult to know. It is not surprising that it is a difficult concept to research. We do, in fact, know more about social role than about the personality development of aged people. Are there predictable age changes in personality? Does bad health affect one's outlook as well as one's intellectual efficiency? Let us look at what is known about personality during the later years.

The most important fact to be noted is that individuality increases, rather than decreases, during old age. Differences among people in personality and in life expeience are clearly more important causes of behavior than is chronological age. It has been said that during old age a person becomes more like himself. It follows that the personality differences among people that we all accept during childhood and adulthood become accentuated, rather than obliterated, during old age. However, this fact should not blind us to the possibility that in addition to individual differences, there may be some changes in personality that are the result of biological aging or the social influences on the aged person.

Active Mastery to Passive Mastery   Dr. Bernice Neugarten and other psychologists at the University of Chicago have carefully studied the personalities of a large number of older people by means of extended interviews, questionnaires, and their responses to psychological tests. They have identified some important differences between middle-aged and elderly adults. The middle-aged people talked about themselves with a bold confidence in their ability to manage whatever came up. Their outer personalities were, of course, greatly varied. However, there was a common thread to their inner attitudes of enjoying challenge, solving complicated problems, and maintaining strong emotional contact with others. They were very closely involved with what was going on in the world about them, and were very concerned about assessing the behavior and feelings of other people and about modifying their own behavior in accordance with what they saw in others.

By contrast, the older subjects were characterized by greater passivity. They sought ways of adapting to the world around them, rather than actively trying to shape their world. This withdrawal from the "active mastery" of middle life seemed related to a loss of confidence in their energy, their ability to solve problems, and their ability to deal with others. They were more concerned with their own feelings than with those of others. They were less concerned with the subtleties of everyday problems or relationships with other people than with maintaining a few simplistic, formula-like attitudes that could enable them to make sense out of the world around them. It also seemed that older men and women became more alike, in that both seemed to be more accepting of their own feelings, allowing themselves more freedom in assuming attitudes traditionally thought to be characteristic of the opposite sex.

The above personality differences are very abstract and represent only general trends, rather than being characteristic of all older people. That is, there are clearly many younger people who do not look upon themselves as controlling their environments, and many older people who do. Also, the Chicago scientists are very careful not to assert that these trends are the inevitable result of biological aging. These attitudes have been taught to our whole society. We are taught over a lifetime that one becomes less potent as one gets older. Thus to become passive is what the world seems to expect.

Disengagement   Other scientists from the University of Chicago observed some of these same traits and went further in trying to reconcile them with some of the observed facts about the social role behavior of older people. Elaine Cumming and William Henry suggested that older people by choice "disengage" themselves from the outer world, and that society, in turn, finds ways of cutting its ties with the aging person. Unquestionably, society does disengage from the elderly: forced retirement, jokes about the old, diminishing recreational and leisure-time opportunities, and so on, attest to this. The realities of biological aging produce similar effects. Friends and relatives die, the older person's energy decreases, and the geographic range of their behavior diminishes. The facts seem pretty clear on this side—people do engage in fewer activities, see friends less often, and go fewer places as they age. Cumming and Henry asserted, in addition, that the inner aspect of disengagement was an inevitable stage of life. Psychologically the older person may become less concerned over what other people expect from him; he can react in a way that pleases him alone, to the point of eccentricity. He is said to have more active enjoyment of his own thoughts and feelings, taking pleasure in being an observer, rather than an actor. He enjoys more the idea of who he has been, rather than who he is, or who he might become. Disengagment, in a sense, is a rediscovery of the self. Among other things, this view admits some truth in the stereotype that old people are more self-centered than are the middle-aged.

Cumming and Henry say that the most satisfying way to age is for the individual to comply with the disengagement that society initiates. Thus, ideal aging means *mutual* disengagement between the older person and society. They suggest that many older people are unhappy because they subscribe to the glorification of youth and youthful engagement in life, while biology and society conspire to make continued engagement impossible. They thus have a continuous and increasing sense of failure in achieving their goals.

Such people certainly do exist. Another completely different research project found a substantial number of people who could be called the "rocking chair" type—relatively inactive but moderately satisfied people whose major pleasures was to watch the passing scene. However, they are in a minority. Later research has shown that for most people, those who are most active are also the hap-

Fig. 10. The enjoyment of being alone is a positive experience for some older people. (Photo by Sam Nocella.)

piest. One researcher clearly pinpointed where disengagement oversimplified the issues: people maintained a positive state of mind when they seemed to cut down on activities and relationships with people voluntarily, but when the same reduction in activity was involuntary, their morale became poorer. This theory calls to our attention two facts: society forces some disengagement on most older people, and some people actively disengage from society. The theory is incorrect when it says that disengagement is a state that makes all people contented.

Disengagement theory should give us renewed respect for the right of the aged individual of reminisce, to brag, to retire, to sit and watch, or to appear to be doing nothing. However, we must be properly suspicious of attempts to use disengagement theory as a rationalization for doing nothing to provide meaningful activity for older people. Until we have a situation where every older person is free to choose from a large variety of activities, or to reject them, we cannot say that the inactive person is that way because he wishes it.

"Basic Needs": Do They Change? Mastery and disengagement describe personal needs that are highly subject to social and environmental influences. If we wished, we could examine more closely a number of other needs to which psychologists have given much attention. We could unquestionably identify an increase in the need to depend on other people as one's own resources diminish. The need to achieve may or may not change, but the opportunities to exercise the need certainly diminish, as do occasions for the effective use of power. The need for social give-and-take may change, but its manifestations are very much a matter of how many friends, neighbors, or casual acquaintances are located within the same physical area as the older person. Helping others is similarly contingent on opportunity. With most of these needs, change is most clearly observable when health declines or when society removes the opportunity to act on them. What could be a more natural reaction to the removal of social and recreational opportunities than a frustrated sense of passivity and resignation? My point is that there has yet been no truly convincing demonstration that these needs change *solely as a function of years.*

Some needs have been called "basic," though no one has ever determined exactly which are basic and which derived. Hunger and thirst and temperature needs remain relatively unchanged, where physical health is good. Sex behavior diminishes as a function of age, as Kinsey has shown, though it is worth noting that at age 60 married men still average almost one organsm per week, and all studies have shown some of the very old population to be still sexually active. Certainly the need for love, respect, and understanding does not disappear, though the preferred means for satisfying the need may change.

"Successful Aging" The weight of the evidence supports the idea that the most satisfied older people are those who maintain their friendships, family relationships, engagement in leisure-time activities, and continued performance of the tasks of daily living. Since these activities, plus gainful employment, are those that occupy all of us over our whole adult life span, we can conclude that it is healthy during old age to continue one's life as one has lived it

prior to old age. This is not what the disengagement theorists originally contended. However, research has demonstrated just as definitively that this activity-oriented way of life is not the *only* one that can be satisfying, as one can see demonstrated in the successful use of the "rocking-chair" life style by some elderly. Neither is the way one lives during old age necessarily to be seen in terms of sharply contrasting positive and negative ways of adapting. Some people's lives are characterized by compromise. Their personality needs may not basically be capable of satisfaction in the world or reality, but this incomplete fulfillment is compensated for by defense mechanisms that shield the person from the full impact of his nonadaptive needs.

These and other personality "types" may have little to do with the process of aging. People are likely to maintain consistent personalities over the years. It is certainly reasonable to think that people who have been outgoing all their lives will deal differently with aging than will those who have been loners. It is altogether too easy to "explain away" a particular personality trait by ascribing it to old age. For any of us who work with the elderly it is much more important to examine the individual in terms of how he copes with the biological and social realities of aging than to ponder at length whether he is showing signs of aging.

chapter 2

The national scene of housing for the elderly

One difficulty with the attempt to offer concrete help to practitioners is that specific information is very likely to go out of date quickly. This is especially likely in the housing field where new technologies and changing political orientations impose both high birth rates and high mortality rates on specific programs.

At the time of this writing, housing assistance to the individual renter, as contrasted to the programmatic project-type multiunit housing of the past 30 years, is the major type of housing on the horizon. Although one cannot predict its viability as the nation's political leadership changes, the immediate future seems certain to maximize the role of private-market housing. A housing-allowance program is now under study by the U.S. Department of Housing and Urban Development (HUD). It proposes to provide cash allowances to people in need of financial assistance, who will then seek housing on the open market. Though its proponents claim that it will stimulate new building, this plan will also clearly require greater utilization of existing housing stock than has been true in recent years. Whether better housing will result is problematic. By encouraging the scattered housing of low-income people some of the ills consequent to project housing of large numbers of welfare families may be avoided.

In the case of the elderly, it is by no means self-evident that their housing situation will be improved by the housing allowance. Some disadvantages for the elderly include:

1. The lesser ability of the most needy elderly to search effectively for improved housing. Without an intermediary such as a housing authority or nonprofit sponsor, many older people are

unpracticed in reading advertisements, taking the initiative to use the telephone, transporting themselves to see a prospective dwelling, protecting themselves from sharp business practices, arranging for moving, or dealing with new landlords.

2.   The unsatisfactory location of much of the available housing stock. The major reason for the programmatic housing types (to be described) was the provision of well-located new housing. Much of the unplanned housing that is now available is in deteriorated neighborhoods or areas poorly located for access to social services, medical facilities, and everyday amenities.

3.   The possibility that the financial effectiveness of a housing allowance will be negated by a compensatory rise in rents. Since older people are differentially represented at the poverty income level, they would be selectively disadvantaged by this outcome.

4.   The lesser ability of the housing allowance program to foster age-dense environments where services beyond the provision of shelter may be easily provided. In Chapter 6, some advantages of housing limited to older people will be discussed. Though not all elderly prefer this kind of housing, demand for it is still far from adequately met. Overemphasis on open-market housing cannot help but make it more difficult for these people to be served.

After more than a year's standstill in any federal housing activity, an interim proposal was made by HUD in January 1974, to extend the regulations of the 1937 Housing Act's Section 23 to allow local public housing authorities to contract with private owners for the leasing of units to individuals and families meeting the usual financial criteria for eligibility for public housing. As in the case of earlier applications of Section 23, HUD would pay the difference between the market rental for the unit and the amount the occupant is judged able to pay (25% of his income). This plan covers both new construction, existing housing in good condition, and the rehabilitation of old housing. Though priority is given to applications for family housing where fewer than 20 percent of the units receive a subsidy, housing limited to older people may get the same priority when as many as 100 percent of the units receive a subsidy. The local housing authority may itself manage the units or the owner may do so. A nonprofit sponsor may function as developer, owner, and manager, under the same conditions as a commercial owner.

Thus, the 1974 extension of Section 23 does allow some continuation of the public housing program. However, in putting more initiative into the hands of the private developer, there is clearly less opportunity for the local housing authority and the federal government to be effective in planning the housing to meet the special needs of the elderly. In the case of the nonprofit sponsor, there is little in these regulations to facilitate his continued involvement in housing for the elderly. No assistance is available either for the extensive preconstruction planning and development costs or for construction loans, which must be sought on the open market. Developments will be competitive, and nonprofit housing groups feel that no such sponsor will be able to undertake the risks involved in using this program since the cost of preparation of competitive plans will rest totally on the sponsor.

Even though the current housing situation is so chaotic, for background purposes it is necessary to review the federal programs that ceased with the moratorium declared in January 1973, as well as other earlier federal programs, and nonassisted types of housing. They will be classified according to their basic administrative and financing arrangements, which may reappear, with variations, in the housing programs of the future. Some states—New York, New Jersey, and Massachussetts, for example—have state-aided programs bearing some similarity to federal programs. Although they will not be described here, the planner should investigate such programs if they are available in his state. The chapter will conclude with a brief look at some directions for meeting the future housing needs of older people.

GOVERNMENTALLY ASSISTED HOUSING PROGRAMS

Direct Grants for Construction   The oldest and most extensive housing program designed explicitly for the elderly was low-rent public housing, authorized for the elderly in 1956 and accounting for 253,000 operating units as of December 1973. While no new housing was authorized under this program between January 1973 and September 1974, new units approved before January 1973 continued to become occupied. Direct grants were made by HUD to local housing authorities, which are independently incorporated organizations whose governing members are appointed by municipal or county officials. The rent charged by authorities to low-income tenants is calculated so as to pay the costs of maintenance and administration. A prospective tenant does not qualify for the housing if his income is above a level set for the particular area in which he lives; the elderly tenant's income is reviewed every two years after moving in, and he may be asked to leave if his income exceeds a level established for those already residing in the project. For a long time there were many people whose income was too low to qualify for public housing. However, the so-called "Brooke amendment" to the 1969 Housing Act stipulated that no tenant may be charged more than 25 per cent of his income for rent. Differentials between this value and the actual cost to the housing authority are made up by supplementary federal payments to the housing authority.

Housing built in this program was produced by the authority itself through most of the life of the program beginning with the purchase of land, demolition of existing structures, rezoning, and construction of the housing. In recent years the "turnkey" procedure was increasingly utilized. This operation allowed the housing authority to negotiate a contract with a private developer to carry out each of these steps himself, on a site agreeable to both and with plans developed in accordance with HUD regulations, the wishes of the authority, and local ordinances. The developer sold the finished product to the authority, which then operated the project in the usual manner. The turnkey procedure was meant to capitalize on the expertise of the developer who presumably had had experience in these procedures, and cut into the sluggishness frequently encountered in such quasi-governmental administrative bodies. The turnkey model was popular, although an empirical test of its efficiency in comparison to the normal procedure has not yet been made.

Since federally assisted public housing began in 1937, it has produced about a million units of family housing. The problems of family housing have been amply documented in the press, particularly in metropolitan areas, where the housing has increasingly been populated by "problem families," one of whose manifestations is a growing rate of juvenile delinquency, including vandalism and extensive crimes of assault. Much of such public housing has been built as high-rise projects in poor urban neighborhoods.

The troubles encountered here have generally been those typical of our cities in general, but some earlier practices in design and siting have been questioned, as illustrated by dramatic examples such as the Pruitt-Igoe project in St. Louis. Built in 1955, this project was located on slum-clearance property still bordered by high-crime areas. The 2764-unit project was built as 16 eleven story high-rise structures. A number of innovative architectural features were introduced, such as alternate-floor elevator stops, which in the service of cost-reduction forced the use of dark stairwells to floors where elevators did not stop. These became a natural location for crime, drug use, sexual activity, and use as public bathrooms. Public galleries on every floor were meant to encourage the development of within-floor small social groups. In fact, they became "owned" by the delinquent teenagers and unsupervised children. As a result, the gain of providing shelter for the poor was not enough to keep Pruitt-Igoe alive. Tenants moved out, vandalism increased, and the project took on the look of a bombed city. After an attempt to salvage some

Fig. 1. Public housing can be warm, attractive, and conducive to a continuation or betterment of earlier life style.

of the project through demolition of some buildings and cutting down the size of the subunits within the high-rise buildings, the decision was made to abandon the total project in 1973.

A surprisingly large number of older people live in public housing units designed for people of all ages—27 percent of all such units were occupied by the elderly as of 1970. Many of these people live in multiple-generation families, others as couples or single individuals. Relatively little is known about their daily lives and how well suited to their needs this kind of housing is, particularly how the family roles of the older person differ, if at all, from those of older people in multiple-generation families living in the community.

A substantial minority (22 percent as of 1970) of all elderly people in public housing live in units which, while designed for the elderly, are located in projects serving people of all ages. Sometimes the elderly live in a single building limited to people 62 and over (or younger physically handicapped people) located near other project buildings serving families. In other situations, structures designated for the elderly are interspersed with those serving families; still other variations include the designation of certain floors in high-rise buildings for the elderly, or of certain units within a floor for the elderly. In any case, these units must meet certain specifications, such as providing extra grab bars in the bathroom, electric outlets of a certain height, and so on; they may be rented only to the elderly or handicapped except in unusual situations. Some of the issues and problems involved in housing all generations in the same physical location will be discussed later.

The larger number of units designated for the elderly are in projects whose occupancy is limited to older people. By all standards, these housing environments seem to have been particularly successful. Frequently the tenants have moved from deprived environments whose physical contrast with the new housing practically guarantees a joyous reception by the older person. For anyone interested in housing for the elderly, required reading should include the story of Victoria Plaza in San Antonio, one of the first sites built for the elderly. Under the inspired direction of Mrs. Marie McGuire Thompson, at that time the San Antonio Housing Authority's Executive Director (later the federal Commissioner of Public Housing, then Special Assistant on Problems of the Elderly and Handicapped, and still serving as a major consultant on housing problems), and with an architectural design by Thomas J. Thompson, Victoria Plaza demonstrated to the country that older people were capable of moving from their homes and forming a new and living society for themselves. The story of Victoria Plaza has been written by psychologist Dr. Frances Carp in a fascinating document entitled *A Future for the Aged* (1966). Though the book is primarily the report of a research project, Dr. Carp writes of the personal and social lives of the elderly tenants in a way that makes Victoria Plaza very real to the reader.

The success of Victoria Plaza and others like it that followed insured the steady growth of this type of housing. The proportion of elderly-designated housing units (EDUs) to family-housing units has gradually increased to the point where in 1972, EDUs accounted for 37 percent of public housing unit production. Thus, in this area, at least, the elderly appear to be receiving long overdue compensatory attention. As it happens, housing for the elderly became the most popular form of building with housing authorities and local communities. From both a management and financial point of view, there are many fewer problems in dealing with elderly tenants than in dealing with younger families. Therefore, from the wider point of view of the welfare of society as a whole, there appears to be some danger of neglect of the housing needs of poor families for the sake of the relative ease of housing the elderly.

Direct-Loan Interest Subsidy Programs   The second most extensive federal housing program for the elderly was the so-called "202" housing, as authorized by Section 202 of the 1959 Housing Act. This program made available direct federal loans at 3 percent interest for 100 percent of the cost of constructing housing for limited-income elderly tenants. Loans were made only to nonprofit organizations able to develop and administer the project for the duration of its life. The program was terminated in 1969 in favor of the 236 program, to be described later, primarily in order to reduce the appearance in the annual budget of the large immediate outlays of federal money required to produce the original project. At the time the program ceased 45,000 units had been produced by the many different church and synagogue groups, unions, fraternal and civic organizations, and groups organized for the express purpose of building housing for the elderly.

Occupancy of the 202 projects was limited to people with regionally varying annual incomes in the neighborhood of $4500 for single individuals and $5500 for couples, as of 1971. No asset limits were set. Since the sponsor had to charge rents high enough to administer and maintain the project, as well as to make mortgage payments, the rent was in the neighborhood of 80–$90 per month for efficiencies and 100–$120 per month for one-bed units. Thus, a person living on welfare would not normally be able to pay these rents, nor would people with no income other than Social Security. Thus the 202 program served a lower-middle income group, by income standards of the elderly (in 1970 only 13 percent of single older people had incomes of as much as $5000). While the public housing program undoubtedly served many poor elderly whose adult-life incomes had been in the middle-income range, the 202 sites were not able to serve many poor tenants until relatively recently. The 1965 Housing Act established the rent supplement programs that provided to nonfederal landlords federal grants of a size that made up the difference between the normal FHA-approved rent and the rent a welfare-level tenant would have to pay for public housing in that locality (now, since the Brooke amendment, set at 25 percent of the tenant's income). Although the law allowed up to 40 percent of tenants in a building to receive rent supplements, an administrative order limited the percentage to 20 percent of units in most cases. In actual fact a relatively small number of 202 tenants were receiving rent supplements, less than 10 percent as estimated by the 1971 housing survey conducted by the Philadelphia Geriatric Center.

Another form of subsidy, the Section 23 leased housing program, has allowed local public housing authorities to rent units in nonpublic housing buildings for tenants eligible for public housing. The tenant pays the local public housing rate, and HUD, through the housing authority, reimburses the owner for the difference between what the tenant pays and the market rental of the housing. Some 202 projects have thus been able to accept some welfare-level tenants. In our 1971 housing survey, administrators of 202 projects differ among themselves in their evaluations of the success of these subsidy programs. While the majority approve of the resulting income mix, a substantial minority do not. Some of the opinions given state that tenants do not look favorably on living with people "who have not put money away for the future."

Fig. 2.   High-rise housing in an urban area can be aesthetically pleasing (Demchik and Supowitz, Philadelphia, architects. Photo by Sam Nocella.)

While 202 occupancy has tended to be segregated by income and race (see Chapter 6), relatively few have ended up with high percentages of tenants who are members of the sponsoring organization. The 202's are not distributed equally across the nation. They flourish in retirement areas such as Florida and California, in the Northeast, in many of the large metropolitan areas, and in pockets in the midwest. The south, except for Florida, has relatively few, and many midwestern, mountain, and southwest areas are quite devoid of them.

The 202 clearly benefits from the continued involvement of the sponsoring organization in the management of the project. There is almost always an activity program, frequently managed pretty much by tenants themselves, but always with some overseeing by the administrator. Official federal policy through most of the lifetime of the 202 program was to encourage independence in tenants by discouraging supportive services such as on-site meal service or medical facilities. While most 202 projects have more common space than the typical public housing project, relatively few were able to obtain federal approval for supportive-service space. Many of those sponsors who did build such space did so without using federal funds for that portion of their building.

Sponsors and housing consultants generally found the 202 program relatively smooth to negotiate, even though the staff serving it in Washington and in the regions was small. There was relatively little red tape involved, and the staff all had the opportunity to become specialists in housing the elderly. The major complaint voiced was the strictness with which costs were controlled, resulting in many sponsors' dissatisfaction with the small allowable size of apartments, common space, and landscaping costs. The success of this drive to keep costs down is attested to by a HUD study showing that the average cost for a 202 unit was more than $3000 cheaper than a public housing unit. For those interested in this comparison, cost differences and end-product differences are compared by category in the appendix to the Senate Committee on Aging hearing of August 4, 1971, "Adequacy of federal response to housing need of older Americans," obtainable from the Government Printing Office.

The direct loans made to sponsors of 202 projects showed in the annual federal budgets as expenditures, not offset by the value of repayments being made, which had become substantial by 1968. These figures thus constituted an embarrassment to whatever administration was in power at the moment and led to the design of Section 236 mortgage insurance-interest subsidy housing program of the 1968 Housing Act.

After a 5-year "death" a variation of the 202 program is contained in the August 1974 Housing Act, but its usability by nonprofit sponsors without substantial start-up money remains to be demonstrated. The 1974 version offers direct loans at the government interest rate (estimated as 8 percent as of September 1974) and not requiring the amount of the loan itself to appear as an item in the annual national budget. The 236 and public housing programs were also continued, and the leased-housing and rent-supplement programs have been better integrated with other federal housing programs.

INTEREST-SUBSIDY PROGRAMS

The 1968 Housing Act created the Section 236 program. This program was abolished by the 1973 housing moratorium and revived again in the 1974 Housing Act. The 236 program differs importantly from the 202 program:

1. It could be utilized by either profit or non-profit corporations.
2. Tenants could be of any age, and no fixed percentage was mandated for the elderly.
3. The sponsor borrowed at the current rate on the open market from private mortgage financers.
4. The federal government made monthly payments to the sponsor based on the number of limited-income tenants living in the project, at a rate so as to lower the effective rate of interest to as little as one percent, and thus to enable the tenant to pay a rental in a range comparable to what he would have paid under the 202 program.

Among the advantages of the program were its ability to offer housing to people who differed widely in age or economic capability. From a political point of view it enabled the production of more units, since only the interest subsidy payments were budgeted to current federal expenditures. A major disadvantage was the greater total cost to the country in the long run, attributable to the difference between the 1 and the 3 percent interest rate (offset by the net cost to the government of borrowing money for direct loans in excess of the amount being repaid). Loan costs in addition to interest—fees and so on—appear to have been appreciably higher under the 236 program. Other disadvantages were that the elderly were not assured of a predictable flow of units earmarked for their use. Although two-thirds of the 236 projects were claimed to have nonprofit sponsors, a profit-making corporation could initiate the project, or a builder could even negotiate the formation of a corporation to initiate it. Therefore, a continuous service-oriented management was not assured. Finally, responsibility for the program's administration was placed within FHA, which is primarily a loan insurance institution, not one with expertise in meeting the wider social needs of older people. Many who have worked with

FHA since the 236 program began have complained of inelasticity, the inappropriateness of the standards invoked for building for the elderly, and the sheer sluggishness of the bureaucratic process as compared to the old 202 procedure. When defending the merits of the 236 program to the Senate Committee on Aging, Assistant Secretary Eugene Gulledge (also Administrator of FHA) made what must have been his major faux pas of the year when he excused a technical error made by an FHA regional office by saying "On any particular subject we have a shelf of regulations which is nine feet in length!"

In any case, the quality of the 236 program in terms of actual performance has not yet been assessed. Through 1973, about 19,000 units that had begun to be processed under the 202 program were occupied after being transferred to the 236 program. As of December 1973, during the 1972 fiscal year, about 12,000 new 236 units were in operation. As of March 1971, about 1500 elderly 236 occupants were receiving rent supplements. Their median income level was $3300 per year, and they lived in units whose average nonsupplemental rental was $105 for all size units.

MORTGAGE INSURANCE PROGRAMS

The 1959 Housing Act provided a mortgage insurance program enabling profit and nonprofit corporations to borrow at market rates to build housing with relatively few restrictions as to tenant characteristics or type of environment provided. A large number of nonprofit organizations, primarily church groups, used this Section 231 insurance program to build "retirement centers" that offered many life-supporting services such as central dining room, housekeeping, and full medical care—from medical dispensary to permanent nursing-home care. They are lush in recreational and leisure-time opportunities, and sometimes extremely beautiful in architecture, siting, and landscaping. Often they required large "entrance fees" beginning around $10,000 and going much higher, in addition to high monthly maintenance charges revised as costs rise. The tenant who paid the entrance fee usually signed a contract giving him the guarantee of life care so long as he maintained his monthly payments. In 1963, however, federal regulations were established that prevented the use of entrance fees, and those 231 projects financed under this program since that time have had to pay for their operation on the basis of monthly charges only. There was some abuse of the entrance fee, with large reserves building up beyond the necessary amount, leading some localities to withdraw tax exemption for these facilities.

A number of profit corporations also utilized the 231 program, frequently with inadequate financial planning. At one point, while only six percent of church-sponsored 231 projects had to be repossessed by F.H.A., 45 percent of those sponsored by profit corporations had failed. This high rate of failure, totally unlike the 202 situation, led to the virtual abandonment of the 231 program long before the 1973 housing moratorium.

Through 1973 about 42,000 units were produced by the 231 program. The location of these 286 projects was heavily skewed toward the retirement areas of the country. Although the number of units produced was thus as high as that under 202, this type of program that benefited the "wealthy" (by comparison) segment of the elderly population died partly because of its inconsistency with national priorities favoring building for the much larger number of less well-to-do elderly.

The foregoing were the major federal housing programs serving the elderly. The remaining programs are less extensive and will be described more briefly.

Rental Programs

The 221 (d) Programs provided insured loans at market rate, or below-market interest rate to nonprofit, cooperative, or profit groups to build or rehabilitate housing for people of moderate income. Statistics have not always been kept on occupant characteristics, but it is estimated that substantial numbers of tenants in these buildings are elderly. About 900 elderly tenants occupied new 221 (d-3) units during 1972 and 1973. Many of the older apartment buildings' populations have aged together in these residences. As of 1969, about 4000 elderly tenants were receiving rent supplements to enable them to live in this type of housing.

The Section 515 Rural Housing Program The 1949 Housing Act authorized the Farmers Home Administration to provide mortgage insurance and direct loans to nonprofit or cooperative groups for building or rehabilitating rental housing for moderate-income people in a rural area. About 700 units were authorized in 1971, and a total of 4000 had been produced as of 1971.

Purchase Programs

The F.H.A. Section 203 Program (conventional FHA mortgages) This program had a low rate of utilization by the elderly—between one and two percent of mortgages were utilized by people 60 or over in 1971.

The 213 Program of the 1950 Housing Act authorized mortgage insurance for cooperative groups or developers who would sell to a subsequently formed tenant cooperative. No special provisions were made for the elderly, and there are no figures available on the extent to which the elderly occupy these units.

The 235 Home-Ownership Program of the 1968 Housing Act provided interest abatement to bring the rate down as low as one percent to a mortgagee. The buyer had to pay a minimum of 20 percent of his income, and the actual interest rate paid was dependent on the amount of his income. As of the end of 1970, about 3300 new or existing homes had been purchased by owners 60 or over.

The 502 Rural Home Loan Program of the Farmers Home Administration (1949 Housing Act) provided home ownership loans for residents of rural areas and small towns. The borrower had to have the financial resources to repay the loan. In 1971 about 3300 such homes were built for people 62 and over, at a total (land plus home) average cost of $11,000.

The Section 207 Mobile Home Purchase Program This is for the most part a program serving the relatively young. According to 1970–1971 figures, only four percent of such loans went to the elderly.

Rehabilitation of Existing Housing Stock

Section 312 Home Rehabilitation Loans (1964 Housing Act) Property owners in urban renewal or code enforcement areas were eligible for direct loans at 3 percent interest to rehabilitate properties. In recent years about 17 percent of the loans have gone to elderly recipients.

Section 115 Home Rehabilitation Grants (1965 Housing Act)   Direct grants up to $3500 were made to low-income (less than $3000 per year, or paying housing costs that exceed 25 percent of income) homeowners for improvements to properties in urban renewal or code enforcement areas. Sixty percent of the 14,000 grants made through 1971 were to elderly recipients.

Section 235 Home Rehabilitation Loans   were made to nonprofit or municipal groups to remodel homes that were subsequently sold to individual household heads under the 235 purchase program.

Section 504 Rural Housing Rehabilitation Loans   were made by the Farmers Home Administration to low-income homeowners in rural areas at one percent interest. Two-thirds of the 4400 such loans made in 1971 were to people 60 and over.

Relocation Payments

Relocation Expenses   are paid to urban renewal relocatees, either actual expenses, or up to $500.

Replacement Housing Purchase Allowance   may be granted, up to a cost of $15,000 for replacement purchase or $4000 for rental.

The extent of the recent utilization of the relocation programs by older people is not known.

NONFEDERALLY AIDED RETIREMENT COMMUNITIES

There are an unknown number of privately financed retirement centers that are quite similar to those described above. Many churches and other nonprofit and profit corporations have preferred to use their own funds for such building, and when doing so are, of course, free to continue the entrance-fee life-care practice if they wish.

Perhaps the best-known retirement villages are the Leisure Worlds of Seal Beach and Laguna Hills, California, and Maryland, and New Jersey, Sun City of Arizona, and so on. Many of these environments have low minimum entrance fees, allow people over 50 or 55 to live there, and many sell detached houses, town houses, or condominiums, rather than rent. The atmosphere in such projects is quite different from that in the life-care retirement center. A premium is put on activity, social interaction, and good health. While full medical care is frequently provided, the required life style, especially that involved in the care of an owned home, seems less congruent with the needs of the person of marginal competence than does the life-care center. We do not yet have adequate information on how the retirement village resident changes as he ages, how he copes with his changing competence, how long he continues to live in an owned residence if he gets sick, or how he makes out financially if he sells his house, especially under the pressure of sudden illness.

It is impossible to estimate the national supply of nonfederally funded retirement centers or retirement village units, since there are no registries or mandatory licensing agencies for such housing. They clearly serve the economically elite segment of the elderly, as well as those in above-average health and with strong social needs.

Older People Living in the Community

While this book is written primarily for those who are concerned with planned or clustered housing, it is important to know something about the 19 million not living in such housing. The range of choice of housing by the community dweller is limited by the constraints of economics and health, so that older sections of the city, older structures in towns, and farmhouses are where they live. At best, this type of living gives them continued opportunity to live in communities, neighborhoods, dwellings and among furnishings that are familiar and comfortable. For these reasons, as well as a diverse set of factors such as social ties and economic reasons, one research project showed that about 70 percent of a group of 5000 Social Security recipients indicated no wish to move. Applying a very stringent criterion for dissatisfaction, Irving Rosow found that only 6 to 8 percent of apartment dwellers in Cleveland were actively dissatisfied with their housing (1967). When questioned about their wish to move, 31 percent of a group of Los Angeles residents, people 50 and over, indicated a wish to move. However, the Philadelphia Geriatric Center studied the housing wishes of a small group of elderly Jewish immigrants remaining in their homes in an inner-city slum. About 85 percent would like to move; about 45 percent owned their own homes, and 100 percent of these would move if they could sell their present homes without financial disaster. Thus, the wish to change residence is highly dependent on one's local situation.

Homeownership Among the Elderly The United States is a country of homeowners, and as might be expected, the longer one has had the opportunity to earn money, the greater the probability that one owns his own home, up to a point at the peak of one's earning years. Where less than 20 percent of household heads under age 25 own their own homes, three-quarters of those in the age 45–54 age group do. This percentage then drops slightly, so that about 70 percent of those 65 and over owned their own homes in 1970.

Large numbers of them may be caught in the situation of needing to stay in their owned homes, for economic reasons, in the face of compelling contradications against remaining. Deterioration of the neighborhood is likely to reduce their mobility and restrict the general richness of their living style, in addition to increasing their physical danger. Frequently neighborhood resources move out as the area declines. In our study of the urban slum mentioned previously, several synagogues and the community center had moved as the larger, more mobile group went to newer areas of the city.

Homeownership does not by any means give one clear sailing. In 1960, about 17 percent of all owner-occupied housing units were rated as dilapidated or lacking in some basic plumbing facilities. While comparable data were not gathered in the 1970 census, about 8 percent of elderly households were lacking one or more of the basic plumbing facilities in 1970: flush toilet, private bath, and hot water. The proportion of black elderly without these facilities was almost four times that of whites. Homeownership is a financial burden as well. As of 1969, the costs of property taxes and labor for home maintenance repairs had increased, respectively, 60 and 89 percent more than the total consumer price index had over the past five years.

The Residential Distribution of Older People More than 60 percent of all older people live in the metropolitan areas of our country, a slightly greater proportion of them in central city areas than in surrounding suburban areas. Not surprisingly, elderly blacks who live in metropolitan areas are 50 percent more likely to live in central city areas than are white elderly. Relatively small proportions of older people live on farms (5 percent) or in rural nonfarm areas (17 percent). We do not have population data on the proportion of older people in deteriorating inner-city areas, but surveys from Model City neighborhoods do indicate that the proportion of elderly is above their national proportion, sometimes radically so.

Composition of Households with Elderly People   Two-thirds of all elderly individuals live in family settings, while one-quarter live alone. Of those living alone, there are three times as many women as men. Looking at the 50 million families counted by the 1970 census, 830,000 contained both people 65 and over and people under 18— most of these probably three-generation families.

It may be helpful to sketch briefly how several different types of older people live, using research data wherever possible, and filling in with informal observation where necessary.

The "Average" Older Person   In spite of the fact that she is pure fiction, the average person is likely to be in reasonably good health. She can move about her neighborhood in or near an urban area without great difficulty, though longer trips are infrequent, unless it is to visit close relatives. In many areas, the only transportation possible is someone else's car. She is likely to live in the same household with one or more family members, though an elderly man is even more likely to have someone share his home. Like average people everywhere, her biggest problem is money. The house is paid for, but expenses appear to rise in advance of periodic Social Security adjustments. Both man and wife fill a substantial amount of the day doing everyday duties around the house. They may watch television about three hours a day. The wish to see more of other people is frequently voiced, though casual contacts with neighboring tradesmen can be satisfying. If older people are fortunately situated, they may richen their lives visiting in a park, attending a senior center, or continuing with earlier-life hobbies. Still, there are too many hours of inactivity. Though by most standards their spirits remain good, depression is a threat, and they may be anxious over the possibility of a catastrophic illness or loss of physical or financial independence. The average older person as an individual is thus pretty much like anyone else, but with somewhat less biological vigor. He must expend more than the usual amount of energy coping with social and environmental situations where he is selectively at risk: low income, poor transportation, and a shrinking social world.

The Rural Poor We need a lot more imagination to picture the way of life of older people who live in villages, farms, or rural nonfarms since the researchers neglect them as much as our society does. The average person in a rural area has an income from $400–$700 less than the person his age who lives in a metropolitan area, and thus even our average person qualifies as poor or near-poor. His deprived status shows in the quality of his housing, which may have few of the comforts we take for granted, particularly if he is black and lives in the South. Most have electricity, but one in three is likely to lack basic plumbing facilities, a telephone, and even more, lack central heat. They don't go many places, including to the doctor, in spite of being in the poorest health of any aged group. They have more disabilities in performing tasks of daily living than any other segment of the older population. The scraps of information available suggest that they may travel less than a third as much as many others, and in one reported locality, their minimal necessary travel costs them 3 percent of their meager income. No good picture of their daily time investment can be created, but in one way, the popular view of the older rural resident seems to be correct: his level of social interaction is higher, and he reports less feeling of loneliness than does the urban dweller.

The Small-Town Elderly Person The older person living in a small town easily qualifies for the classification "poor." She is highly likely to own her own home and even to have excess space in it—sometimes a substantial burden. On the other hand, her greater likelihood of being able to live on the ground floor is an advantage to the disabled, as compared to urban dwellers and their more frequently unavoidable stairs. She is also likely to be equipped with the most important household facilities, though it must be emphasized that the disadvantage of the black elderly noted in other areas is undoubtedly present here as well. Her health allows her to be independent in most ways, though she is measurably less independent than the urban dweller. Even though she rates her own health as less good than that of the average senior citizen, she receives less health care. The generally sparse nature of services in nonmetropolitan areas, especially the transportation that links the person to the services, puts her more on her own. On the other hand, there are clear compensations to her financial and health-care deprivations. Children and other relatives are more likely to live within day-visit distance, and most friends are local. The small-town resident has a higher amount of social contact than any other group does; daily contact with both family and friends is the rule. Since small towns have somewhat higher concentrations of older people than do urban areas, the senior adult's total social integration is aided. She is likely to belong to a formal organization, particularly a church. The balance in the ledger resulting from this combination of resources and deprivations is difficult to assess. There is no evidence that the morale of the small-town resident is any better than that of older people in the nation at large. Some feel, however, that the problems of income and medical treatment are potentially soluble, and that their higher level of social contact is an asset which allows them greater possible life satisfaction than other groups.

The Poor Inner-City Resident   Like the aged in general, the inner-city resident in most areas largely owns his own home, but he is more likely to rent his home than others. The condition of the renter's dwelling is substantially poorer than that of the owner. On the other hand, the renter can get out more easily than the owner. The homeowner thinks constantly about how he can better his housing condition. Thinking about how to unload the old house, the unimaginable cost of a new place, the imponderables of a new neighborhood, and the lingering attachments to the old, takes time—and the passage of time brings further deterioration of the neighborhood, house, and owner, increasing the difficulty of making the move. Thus most slum residents become used to living in dehumanized, ugly, and threatening surroundings. Black and white aged alike go about in constant fear of physical attack. The general neighborhood disorganization makes any trip out at night or even a daytime walk an anxiety-arousing experience. Whether realistic or not, fear drastically reduces the person's behavioral space. Social activity, self-maintaining errands, and basic necessities such as medical care become more difficult in the vicious circle of increasing isolation and decreasing services. The inner-city resident is much more likely to

Fig. 3. The older inner-city resident frequently has access to many resources, but his neighborhood may be unattractive and even unsafe.

suffer from loneliness, alienation, low morale, and mental illness than other groups.

LOOKING AHEAD

Thus far, the country's major response to the various community housing problems mentioned has been the generally successful group housing programs described earlier in this chapter. Compared with

Fig. 4. The inexpensive row houses on the left were each remodeled by the Philadelphia Geriatric Center to house three relatively independent older people. (Photo by Mort Savar, Lindelle Studios.)

public housing and the lower-middle income programs, the programs that facilitate an individual's ability to choose continued integration in a community with residents of all ages have been a drop in the bucket. Thus, federal policy seems deliberately to have fostered segregation of older people and whatever degree of institutionalization comes inevitably from clustering sizeable numbers of people together into the same organizational unit.

As stated elsewhere, neither age segregation nor bigness is inherently bad. What is bad is our natural tendency to assume that whatever seems to be good should be copied everywhere for all people. Relocation payments, rent supplements, leased housing, and housing allowances are means of increasing individual options, and therefore should certainly be provided.

The future of planned housing will have to include many other variations on the theme of facilitating continued community residence, however. It is in this area that the prospective sponsor has the opportunity to be most creative, though the means for being creative seem to have been removed by the 1973 moratorium. Without going into depth in any area, some possibilities for the future include:

Community Housing Rehabilitation   In some cases, a sponsor can provide units more cheaply by rehabilitating existing housing with the needs of older people in mind. This housing can be scattered and totally blended with the community, being a "project" only in the sense that administration, maintenance, and a social program for tenants are centralized. This approach lends itself ideally to helping rescue a neighborhood from decline. In other instances, as in an "intermediate housing" program sponsored by the Philadelphia Geriatric Center, homes may be remodeled into apartments, clustered in an area adjacent to, but not intimately associated with, an institution for the elderly. In this example, institutional social and medical services are available for emergencies, but otherwise in-

Fig. 5.   The community housing (right center) is located near the parent institution but clearly is not a part of the institution. (Photo by Sam Nocella.)

Fig. 6. This shared sitting room complements the private full apartments of each tenant. (Photo by Mort Savar, Lindelle Studios.)

dependent living continues. This model could be utilized under the 1974 Section 23 housing regulations, though as mentioned earlier, it would be very difficult for the nonprofit sponsor.

The Housing Broker Organization In almost any area, there are older people with too much space and others with no suitable place to live. A broker with the additional capability of offering remodeling services linked with a socially oriented administrative structure could add considerably to the options available.

The Boarding House The boarding house of legend still lives in some areas, but their quality is not controlled and there are few inducements for socially motivated organizations to undertake sponsorship of such projects. One of the problems is local regulation. The entry of some nonprofit sponsors into this field should help to establish standards and begin to serve a great need.

The Halfway House   A variant of the boarding house is a more protectively oriented living situation. Discharged elderly mental patients, alcoholics, or mental retardates can live without major medical facilities but with the assistance of a housekeeper.

The Home Repair Service   One barrier to people's remaining in their own homes is the lack of reliable repair and home rehabilitation services. Their vulnerability to fraudulent repair practices is well known, and they are frequently without the knowledge to avail themselves of HUD home rehabilitation grants and loans. An agency that could provide fairly priced small assistance (plumbing, heating and electrical repairs, and minor carpentry) and financially assisted larger repairs would add significantly to the solution of the total housing problem.

The foregoing has been quite sketchy and is not meant to be a substitute for the complete familiarization that can be gained only by absorbing the information contained in the great variety of publications available from HUD. A visit to the HUD Regional Office can usually locate the most important of them, though one always finds that there is relevant material in the offices of program personnel in Washington that nobody else has heard of. Since change is the name of the game today, the prospective sponsor should make certain to keep in touch with current housing legislation and regulation changes.

chapter 3

Some principles of planning and operating housing for the elderly

The previous chapter has noted the diversity of the older population while indicating some ways in which the older population as a whole differs from younger people. Later chapters will repeatedly refer to these facts about older people and attempt to relate them to specific design and administrative problems. However, it may be helpful to think first about some general principles that may be useful in establishing both the larger goals of housing and in making more specific decisions about structure and the handling of day-to-day problems.

1. THE PHYSICAL ASPECTS OF HOUSING ARE RELEVANT TO THE ACHIEVEMENT OF HUMAN GOALS IN HOUSING FOR THE ELDERLY.

Many people in the helping professions become used to accepting the idea that one's physical environment is of only marginal relevance to happiness. It is not at all difficult to enumerate cases that seem to prove this point. The most thriving business in psychiatry is among the wealthy, who are relatively free to choose their own physical environments, yet seem to be not much better in achieving peace of mind than the poor. Visitors to impoverished countries are always surprised and delighted to find the "poor-but-happy" phenomenon, and will contrast it with the apparent decline in life satisfaction that occurs as formerly deprived people move slowly toward the gratification of physical needs.

The psychologist would probably agree that for most people, happiness or life satisfaction depends on a large number of factors, only one of which is the physical environment. He would further emphasize the extraordinary capacity of the human being to find a way of coping with a wide variety of environments, including stressful ones. The "happiness" of the poor in an underdeveloped country would be seen as partly in the mind of the visitor—a contrast to the visitor's expectation that no one living in poverty could ever smile, for example. Another explanation would lie in the fact that the average person is equipped with physical and psychological capacities that enable him to "rise above" his environment. The psychologist would certainly consider it an open question whether the inner experience of happiness or life satisfaction differs greatly among average people in a variety of environmental situations.

Two factors can heighten the likelihood that the individual's well-being might be affected by his physical environment. One factor is the strength of the physical stress imposed on the individual by the environment. No person is immune to the effect of excessive heat, excessive cold, extreme sensory deprivation, or unsanitary conditions. It is more difficult to think of situations when the environment is so *good* that everyone's state of mind improves! In fact, it is possible that sometimes that exact opposite might occur, as it did when a scientist created an artificial Shangri-La for a species of bird that had been used to struggling for a living in a relatively barren environment. When the experimenter suddenly introduced an oversupply of food, always-available nesting material, and freedom from natural enemies, this welfare state resulted in a deterioration of the personal and social habits of the birds, including a colony-threatening reduction in birth rate. We conclude that there is both a threshold of stress beyond which most people's tolerance does not extend, and also that there is some evidence in favor of the "too much of a good thing" phenomenon.

The second factor that may enhance a person's susceptibility to environmental influence is a low level of personal resources. This generalization states that the less competent the individual in any area, the more likely it is that his behavior will be governed by his environment. The poverty-stricken individual has less freedom to compensate for environmental stress, such as seasonal changes, a depressed economy, or crime in his neighborhood. The psychotic individual may be more vulnerable to exploitation by his more competent peers. The older person in a large number of ways is more at the mercy of his environment than is a younger person. He is more likely to lack both physical stamina and economic means, and he has fewer social resources as the result of negative stereotyping of the elderly, social isolation, and so on. In a very real sense, then, environmental influences that the person with average competence might adapt to or actively counteract may well limit the adequacy of behavior in which the older person can engage.

2. ONE GOAL FOR SOCIETY IS TO PROVIDE ENVIRONMENTS THAT WILL CHALLENGE A PERSON TO PRODUCE HIS BEST.

The bird welfare state is only one of many examples that can be found to support the idea that a lack of exercise will risk the loss of skill. There seems to be increasing evidence that daily physical exercise is associated with longer life, while the sedentary life makes one more vulnerable to the effects of brief extreme exertion. For some organisms, a severely limited dietary intake during a critical developmental period actually seems to increase their lifespan. It is a well-documented fact that suicide and homicide rates decrease in times of national stress, such as during the enemy occupation of central European countries during the second world war. Some people feel, conversely, that material comforts are so relatively accessible today that an overreaction against the typically American achievement motive has occurred among the young—one that threatens to destroy the country's initiative.

Some of these ready examples are oversimplified and certainly of questionable validity when applied to humans. However, recent experimental work in the psychology of motivation has revived the notion that the need to explore is sometimes as strong as the need for security. Under some conditions, both animals and people will deliberately upset a state of security to create tension. Curiosity appears to be born of boredom, and boredom is frequently the feeling state that results when all needs are too well satisfied. One experimental psychologist taught his rat subjects that they would be rewarded with food by pushing a lever. An alternative response was offered by another lever that would reward them with a chance to explore a new part of the cage that was unfamiliar. The novel experience won the popularity contest, so long as the rats were not starving.

We know relatively little about how older people might respond, given the choice between food and a new maze! However, we have a duty to take very seriously the idea that curiosity, exploration, and novelty may, under the proper conditions, excite the older person every bit as much as they do rats and younger people. How much of the environment that society creates for older people is based on the assumption that older people as a class prefer the familiar, the unchanging, the simple? Certainly a near-poverty income, a lack of public transportation facilities, or a lack of protection from crime are deterrents to the acquisition of new skills and the growth of self-fulfilling interests. A corollary principle that may at first seem to be in conflict with the environmental challenge principle is:

3. A MAJOR GOAL IS TO PROVIDE SUPPORTIVE ENVIRONMENTS THAT WILL HELP MAINTAIN ADAPTIVE BEHAVIOR IN THE LESS COMPETENT ELDERLY.

Most social welfare programs are supportive, for example, public assistance payments for the financially dependent, protective services for the mentally incompetent, or nursing home care for the physically incompetent. While these welfare measures are obviously designed for good purposes, we are in fact both individually and as a nation most ambivalent in our feelings about giving and receiving such support. The national welfare system has been questioned. Does the easy availability of public assistance cause or at least encourage dependence?

In the case of the elderly this ideological conflict is perhaps less marked. The public stereotype of the elderly regards them as dependent, and therefore in one sense is more "accepting" of their need for welfare measures. However, the conflict remains in a slightly different form even when the most thoughtful planners design services for the elderly. The problem is to determine when a supportive environment is best and when a challenging environment is best.

A distinction has sometimes been made between *therapy* and *prosthesis*. Therapy is treatment which has the potential of permanently changing the individual so that his functioning is not limited. Therapy is thus applied for a limited period of time; when the individual is cured, therapy ceases and he continues in good health. Penicillin is therapy for an infectious condition, and immobilization with a cast is therapy for a broken bone. On the other hand, there may be conditions which are resistant or completely unamenable to permanent cure. Some such conditions lead to permanent disability. However, many can be partially or wholly compensated for by the continuous application of an aid that minimizes the condition. For most wearers, corrective lenses are prosthetic devices that bring the functioning of the eyes completely up to a normal level. Yet, in the majority of cases, the improvement in eyesight comes only while the glasses are worn; there is little permanent improvement. A leg brace for a polio victim is an example of a prosthesis that greatly increases the ability of the wearer to live a normal life, but does not elevate his functioning to the level of those with normal leg muscles. Much rehabilitation work involves identifying the deficit and creatively prescribing a prosthetic measure whose continued use will allow relative freedom of living style. The prosthesis need not be a physical object that is attached to the person, as in the case of glasses or a brace. By our definition, insulin is a prosthesis, since it does not change the basic diabetic condition, yet it maintains the physiological balance that makes the difference between life and death. A disability pension may be looked upon as a prosthetic device that compensates for lost earning power. A total environment or a single aspect of an environment may act as a prosthesis. A prison acts as a prosthesis for the antisocial behavior of the criminal whose crimes are repeated (theoretically, the same prison is supposed to be "therapeutic" for the first offender). A more limited environmental prosthesis is the elevator, whose availability removes the risk of a heart attack from the afflicted person who must live on the fourth floor.

The concept of prosthesis may be applied to this issue of how supportive the environment should be in order not to risk the unnecessary loss of independence. The critical decision seems to rest on the proper matching of the capacities of the individual to the amount of support offered him by his environment. The psychologist Eva Kahana has referred to this condition as "person-environment congruence." One aspect of the task involves the very careful assessment of the degree of the older person's disability, the extent to which "treatment" may be expected to result in permanent improvement, and the extent to which various types of prostheses may be expected to result in the continuous maintenance of a higher level of functioning than would otherwise be possible. The other aspect of the task involves the design of the proper prosthetic device, service, or environment to do the best job. The most important conclusion to be drawn thus far is that a prosthetic measure may be as necessary and lead to as positively fulfilling a result as therapy. To conclude automatically that a supportive service caters to dependency and therefore should be withheld is to deny that some disabilities are fixed and incapable of cure; it also denies the right of the incapacitated to the satisfaction of their human needs.

The chapter on social and psychological aspects of aging was careful to emphasize that there are few disabilities intrinsic to aging. However, it also pointed out a few areas where a negative age change does occur, and many instances where older people are unable to function at an optimum level because of their health conditions or our social rejection of them. The net result is that increasing proportions of people suffer these impairments as chronological age increases. Therefore, on a statistical basis there will have to be more supportive services as people grow older. Later on, the specific use of supportive services within the context of the housing environment will be discussed at length. At this point, it seems worthwhile to list for the reader's consideration a variety of personal impairments or social deprivations that may reduce the older person's ability to cope with problems and thus would raise the question as to whether additional services might be required to prolong independence in other areas.

Personal impairments:
1. Physical illness—the acute and chronic illnesses of old age.
2. Mobility—arthritic pain, fatiguability, paralysis, cardiac problems, lessened energy.
3. Self-care—deficits in ability to groom, control of bladder and bowel, food preparation, dressing, and other behaviors (usually secondary to physical or mental incapacity).
4. Speed—slowing down of the ability to move one's muscles,

to respond to signals from the environment, to make decisions regarding how one should behave.

5. Mental status—impairments in memory, ability to learn new behaviors, or to think abstractly.
6. Psychological adjustment—anxiety, depression, excessive dependence, antisocial behavior, alcoholism, suicidal thoughts.

Social deprivations:

1. Low income.
2. Inadequate housing.
3. Poor nutrition.
4. Crime-ridden neighborhoods.
5. Lack of public transportation.
6. Enforced retirement.
7. Lack of continued educational opportunities.
8. The steady move of recreational resources to suburbs and resort areas.
9. Centralization of medical resources and their consequently increased distance from the older person.
10. The concurrent growth of the small family, smaller dwelling units, and decline of three-generation living.
11. Loss of friends through death, lowered mobility, and migration.
12. The youth culture and anti-elderly stereotyping ("ageism").

Not all, or even most, older people have all these disabilities, and they are not necessarily the result of old age alone. However, if you are in the age range that society has defined as "old," you are likely to have the fullness of your life limited by many of the above deprivations. Therefore, in order to prevent your whole life's being limited by one or a few of these sources of disability, a prosthesis may bring up your ability to perform just enough to allow you to engage successfully in the others. A particularly good example is provided by the person with a relatively minor physical defect that limits her ability to move freely in and out of her third-floor walkup apartment. A weekly visit by a jitney, with a driver to help her up and down the stairs, may be the prosthesis that will make all the difference to her in allowing her to shop so as to meet her nutritional, grooming, and housekeeping needs; to visit a medical center; and to engage herself socially with other people her own age who utilize the service.

The next major principle for planning speaks partially to the question of *whom* should be challenged and *whom* supported.

4. A GOAL FOR PLANNING SHOULD BE TO PROVIDE THE OLDER PERSON WITH THE WIDEST RANGE OF ENVIRONMENTAL OPTIONS, FROM THE MOST LIFE-ENRICHING TO THE MOST LIFE-SUSTAINING.

Challenge and support have been suggested as equally appropriate, depending on the need and capacity of the individual, and the amount of challenge or support involved. How does the person become matched with the environment, or environmental aspects, that can give him the most satisfying life?

The most important aspect of the answer is that most people, if given the appropriate range of choice, will themselves choose what is most consistent with their needs. Whether a person is rich or poor, black or white, old or young, he will normally strike a balance between choosing an environment that is interesting (challenging, life-enriching) and one that is easy for him to live in (supportive, life-sustaining). Under ideal conditions, these two polar opposites may not be mutually exclusive. The ideal of middle-class life seems to be an environment where cultural and educational opportunities are high, occupational advancement opportunity is high, and changes of scene possible—all of these generally consistent with environmental challenge. On the other hand, the same environment may in other ways be supportive—labor-saving devices, high levels of municipal services, access to babysitting pools, and so on.

A growing segment of adult society seems to be moving toward achieving this blend of challenge and support. There seems to be no reason why the elderly should not be included in this surge toward the good life. The more that the average older person can choose whether he wishes to live in suburb or city, in a high-rise or low-rise, keep his private physician or use a "house" doctor, be in the neighborhood coffee klatsch or stick to himself, the more likely is it that he can achieve goals consistent with his own needs.

This principle does appear to accept the social value of middle-classness. There are, however, four situations to contend with that deviate from this model of the great, well-fed middle. These four situations are those that arise when the statistical minorities of highly competent and highly incompetent older people choose situations that are extremes of challenge on the one hand, and support, on the other, as shown in Fig. 1.

Two of these four situations represent positive outcomes:

1. High Competence-High Challenge   Many of the people who represent our ideal of the full use of resources during old age fit this description, and their behavior is clearly identifiable as *creative*— Picasso, Pablo Casals, Marshal Tito, or Justice Douglas are public figures who come to mind as representing this elite group of gifted people in their ninth decades of life who appear to search constantly for new problems to solve. On a lesser level, we all know individuals who fit into this category.

For example, Mrs. A. is the 82-year old widow of a physician. Her health is robust, and she has utilized the years since her husband's retirement and death to "become" some of the things her earlier culture-bound acceptance of the female role has not allowed her to be. She continues some of her old associations in her church league and her women's club, but she does so in a way that makes their memberships hold their breath at times. She reportedly scolded the business meeting of her club loudly for spending an hour deciding on the decor for a party for themselves, while not mentioning the recent assassination of Martin Luther King. She took on an emergency task in her son's office at a time of help shortage, and has stayed for five years as a part-time telephone solicitor, insisting loudly on periodic salary increases for herself.

Old age as socially defined frequently forces such people to look actively or create for themselves environments that are consistent with their needs to explore and conquer. For the most part they do

	High Challenge	High Support
High Competence	Creativity/More challenge	Atrophy/More challenge
Low Competence	Self-defeat/More support	Dependence/Stability

Fig. 1.

so themselves, and will not need the assistance of the professional. However, on a societal level, there is always the need to expand the opportunities for such challenge, so that those ready to choose may do so. Thus, on Fig. 1, the prescription is for "more challenge," in the expectation that the gifted will choose it.

2. Low Competence-High Support Some of the people with multiple deficits and deprivations are fortunate enough to have available situations that provide them with compensating support. For the most grossly impaired, living in a superior nursing home will probably constitute the best match of capability with environment. Contrary to public opinion, there do not appear to be immense numbers of people misplaced in institutions. About half of nursing home residents are mentally impaired and even larger proportions have major physical impairments. Research done at our Center by Mrs. Elaine Brody has underlined the importance of the older person's own assessment of his capabilities in determining whether he applies for admission to the institution. The wish of family members about institutionalization, and various situational factors were each much less critical to this decision than was the client's own attitude. This indicates that even the poorest-off person retains a relatively realistic view of the amount of independence and challenge he can tolerate, and screens himself out of situations that are potentially too demanding.

Families serve as the major resource to furnish the high level of support required by physically or mentally impaired people. By our best estimates as many incompetent older people live in the community with a supporting family member as live in institutions.

Housing, social service agencies, senior centers, homemaker services, outpatient clinics, and so on are other types of supports for the older person of lesser degrees of impairment than those in or ready for institutions.

The other two situations shown in Fig. 1 represent mismatches, and therefore may call for more active intervention from other people or agencies than did the matched situations.

3. High Competence-High Support People may sometimes choose environments for themselves that are overly provident. Some people look on the bourgeois life style as a whole as being a stultifying limitation to the full realization of self. Examples of overly supportive actions in behalf of older people are unnecessary institutionalization, giving up an independent household while undergoing the temporary anxiety of bereavement, or a preference for being driven rather than driving one's own car. Most of these situations involve the person's being motivated by dependency needs that are inappropriate to his general level of well-being. Through the lifespan, most people are vulnerable to the seductiveness of the over-good life. Like the welfare-state birds, we may all have a price for which we would relinquish the need to strive. People who give up challenging situations and allow their skills to atrophy are probably those with a reduced level of confidence in themselves and their capabilities.

For these people, the planner and the professional have to think in terms of both therapy for the self-doubt that leads such people to wish to be dependent and environmental programming that will exercise their skills. In the rehabilitation field, the best work has seemed to come when the task assigned to the patient has been just one step ahead of the patient's present capability. The patient who never leaves his chair is urged to raise himself half-way and then to sit down. When he succeeds several times in this task, he is then urged and praised when he can stand upright while still holding onto his chair. Then follow successive stages of letting go of the chair arms, moving one foot forward, standing a foot away from the chair, moving away from the wall, and so on. The person experiences more hope and a greater sense of reward at successive stages when the goal is minimal, rather than when he is repeatedly told that he must do the whole task, for example, learn to walk.

The same considerations apply to the less impaired person in other situations. His anxiety may be temporary, as when faced with an external stress such as an urban renewal program forcing him to relocate, or the loss of a spouse. The provision of opportunities to meet challenges of graduated magnitude may be an essential task of planning.

An example of a person whose anxious dependence led him to choose an overly-provident environment is Mr. F., a person who was hospitalized as a schizophrenic in his late twenties, and stayed in the mental hospital for a number of decades, while his family gradually built lives that excluded him. He is a fairly intelligent person whose overt psychotic symptoms ameliorated with time and the advent of tranquillizing drugs. As the hospital environment more and more became the only environment in which he could imagine living, he half-consciously built a life for himself there that would maximize his comfort and minimize his chance of undergoing stress, that is, facing the outside world again. He became a messenger and performer of small errands for two hospital buildings that housed chronic patients who were physically ill. The professional staff of the buildings where he worked was medically oriented and paid no particular attention to the anomaly of this patient's apparently high level of performance of his errands and his presence as a patient in a nearby chronic ward of physically active patients. The personnel of his own ward of residence, on the other hand, rarely saw him and simply assumed that his illness remained active, while not interfering with his daily work assignment. In short, Mr. F. proved to be a master at manipulating his own image so that his supports were prolonged and his comfort maximized. Only when the recent (in the past five years) move to clear out the mental hospitals occurred did a searching psychiatric assessment reveal how well he was performing his tasks. The state where he lived was fortunate in having a carefully planned housing project for older people, one of whose purposes was to mix community-resident elderly in need of housing with elderly discharged mental hospital patients. Mr. F. was extremely resistant to the idea of leaving the place that had been home for him for so long. In spite of the fact that his bed was in a room with six other people, that he was allowed only three shower times per week, and had to make do with "state" clothes from a common bin, his feeling of well being was maintained by the predictable, protected atmosphere of the institution. In actual fact, he had no choice about leaving, in the wave of mass transfers. In his case, unlike many others who moved out to nonhospital locations, he was lucky. After a period of anxiety and seclusiveness he gradually expanded for himself the range of his movement. Eventually, he came to be able to appreciate the ability to smoke a better brand cigarette, the less institutional meals, and the self-chosen clothes his welfare allotment provided.

In Mr. F.'s case the prescription was clearly one that raised the level of challenge offered by the environment. Intervention—meddling, if you will, in a somewhat clumsy way—by professionals was accomplished so that the challenge stayed within the limits he could tolerate.

4. Low Competence–High Challenge   The other problem situation is one where the individual seems deliberately to choose more stress than he is equipped to deal with. Frequently this is done by people whose lives have been characterized by a high degree of independence and espousal of the virtues of self-reliance. It is very important to remember that today's older generation looked upon work, achievement, and independence as the ultimate personal goals. This generation, in its encounters with emigration to a new country, with social stratification more rigid than we experience today, and with the rigors of economic deprivation culminating in the great depression of the 1930s, is perhaps the least inclined to accept the appropriate and necessary dependencies of old age. Sudden loss of income, or especially the onset of ill health, may be intolerable to the self-images of many of these older people.

The result may be that they cling inappropriately to a life style that is self-defeating, either because their basic needs cannot be accommodated, or because their behavior is no longer adequate and keeps reminding them of their failures.

Mrs. G. was "discovered" by a social worker who happened to be walking on her day off through an automobile dump in a rural area. Mrs. G.'s face was visible through the window of an abandoned school bus, and the social worker quickly realized from the steps, curtains, and hanging wash that this was home for the lady. On investigation, Mrs. G. was found to be undernourished, with a number of untreated medical conditions. She had lived year-round in the bus for several years after having been evicted from her room in the nearby town for nonpayment of rent. She occasionally received a check from a niece in another state, but had no other income. The owner of the dump tolerated her presence and gave occasional but undependable assistance. She heated the bus with a small space heater in the winter, and with great effort scavenged the remainder of her livelihood. Although she was somewhat depressed, she was not hostile to the social worker and eventually was able to be persuaded to use a welfare allotment on a room in a small community where her needs were considerably better provided for.

The prescription here was clearly for more support. Was Mrs. G.'s life in her bus self-defeating? Certainly, in the sense that her life was threatened! The picture is not so clear from the point of view of her psychological adjustment. Her depression was at least partially due to her poor food supply. Walking and lifting constituted unpleasant tasks for her, and she was as cold as anyone else would be in freezing temperatures with inadequate heat and clothing. On the other hand, her day was filled with tasks that were very clearly "meaningful"—quite an understatement! Mrs. G. represents one of those puzzling people for whom the provision of more support seems mandatory; yet there was a great risk of destroying her sense of purpose by moving her to a comfortable surrounding.

There are other people who will consciously or unconsciously choose an environment that is too challenging for them on the assumption that others will take care of them. As contrasted with the anxious dependence of the competent person who chooses a sustaining environment, this behavior is deliberately manipulative. The psychologist might call this behavior sociopathic—the use of others to further one's own needs without regard for the wishes and rights of others. Again, it is difficult to draw the line between what is "normal" manipulative dependency and what is inappropriate enough to be countered by professional intervention. The question of screening applicants for housing will be discussed at greater length later on. However, a frequent situation where the older person, her family, and her physician may conspire in this kind of manipulation is in the effort to obtain admission to a housing project without revealing the existence of a physical or mental condition that might otherwise disqualify the person. There are, certainly, instances when the professional had to intervene to prevent the creation of a situation of excessive dependence, whether to protect the aged individual or the state of well-being of the social environment in which the person may move.

These, then, are two problem situations where the individual may make the wrong decision about where he belongs, and where the intercession of a professional, a service, or a prosthetic environment may be in order. We also see that the two unusual but ideal matching situations require the continued provision of challenging or sustaining environments. The great majority of people fit into none of these extreme matching or mismatching situations, but ideally would find modest satisfaction living with their limitations and enjoying the moderate stimulation and the moderate support that the average life situation gives—if, that is. The "if" is a big one, familiar to blacks, Indians, Appalachia residents, mental defectives, and other disadvantaged groups, in addition to the aged. The "if" refers to the availability of choice by the person, typically not extended to underdog individuals. Too often, even if services are designed to counteract some of the inequities, they are tailored to fit only one kind of person, frequently the kind the service deliverer *hopes* to give service to. Thus, occupational therapy services frequently are beamed primarily to people who have learned during earlier life that artsy-craftsy activities are acceptable, and not to the working class male; the social life of a senior center is geared to large group activity and not to the retiring person who can interact only one a one-to-one basis; or the housing environment is designed to offer some choice to the person, such as which floor of a high-rise he occupies, but not a choice of the supportive services he utilizes.

Great financial and manpower resources are required to provide an adequate array of facilities from which the older person can choose. Some specialization is required in the interest of efficiency, but far too often the need for diversity is not seen by planners and workers even when diversity is possible. In short, older people's independence can be prolonged simply by making many different types of environments available to them. Their own extraordinary capacity to cope with life would stay much better-exercised this way than in the case of the model where a single type of service is provided into which people of greatly diverse needs must be fitted.

The foregoing general principles will be discussed more concretely later as they relate to housing specifically.

PART TWO

The Planning
and Designing Phase

chapter 4

Is there a need for a new project in your area?

The success of most housing developments for the elderly would seem to make the title of this chapter almost an academic question. However, there are a number of factors that may affect the need of a community for new housing, and they are worth some attention at this point. The issues discussed here relate primarily to need, rather that to economic feasibility from the viewpoint of the sponsor. The economic considerations will have to be discussed by others more expert in these matters.

However, the question of need is intimately related to the financial status of the potential tenant. Very plainly, older people with comfortable incomes have wide ranges of choice as to where and how they live. It seems reasonable to suppose that an adequate income can buy or rent housing on the open market that has many of the desirable features that we try to build into our specially planned housing for the elderly: labor-saving conveniences, safe location, proximity to community facilities, and so on. In addition, open-market housing may spontaneously become housing for the elderly. Many new high-rise buildings in urban locations attract older people disproportionately, so that the advantages of living near people one's own age are added to those mentioned previously.

Nevertheless, the obvious success of much housing built for the high-income elderly attests to the strong need for good planned living among the affluent aged in spite of the many options open to this group. Adequate figures are not available to determine whether the percentage of affluent aged who choose age-segregated planned housing differs from the percentage of middle- and lower-income people who choose similar housing under free-choice conditions. We do have to assume that the need for this type of housing continues to be strong, however, seeing how rapidly new centers fill.

It is of interest to look at the federal government's experience with the 231 program—its major high-income housing program. As was mentioned previously, the failure rate among profit corporations was far greater than among religious organization sponsors. There may be purely economic explanations of this difference in success. However, one major reason for the financial success of the religious organizations may be their commitment to service as well as to balancing the books—really good service apparently sells well. In spite of the basic contradiction of a service organization's expending so much energy in serving the elite, as most 231 sites do, the fact is incontrovertible that the environments provided in "nonprofit" retirement centers are superb in both sustaining and enriching the lives of their tenants. This commitment cannot help but make a difference in the ability of such a project to maintain occupancy. The cooperative, where the tenants actually own both their own property and the organization that provides maintenance, services and activities, has a similar capacity to attract a steady flow of occupants through offering good service.

In summary, the mere existence of a variety of open-market alternatives for living has not prevented planned housing for wealthy older people from also being successful. The most important consideration seems to be the quality of living provided. There is no indication that the market ceiling for good housing has been reached. In fact, the coming years will no doubt bring an increased proportion of the elderly who can afford relatively luxurious living. Our hope is that profit-oriented sponsors can learn from the successful nonprofit sponsors' experience and ultimately assume the major part of the task of serving the affluent in a humane and mutually beneficial way, leaving the nonprofit sponsors more free to develop their expertise among people in greater economic need.

The evidence is clear that among the major segment of the older population whose income is low to moderate, there is a great need for good housing. While the percentage wishing new housing is not impressive (on the basis of several researchers' estimates, an average of around 25 percent of elderly people state that they would like to move, or are dissatisfied with their present housing), the numbers are very high. Knowing the very strong tendency of all people, but especially the elderly, to express overt satisfaction with whatever their present situation is, there is no question that this percentage represents a minimal estimate of need. At our Center, we studied intensively a group of elderly Jews who had lived in a strong urban ethnic community most of their adult lives. The area had relatively recently moved downhill economically and developed a very high crime rate, so that most of the original residents had moved away. The inappropriateness of this situation for the elderly was very clear, and here there was no question: 88 percent would like to move if various realistic barriers were removed. Similarly, Drs. Maurice Hamovitch and James Peterson at the University of Southern California have found some evidence suggesting that the need for new planned housing is greater among older people with few immediate family ties. Thus, the amount of housing dissatisfaction varies greatly according to the situation.

Let us accept the conservative estimate of the percentage of older people who actively wish new housing as 20 percent. In numerical terms this is four million people. We may contrast this number with the 600,000 who now live in specially planned housing for the elderly, by the best estimates now available. Plainly, there is plenty of room for new recruits to both planned housing and nonplanned but improved housing in ordinary communities.

CHARACTERISTICS ASSOCIATED WITH NEED

Deprived Urban Neighborhoods Every urban area has neighborhoods such as the formerly Jewish area that we studied. Unquestionably, the size of the pool of potential applicants in such urban centers is relatively high, though perhaps not so high as the 88 percent of our subjects who said they would like to move. As everyone knows, despite the grim dissatisfaction of many people with their living situation, they will resolutely resist the attempts of "better-informed" relatives, social workers, or friends to get them to leave. Innumerable reasons will be found by some older people for not accepting a new home. Thus, the mere presence of poor elderly living in an urban slum will not guarantee filling a new project quickly.

Social Deprivation Planned housing now in operation serves far more than its share of older people living alone. The greater death

Fig. 1. Many older people are reluctant to move from a familiar neighborhood despite its many disadvantages.

rate among males assures the gross overrepresentation of widows in such housing, and widowers and never-married people of both sexes are disproportionately housed here, as compared to their number in the country's population as a whole. Whether in single-person households or not, many older people are attracted to planned housing for the elderly because it offers the promise of contact with other people. For some, housing is seen as therapy for loneliness and a sense of isolation. For others, the social contact simply adds an extra positive dimension to their lives. In any case, unquestionably where there are more physically or psychologically isolated older people there will be a greater housing need. Whether one can identify the existence of such people in a way to help plan whether housing is needed in a community is another matter. It is clear that inner-city areas have more such people residing in them. One of the most familiar findings from older social research is the likelihood of finding more isolated people of all kinds, including elderly, as one moves closer to the central business district of a city. Older suburbs will increasingly present a similar problem.

Geographic Location   In addition to the central-city geographic clustering of isolated older people, some sections of the country have greater concentrations of older people than others. In Florida, for example, 14.5 percent of the population is 65 and over, as contrasted with the national average of 9.9 percent. This figure may be compared to Nevada and New Mexico which have elderly populations of only 6 and 7 percent.

There are, of course, definite "retirement areas" in the country. Migration to a favorable climate or to a location where living costs are relatively low (the two phenomena sometimes occur together) has increased over the years of this century, and in some instances has markedly affected the age composition of the population of whole states such as Florida. In other states, such as California and Arizona, significant in-migration by the elderly has occurred in certain areas, but because of the relative "youth" of the state in historical development, the proportion of elderly remains below the national average.

With the exception of the retirement areas, there has thus far been relatively little tendency for specially designed housing for the elderly to be built in proportion to the elderly population of the larger geographic areas. Thus far, local custom and political orientations appear to have been more important determinants of where such housing is built. Though there probably will come a time when the states or regions with high proportions of elderly who have not built significantly for older people will catch up, for the time being, census figures on age for states or large portions of states do not provide an adequate guide to housing need. On a municipal or county level, however, the existence of an aged population whose proportion is significantly higher than that of the national average— say 12 percent of more—may be taken as one of several criteria for assessing need.

Retirement areas will, of course, have high proportions of elderly residents. Almost all such areas have already built disproportionate numbers (with respect to the rest of the country) of 231, 202, cooperative, and privately financed senior housing, as well as public housing, where the local political situation favored it. At least in the case of low or lower-middle income housing there is as yet no indication that the market is saturated in these areas.

Rural and Small-Town Residence We know too little about the style of life of older people living in rural areas. We have mentioned previously that they appear to be environmentally deprived, but perhaps somewhat compensated by stronger social networks. The problems of location of housing environments where people are not clustered as in cities are substantial, and we have too little knowledge as yet to suggest what indications of low or high housing need one may look for in those areas.

As a national phenomenon, 202 and 236 housing is strongly oriented toward medium-sized and large metropolitan areas. However, exceptions are very important to note. Iowa, for example, has a relatively large number of 202 projects, located in towns and small cities. These have been financially viable, and it may be of interest to prospective sponsors to learn from some of these operations how they have gone about the process of recruiting tenants. Low-rent public housing has also proved its value in rural and small-town locations in many states. In Texas, for example, the 1970 HUD directory of public housing lists 288 projects in 121 different localities. Of these, 146 projects contained less than 20 units each that were specially designated for the elderly. The availability of federal funds for building in these predominantly rural areas has uncovered the strong need for public housing and has proven the feasibility of providing such housing in small quantities. Other federal programs discourage or prohibit building projects with so few units. It is time for HUD to give specific attention to the study of this type of housing as provided by public housing authorities, with a view toward developing ways to enable local nonprofit groups and small housing authorities in other parts of the country to do the same. Clearly, there will be few large-scale projects that can succeed in the Great Plains, but smaller developments that do not require people to move far from their lifetime homes ought to be possible, given federal expertise and willingness to subsidize if necessary.

In any case, before assuming a need that can be translated into successful recruitment in sparsely settled areas, very concrete information will be required. This may mean a formal survey of the potential applicant pool, possibly done through volunteers using a standardized interview. For anyone planning housing, such a survey can provide valuable information. However, one must recognize that the real meaning of such survey data is not given by the number who say "yes" to a question like "if the Lions built a garden apartment development for older people in Zenity, would you like to live there?" One has to realize that many say that they are satisfied with what they have, or express a disbelief in the possibility that such a project could really eventuate. Others may say "yes" because it seems like a "nice idea" but would never dream of moving when the time comes. We estimate that even among people turning in preliminary applications for elderly housing half to two-thirds may never actually move in. Thus, it would seem, on the basis of an educated guess, that at least twice as many expressions of interest in becoming a tenant should be found on a preplanning survey as the number of units to be considered. Appendix 4 gives some sample questions that may be useful in assessing housing need and potential interest in moving into such housing.

Membership in Sponsoring Organization The local organization has a readymade pool of potential occupants in its aged members and relatives of members. The larger this number, obviously, the more tenants the sponsor can count on. However, it is most unusual for any sponsor to be able to count on a majority of its tenants being recruited from among its own members. The rule is, in fact, that very small proportions of their members will be tenants. We do not have good research data on this question, but one city affords three illustrative examples. One project is sponsored by a major union and has a reasonably good location, but it began occupancy with about 15 percent of its tenants being retired union members. Another major union sponsored housing in an excellent center-city location, near a long-standing and successful union health center and senior activity center. Somewhat more than half of its original tenants were union members. Finally, a flourishing Mediterranean ethnic community group opened a project in a very desirable center-city location about 15 blocks north of its home neighborhood of ethnic concentration. Much to the chagrin of the sponsors, very few of its members applied; at one point early in its history, 90 percent of its tenants were Jewish! Thus, one must have definite assurance of the likelihood of obtaining tenants from outside one's own organization.

Subgroup Membership   There is some evidence that planned housing is especially attractive to Jewish older people. The recruitment of minority elderly will be discussed later, but it may be mentioned here that rents are generally too high for any large percentage of the deprived minorities—black, Spanish-speaking, or American Indian—to be able to pay themselves, aside from public housing or the rent-supplement program. On the other hand, the presence of these people in large numbers in public housing suggests that the need is strong and that economic considerations, rather than personal preference, may limit their presence in private-nonprofit housing.

Special Need Situations   We shall probably never again see urban renewal involving such mass disruption as took place in the decades following the Second World War. However, the need for relocation on a smaller scale will always be with us. This situation may frequently occur in areas of high concentration of older people. Plans for demolition are generally made far enough in advance to give an authority or sponsoring organization time to include the relocatees in their plans. Any news of impending renewal should alert agencies to determine the numbers of older people who might be affected and to begin thinking in terms of building or rehabilitating housing for them.

Another special need situation involves serving the discharged mental hospital patient. Unfortunately, many projects take a dim view of considering such people as tenants. However, a growing number of patients whose problems include lack of practice in social skills, rather than active psychiatric symptoms, are being discharged into the community. Ohio has adopted a most creative approach to serving these patients in building "Golden Age Villages" in Toledo and Columbus. These are public housing projects built under the public housing authority and operated by them, with the joint sponsorship of the state mental health office. The projects are located on busy streets at the edge of mental hospital grounds, yet far enough removed from other hospital buildings to avoid "infection" from the mental hospital atmosphere. The majority of tenants come through the normal housing authority rental channels, but a substantial minority are elderly dischargees from the hospital. The city recreation department provides an activity program, and the hospital provides regular mental health and other services, in a most unobtrusive way. This is a most successful model which deserves serious consideration.

Another special-service group is seen in the physically handicapped tenants of the Highland Heights public housing project in Fall River, Massachusetts. This project has an intimate association with the neighboring local hospital, so that not only is full outpatient care made specially available to tenants, but also sheltered care is provided within the housing site, in the form of visiting nurse, homemaker, and other services.

ESTIMATING NEED FROM NATIONAL DATA

A gross estimate of local need may be attempted by taking account of the locality-specific factors previously described and going on to determine how closely the planned-housing stock of the community approximates the national average. The estimated 600,000 specially planned units in the country as a whole average out to about 30 per 1000 elderly population, considering people of all income levels. Furthermore, in 1971 there were 125 on waiting lists for 202 and public housing for every 100 tenants. Thus, one might suggest a minimum-need rate among the elderly living in similar geographic areas as in the neighborhood of 70 units per 1000 elderly population, with need being highest in the lower-income groups. It is probable that rural and sparsely settled areas of the country would have considerably less need than this, however. Waiting-list size can be taken as only a rough approximation of need, of course. The growth of possibilities is likely to accelerate demand in the near future. There is good reason to feel that many older people in need of housing simply do not apply because they are discouraged by the

Estimating Need for New Housing

Indicators of High Need	Indicators of Low Need	Comments
High local concentration of elderly		National average: 9.9% of U.S. population is 65 or over.
Many high-income elderly		Housing costs of $300 per month require $12,000 annual income.
Many middle-income elderly		Nonprofit sponsor with long-term management commitment required.
Many low-income elderly		Near-poverty single-person income for 1973 = $2800. Monthly rental = $60 for this income. Major subsidy required (public housing, rent supplement, housing allowance, Section 23 leased housing).
High general population density. City-center land available	Sparse population (rural, small town)	Sparse population requires smaller project, careful determination of old people's willingness to move.
Many elderly single-person households		Possible need for more supportive environment than in case of couples.

Traditional retirement area	All income levels, but probable selective appeal to higher-income groups.
Poor condition of local housing stock	Rehabilitation as an alternative to new construction.
High-crime area	Location, security, and access of increased importance.
High concentration of aged members of sponsoring organization	However, % tenants who are members is usually quite low.
High Jewish elderly concentration	Some evidence of selective appeal of planned housing to Jewish subgroup (all income levels).
High black elderly concentration	Blacks constitute 7% of aged population in U.S. Black aged have lowest income and require high subsidy level.
Large waiting lists for existing senior housing	Vacancies or small waiting lists — Estimated average list = 125% of filled units.
High demand revealed by consumer survey	Caution required in projecting actual application flow from preference survey data.

size of current waiting lists. There is always attrition from any application or waiting list, however, which would offset to some extent the underestimation of need.

The foregoing comments have been necessarily general, based more upon social science than upon really concrete and sometimes all-important economic considerations. For pragmatic planning there is no substitute for an extended series of conversations with business and real estate leaders, the local and regional planning commission, and people with experience in giving geriatric services, especially those who are already engaged in housing operations. Finally, for most sponsors, a housing consultant will be necessary—almost no one else has the assembled expertise to put together all of these sources of information to lead to a decision that melds the social objectives of a housing program with economic and bureaucratic realities.

chapter 5

Locating a
housing environment

Most of the nation's mental hospitals were built in the serene countryside, on the theory that a retreat from the noise, demands, and clutter of the city would be therapeutic. Although many institutions for the elderly have been built with the same thought in mind, housing is new enough to have escaped the worst of this quietistic push. However, decisions regarding location are still apt to be made capriciously or opportunistically, partly because of general lack of knowledge regarding what is desirable. Our ignorance is still notable, but we do have some mistakes and some successes of others to guide us. One thing is certain: we shall rarely have the ideal site. Thus, rather than trying to specify only the ideal, we shall attempt to speculate on the consequences that might follow if one compromise or another is made. The entire physical design process involves many such tradeoffs, a matter with which design professionals are very familiar. The other matter we shall concern ourselves with is ways whereby compensations for various undesirable situations can be programmed.

THE BASIC QUESTION: URBAN, SUBURBAN, SMALL-TOWN, OR RURAL LOCATION?

Sometimes an organization really has wide latitude of choice of location. Many sponsors have begun with a given amount of available money and have had to decide how to balance off the lower cost of land outside the city with the corresponding loss in range of facilities available as one goes further away from the center of the city. This question has been considered to some extent in the previous chapter. In this context, however, it is the effect on the tenants, rather than the marketability of the housing, that concerns us. The most successful rural housing environments that I have seen are those that are wealthy enough to build within their own perimeters those facilities that might be available in more urban areas. Stores, barbershop, beauty shop, snack bar, dry cleaning, church, medical service, and some organized recreation are only the most basic. The most flourishing would add specialty stores, infirmary, swimming pool, repair service, domestic services, and so on. In short, the burden is really on the rurally located project to bring in all of the required services. Since most services are bound to have relatively low utilization rates, this could be prohibitively expensive.

On the other hand, a town does not have to be very large to contain enough of those basic services to suffice for most tenants's needs. The fact is that every observer of the scene of housing for the elderly is likely to be surprised by how few tenants use whatever local facilities are available. The percentage that utilizes various resources varies widely, but except for medical care, a small grocery, and perhaps a church, the majority will be nonusers. Therefore, building in locations that add successively more of such facilities will certainly be adding general enrichment, but to a successively smaller additional proportion of tenants. Thus, the planner will have to decide whether he will build for the bare minimum of enrichment, for the maximum, or somewhere in between. The needs of his potential target population would probably be one major determinant of where on the local-enrichment continuum he would locate his project. A cosmopolitan, urbane elderly group would contain more people who would feel deprived in a resource-sparse location, where people used to low availability of facilities, low levels of environmental complexity, and much free time might not be bothered so much. In any case, since only a minority will spontaneously participate in many of these activities, a major operational problem is likely to be that of encouraging the use of what facilities there are.

The suburbs vary widely in their suitability for housing the elderly. Frequently even the basic physician–store–church are less accessible there than in a small town. Part of the rationale for suburban growth has been to keep wide physical boundaries between commercial and residential facilities, so that much land that might be used for housing for the elderly is miles from any store. Add to this the fact that public transportation has been unable to survive in many suburbs, and you may well pause before leaving the bustle of the city.

Good suburban locations may be found, however, since some land use patterns may make local approval easier to obtain near commercially zoned areas, where shopping and recreation are within walking distance.

Mrs. Marie McGuire Thompson, the Department of Housing and Urban Development's former long-time advocate for the elderly, has suggested that the possibility of building housing for the elderly in new suburban shopping centers be considered. The option of window shopping has become more and more difficult to provide outside of center-city areas. The shopping center provides not only the shopping facility, but also the chance to watch activity of other people. Mrs. Thompson suggests that developers be approached by prospective sponsors regarding their willingness to include an area with protected access to house the elderly. Such a location would do much to counteract the growing risk that the next generation's elderly will be prisoners in their suburban single-family homes. Planners have already acknowledged the desirability of building into these new shopping center areas a population that will be physically present beyond shopping hours—that is, hotels, apartment houses, theaters, and so on—and housing for the elderly would constitute a welcome addition to this population.

Some sponsors are bound to receive as a gift acreage in the far reaches of the metropolitan area, or to be unable to resist a bargain. What then? The sponsor should as a bare minimum insure that a genuine store operate on the premises, that a pool of physicians' names (willing to make house calls) be maintained, and that enough administrative support be given to maintain a weekly religious service and a weekly recreational function. Many isolated projects, if they do anything about shopping, handle it as an infrequent emergency need, and may provide only an undependable volunteer shopper service or an equally undependable volunteer driver service. If this is really all that is possible, it is better than nothing, but for a relatively small additional expense and effort it is possible to maintain a buying club, cooperative, or marginally profitable house-supported store. The opportunity to look over even a very small stock, to buy after choosing, and to see other people while doing these

Fig. 1. A small store on the site not only provides a basic resource for the tenant, but also encourages social interaction among tenants and among age groups. (Photo by Sam Nocella.)

things, is far more satisfying than having others take primary responsibility for one's shopping. Every sponsor who does not have such a store within easy walking distance should look carefully to find some way of maintaining a genuinely functioning store on his site.

A possible consequence of being in an isolated location with few on-site facilities is that the project may differentially recruit people with few outside interests, or those who are at one and the same time too limited in competence to miss the outside facilities and too passive to be concerned about the lack of on-site facilities. This factor should be borne in mind in selecting people for admission (see Chapter 10, Initiation into tenanthood).

LOCATIONAL CRITERIA AND URBAN FACILITIES

Most housing sites are urban because that is where the aged population lives. Thus, the least that can be said for locating in a city is that there is an assured need. Sites in cities are scarce, however. Over the years during which the federal public housing program has operated, all too frequently sites have been located on land that was deemed worthless for anything else, or in demolition areas where conditions were not right for more expensive housing redevelopment. Location with respect to service facilities is thus only one aspect of the problem.

Since relatively small proportions of the elderly drive, walking becomes increasingly their main source of transportation. This is particularly true for the low-income group and for women, who are greatly overrepresented in housing for the elderly. There has been great interest among planners in ideal distances from housing to various facilities. The planner Paul Noll, then with the Philadelphia Housing Authority, asked a number of public housing managers what they considered the limits of this distance to be. The following results were obtained*:

Facility	Critical distance
Grocery store	2–3 blocks
Bus stop	1–2 blocks
House of worship	¼ to ½ mile
Drug store	3 blocks
Clinic or hospital	¼ to ½ mile
Bank	¼ mile
Library	1 mile
News-cigar store	¼ mile
Restaurant	¼ to ½ mile
Movie house	1 mile

* From Niebanck, P. L. *The elderly in older urban areas*. Philadelphia: University of Pennsylvania, Institute for Environmental Studies, 1965, p. 65.

Fig. 2. Proximity to a few basic services fosters continued engagement with the world outside the housing site.

These distances were not obtained from tenants, nor related in any way to tenant behavior, but they have been frequently cited as guides to practice. Since they are merely the opinions of administrators, great caution is in order in accepting these distances literally. On the other hand, in the absence of information relating amount of actual use to distance, the list may be useful as a rough guide to planning.

It may also be useful to know the most usual frequency with which older people in 12 urban housing sites studied by the Philadelphia Geriatric Center performed various tasks:

Eat at a restaurant	Less than once a month
Read	2 hours per day
Watch TV	3 hours per day
Leave the neighborhood	2–4 times per week
Sits outdoors (good weather)	3 hours per day
Leaves the site	5 times per week
Shops	2 times per week
Uses public transportation	"Not at all" (most frequent response); of all who ever use it: 1–2 times per month

It is by no means certain that closeness to these and other facilities will insure high use. It is, however, certain that increasingly greater distance will bar increasing numbers of people from ever using the given facility.

There is a great variety of compensatory mechanisms for greater-than-ideal distance to essential services. Perhaps the most important (in rural, small-town and suburban, as well as urban settings) is transportation. Much has been written about transportation prob-

Fig. 3. Proximity to transportation is a basic necessity. This elevated train stop presents a major barrier to tenants in a nearby project by virtue of its steps and obvious security threat.

lems of the elderly. An obvious conclusion from some of the research is that the automobile is the most satisfactory method for those who are physically and financially capable of maintaining driver status. Being transported in someone else's car is also a frequent solution, although the dependence on others causes both realistic and psychological difficulties. Those who use public transportation most often are most critical of it. Various problems associated with public transport include:

- Sparse geographic coverage
- Infrequent scheduling
- Increasingly high fares
- Unpleasant waiting conditions
- Danger of physical attack while walking to stops
- Difficulty mounting the vehicle
- Uncomfortable ride
- Inadequate information and orientational aids

Despite such difficulties, nearness of housing to public transportation can make all the difference in the world to the richness of experience in the life of an aged tenant. Thus, if an area has any public transportation, this would seem to be one of the most critical locational criteria. The actual walking distance that can be tolerated is not only a matter of the physical condition of the older person, however. Where the weather tends to be generally good, the terrain flat, the landscape pleasant, and the neighborhood safe, tolerable walking distance can be longer.

Relatively little has been done in mobilizing the more active and independent tenants of a project to form a helping agency for their less independent neighbors. There is national political support for the general idea of volunteer, as opposed to governmental, welfare efforts, and for a while the prospects seem good for federal funding of projects that attempt to utilize tenants for assistance in such activities as transportation, shopping, home care, and so on, for other tenants.

Other devices may be utilized in compensating for facilities that are lacking. A clerk may be saddled with the extra task of keeping a supply of stamps to sell to tenants. A check-cashing agency or bank messenger may be persuaded to make a regular on-site call on

Social Security day. The now-famous Grey Panther group in Philadelphia, led by Miss Margaret Kuhn, held a confrontation with a bank president to demonstrate the direct relationship between the bank's offering free checking accounts to older people and their freedom from risk of attack after cashing their Social Security checks. A tenant council with no budget at all may still put on a full year's program with films obtained free from public libraries and commercial publicity offices. Bookmobiles will make stops at a housing project, sometimes with special audio and visual materials for the handicapped. Dispensing machines for snacks, newspapers, or cigarettes may be installed. The moral is clear: if a remote location is necessary but would result in the deprivation of life-sustaining or life-enriching opportunities, it is incumbent on the sponsor to seek some alternative means of taking the tenant to the facility or the facility to the tenant.

NEIGHBORHOOD LOCATIONAL CRITERIA

Just as important as service facilities are the social aspects of location, which are primarily what is meant when we say "neighborhood." The most salient social aspect where older people are concerned is the safety or the crime level of the neighborhood. Recent studies of older people in high-crime areas have demonstrated the lowering of morale and the eroding of self-maintaining and self-actualizing behavior that arises when older people live here robbery, burglary, mugging, and worse crimes are frequent. Although the actual incidence of such crimes may be relatively low, the older person is more vulnerable than others, and the psychological effect of a single publicized crime in inestimably great. Realization of the problems involved in building in the inner city has made both HUD and sponsors very cautious about the choice of location for new housing for the elderly. Some details of design that may compensate for the risk of a bad location will be considered later (Chapter 7, Designing the Building).

Closely related to the search for a "safe" area is the search for locations that will foster integration and service to diverse groups of people. Too frequently, the crime problem and other social disorganization exist acutely in ethnic areas of the city whose century-old neglect has produced almost insoluble problems. Before the housing

Fig. 4. Too much public housing is located in areas showing the results of vandalism, physical deterioration, and crime.

moratorium of 1973, in an effort to encourage mixing of minority and majority groups, HUD made it very difficult to get approval of a site for federally aided housing where the probability of occupancy by a single ethnic or racial group exists.

In practice, this resulted in a disappointing and unfortunately increasing number of unsuccessful efforts to locate public housing in white or middle-income areas, and many HUD disapprovals of projects located in black areas. As will be indicated in Chapter 6, it seems clear that the battle to penetrate white impacted areas has to be fought relentlessly. However, it also seems very clear that there is now, and will continue to be, such a major need for housing by minority-group aged as to justify the concurrent building of projects in areas where few whites may choose to apply. In addition to the need being very great, there is also strong justification for the right of a black sponsor to build in a location that will maximally serve the black community, even if there is little hope for recruiting many white tenants. Finally, as long as there is a need and some blacks prefer to live in all-black projects, it seems impossible to refuse to build them. Unquestionably, aged blacks who live in high-crime areas in deteriorated housing are at much greater risk of assault than they would be living in the same area but in an organized housing environment with its many protections.

We shall deal later in the chapter on housing design with some structural compensations for lack of neighborhood security. Here, we need to emphasize the importance of considering security a normal part of operational costs. If one must build where security is poor, guards must be hired. Again, tenants themselves may augment security. My social worker colleague, Mrs. Elaine Brody, has described an apartment dwelling in New York City whose 70-and-over tenants maintain a rotating lobby guard of four elderly ladies until midnight every night. A marauder would have no trouble overpowering them physically, but the sight and potential sound of the four guardians constitute a potent deterrent to a mugger.

Crime is, of course, by no means the only consideration involved in neighborhood choice. A sponsor may have strong positive reasons for wishing to locate in an ethnically or racially concentrated neighborhood. The local church may wish to facilitate its own elderly parishoners becoming the core of its tenant population. Had the Mediterranean ethnic group, described earlier, built its housing in the ethnic area rather than in the city center, it would undoubtedly have served a larger proportion of its own group. To our way of thinking, there should be room for any sponsor to take as his first goal that of serving its members who are known to be in need, since experience has shown that no project is likely to achieve an occupancy level even as high as 50 percent of its own organization's members. On the other hand, *all* of our research evidence favors the idea that social relationships among different ethnic and racial groups are exceptionally good within a housing project limited to the elderly. Therefore, it should be incumbent upon the sponsor to actively seek

Fig. 5.(a)   A resource-poor site location.

Fig. 5.(b)   While one of the site's boundaries was once a retail area, resources have moved out.

Fig. 5.(c)   The residential surroundings are similarly devastated.

diversity, especially if his original neighborhood site choice results in an overrepresentation of one particular group.

Physical features of neighborhoods may sometimes be factors in site choice independent of crime or other neighborhood social characteristics. Areas where widespread condemnation or demolition has occurred may be especially threatening to older people if other types of community growth do not occur simultaneously. For the most part, retail development is a positive factor, but industrial, and some other commercial uses, such as used-car strips, wholesaler areas, and so on, are definite contraindications to location.

A single particularly usable feature may make up for some minuses. One of the sites we have studied was located two blocks from the boardwalk in an ocean resort. The boardwalk constituted the tenants' major living space for a good part of the year. They seemed perfectly willing to endure living in an area full of condemned buildings, marginal businesses, and razed blocks for a couple of years, with this unusual resource as compensation. A large shopping center being within walking distance makes most tenants willing to cope with traffic-crossing problems.

In general, proximity to a park is a decided asset. A good illustration of the effectiveness of a park in amplifying the meaningful activity of older people is the MacArthur Park area of Los Angeles. There are a number of inexpensive retirement hotels within a several-block radius of this park. Although not a large park, it is most varied, containing both flat and gently sloping terrain, a lake with ducks and swans, an amphitheater, a children's play area, benches located in sunny and shaded spots, sidewalks on the perimeter allowing the park occupant to watch either park or busy street activity, public restrooms, a game area with picnic tables and game equipment, a snack stand, and adequate surveillance by both police and park staff. Another favorite spot for older people is the area of benches on the narrow median strip of upper Broadway in Manhattan. The air may be bad and the scenery unexciting, but the high density of people and vehicles affords a constantly changing

Fig. 6. Location near a safe park is a decided asset. The provision of portable chairs for those who wish to seat themselves advantageously is a good investment. (Photo by Sam Nocella.)

show. One of Philadelphia's worst slum areas borders on the largest within-city park in the country. For the most part, timid people stay out of the park, but the short stretch that borders the area where many old people live is used heavily. Enough benches are clustered to encourage their use for social purposes, and a park guard occupies a small structure in the midst of the benches. Further, the structure contains a toilet, and there is a moderate amount of automobile and pedestrian traffic to create interest. Thus, security, interesting behavior to watch, and the availability of a toilet seem to be necessary features to make a location near a park work. Negative features would include heavy vegetation that could give cover to criminals, lack of surveillance, proximity of teenage gathering places, lack of seating, or lack of "action."

A housing environment can intervene to change a park. Many cities would be willing to make physical or administrative alterations in order to render an existing park more usable by the tenants of a newly built housing project.

Under many of today's conditions, proximity to a school could represent a hazard. People have speculated that older people would enjoy being able to watch a school play yard, or be close enough to be able to speak to children as they walk to school. This might represent wishful thinking, since many instances come to mind where harassment by a few children creates in tenants an overwhelmingly negative view of the children as a class. Under some conditions, as with a midcity New York building where an upper-floor lounge looks down upon a fenced playground of a nearby school, the effect can be positive. In this case, there is no ground-level outdoor seating for the elderly, so actual physical contact is impossible. In another creative solution, architect Louis Gelwicks of Gerontological Planning Associates, Santa Monica, California, is designing a combination nursery school and nursing home, building the two so as to be able to control totally the amount, type, and timing of interaction between the two groups. Again, an important aspect of his plan is provision of a glass wall through which the elderly may watch the children playing, but without physical access. In the more usual urban situation, however, a nearby school is likely to cause unwanted noise and make older people avoid outdoor spaces at school transit hours.

A close look should also be taken at the location in relation to delinquent teenager hangouts. Sometimes these spots can be altered by intervention of the police. Some business establishments may attract moderately undesirable, rather than criminal elements; they may be more difficult to deal with. This situation might, on occasion, be bad enough to veto a proposed site.

It goes without saying that many people choose a residential area for its climate. Thus, regions that are warm and low in humidity have an appeal that may be the deciding factor for some people. On the other hand, older people do live in every climate, and there is often great reluctance to move to a distant location simply for the climatic advantage.

A London group decided to build a retirement project in the seacoast town where many members had typically vacationed during their adult lives. To their surprise, very few of their London members were willing to make the move; to stay alive financially, they had to open up the project to the public. Thus, our general advice to a planning group is to stay local and resist the idea of appealing to the very low migration urge (or capability) that older people have.

Are there areas whose climatic or atmospheric conditions contraindicate building? The answer probably cannot be provided by looking only at how bad is the condition. If there are enough older people in the area with the resources to use a new housing environment, this will usually be a sufficient reason to decide to build. There may be some unusual conditions where a difference of a couple of miles may bring purer air, or less cold wind, and by all means extra effort should be made to choose the better condition. For the most part, however, it will be better for older people to live in good housing in a damp, polluted area than to live in bad housing in a damp, polluted area.

We know relatively little about the effect of terrain on the living habits of older people. Many physicians have praised San Francisco as a habitat for the elderly because the hills force them to maintain their muscular skills. However, data support neither these exercise advocates nor their opposite numbers, those who shudder at the thought of building on more than a 5 percent grade. Again, other things being equal, it is better to have no barrier for the marginal people who are forbidden to climb or too weak to do so. The project that is built on a 10–15 percent grade must realize that it should not accept physically marginal people as tenants, and that it might have to find earlier institutional arrangements for tenants whose health declines than they would if located on flat ground. On the other hand, it is also possible to design a structure or organize services so as to minimize such a barrier. A two-level domicile may allow the higher level to be used as an entrance and the lower as an exit, if the within-unit steps can be managed. One-way transportation to shopping areas is somewhat easier and possibly cheaper in man-hours to supply than two-way transportation, if the necessary route is too steep. The housing environment that is remote and therefore necessarily self-sufficient may not have to concern itself at all with the fact of being located on top of a mountain.

Without really knowing whether there is any change in response with age to the continuous presence of natural beauty in our surroundings, it is clear that older people in general look for such locations when choosing a residence and feel repeatedly reinforced in their pride over the setting as visitors come and admire the view. Traded off against a safe neighborhood, a dwelling unit with full plumbing, or easy availability of medical care, the visual esthetics of mountain, river, or lake may seem insignificant. In fact, there is some reason to think that for most people the beauty of their own dwelling unit, building, or immediate surroundings is far more important than the larger-scale environment. However, there will be some tenants especially sensitive to natural beauty. Coming generations of older people are likely to have learned a wider range of esthetic response than the current work-oriented generation, and especially to have become used to the idea of being able to exercise an option in choosing a visually satisfying larger environment. We have heard design discussions where doubt was expressed about whether the older tenants would even notice the eyesore cement factory in the middle of a view; this seems to represent age-stereotyped thinking at its worst. There probably are many more opportunities than we think to choose a location in such a way as to capitalize on its vista or topographical variations.

It seems hardly necessary to comment on natural hazards, which are usually apparent to everyone, and to which we frequently overreact by imposing more restriction than necessary on people's behavioral space. Obviously, sharp drops and deep water need railings; steep climbs need handrails and resting stages; heavy or unexpected

Site Location Criteria

Locational Characteristics	Advantages	Disadvantages	Comments
Urban	Near services, amenities Many potential tenants	High land cost Urban problems—crime, etc.	City-center location most likely to enrich life.
Suburban	Pleasant environs Moderate land cost High future need	Transportation poor Fewer services Amenities more dispersed	More suitable for higher-income people with better access to transportation and amenities.
Small town	Pleasant environs Low land cost High social integration	Must depend on drawing tenants from large radius Sparse services	Many successful projects in towns under 25,000.
Rural	Low land cost Few social problems	No services, amenities Distant from friends, relatives Ingrown social structure	Most successful rural locations provide complete service and amenity package—therefore, primarily for high income.
Middle- or high-income area	Many	Risk of community opposition	Federally assisted housing arouses anxiety about racial integration.
Racially impacted area	Potential tenants in great need High neighborhood familiarity	Potential crime risk Risk of racially homogeneous tenant population	Extra effort, as well as financial risk, necessary to insure racial mix. But even if tenants are homogeneous, it may be justified as improving housing for those in greatest need.

100

	Advantages	Disadvantages	Comments
Resort or retirement area	More social opportunities / Pleasant climate, scenery	Higher land cost / Requires relocation to unfamiliar area	Generally favorable experience with such housing
Proximity to retail shopping, services, enriching opportunities	Engagement with outer world facilitated	Few	Tenants willing to walk 4 to 8 blocks in safe neighborhoods.
Proximity to public transportation	Many	Few	If not within 2–4 blocks, housing should supply to important locations.
Industrial, nonretail commercial area	None	Security threat / Distant from services, amenities	
Much pedestrian traffic	Usually safer / Pedestrians interesting to watch	Some pedestrians may be security threat	Crime rate of area and security design of housing will usually determine if proximity to pedestrains is desirable.
School	Possible enriching resource / Encourages interaction of young and old	Source of noise, annoyance, security threat	College most likely to add to enrichment. Combination of high-crime area and nearby public school should be avoided.
Hospital or longterm care institution	Easy access to wide variety of medical services	Atmosphere of sickness	Housing should be located in physically separate area or block, or with visual divider like trees, etc.

Site Location Criteria (Continued)

Locational Characteristic	Advantages	Disadvantages	Comments
Park	Pleasant sitting and watching, social access, recreation	Sometimes a security threat	Most park areas near housing can be made secure by adequate surveillance.
Bar, liquor store	Few in US	Security threat	In high-crime areas, liquor stores may be scene of holdups.
Church, synagogue	Religious and social enrichment	None	One of the most utilized resources if 1–0 blocks distant.
Heavy automotive traffic		Safety threat	Coordination necessary with police and planning officials on traffic signals, speed and turn regulations.
Environmental barriers			Disqualifications: shopping area requiring unprotected traffic crossing. Steep grade necessary for access, in absence of transportation. Lack of sidewalks; slippery walks in winter.
Unusual resources	Mostly positive		Bodies of water; distant and nearby scenery; senior center; boardwalk.

traffic needs engineering for pedestrian use of the area. But some less obvious hazards may require foresight in planning. Cold weather combined with poor drainage may lead to slippery walks or traffic crossings that may immobilize both tenants and staff. Being in a local fog pocket produce sudden conditions that catch tenants unaware and make it difficult for them to get home from a trip off the site. Prevailing winds may interact with building design to produce a walkway unusable in cold weather, or a noise problem within the dwelling unit.

It has obviously not been possible to suggest a solution for every site difficulty. However, a project faced with an undesirable situation should look among its own resources and those of the local governmental and private agencies for help in neutralizing a natural hazard or amplifying an asset. It is necessary to think about the pluses and minuses together and weigh the possible net outcomes, rather than to look at a single aspect of siting without regard to other considerations. The same principles apply just as strongly to the other design problems to be considered, the designing of the social milieu, the service environment, the building and the dwelling unit.

chapter 6

Planning the scope of a program: whom shall the housing serve?

WHAT LEVEL OF HEALTH?

When the federally assisted housing programs were new, official policy stood strongly in favor of planning the housing as housing alone, without additional services. Part of the reason for this stance was financial. To give federal subsidies for supportive services was seen as offering opportunity for limitless demands on public funds. Thus, housing authorities and nonprofit sponsors were encouraged to some extent to seek local support for anything beyond the shelter aspect of housing. However, a more profound basis for discouraging on-site supportive services was seen in the desire to limit occupancy to fully independent older people. The idea was that since there were nursing homes, homes for the aged, and mental hospitals for the sick, the healthy segment with acute housing problems was the most needy target group. This viewpoint did not do justice to the fact that "health" and "independence" are very long continua, and that some older people move from the healthy toward the unhealthy side during the time they are living in planned housing.

In practice, many projects developed stringent criteria limiting admission to those people in excellent health. There were a large number of older people who were generally healthy, but whose mobility was limited somewhat, and who were therefore excluded as tenants. Many professionals in housing like to think of their own tenants as uniquely healthy (see Chapter 9 on the "Marine Sergeant" attitude), as contrasted with the sick old people elsewhere. Thus, a tendency to look at health as a desirable and sickness as an undesirable tenant quality developed, to the point where the administrator might be made very anxious by the presence of the marginally healthy tenant. One of the short sighted aspects of this rigidly defined policy favoring independence is that it made more difficult the handling of tenants whose health declined during the period of their residence. We still do not have a clear picture of how environments age; that is, do replacements of the original tenants tend to match the latter in health and other characteristics, do they tend to match the surviving original group, or are they less capable than either? Nevertheless, it is certain that some of those who age in such a community do decline in health and therefore require different treatment or a different environment from the one initially designed for the housing. Some managers respond to this situation by initiating the early transfer to other locations (to live with family or to an institution) of people who decline in health. Recent evidence showing the risk to life and health of relocating older people has made people justifiably cautious about moves where other alternatives are available. A cautious administrator may go far out of his way to prolong the time of residence, calling upon family, staff, and outside agencies to provide support when the tenant's personal competence threatens to fail.

Other administrators may concern themselves with redesigning the total environment so that organized, rather than inefficient individual stopgap, measures may be applied. Unfortunately, giving services requires space, and without prior planning, later changes may be difficult. Therefore, it is extremely important to think early about how many and what type of services may be included. If the decision is made not to include the service, there should at least be a hip-pocket plan available for the service *if* it is later wanted.

It is very important to realize that the decision about services will influence what type of tenant applies to the housing. Our own research has indicated that housing offering supportive services recruits tenants who are somewhat less independent than those who enter sites without services. This is no doubt caused partly by service-oriented housing sponsors' being willing to deal with the problems of people who need more than the average amount of support—they probably apply less stringent admission standards of physical and emotional health to applicants. On the other hand, it is certain also that people themselves are in general capable of searching among environmental opportunities and finding the environment that best suits their own level of competence. Thus, both sponsor and elderly tenant are likely to behave in a way that maximizes the congruence between the tenant population's competence and the level of support offered within the housing. The original decision regarding service level will therefore exert a major influence on the long-term character of the housing. If a sponsor is not willing to bear responsibility for tenants whose competence is less than average, he should build housing that offers apartments and social space, and count on devoting his energy toward maximizing the richness of the lives of his well-functioning older people. If he builds housing alone, he is certain to have to make more early, and painful, decisions to ask tenants who decline in capacity to seek other arrangements. It is incumbent on him to include in his brochures and early publicity some statement alerting potential applicants to the fact that continued occupancy is contingent on the maintenance of good physical health.

To make the decision to serve primarily the well is certainly the right of the sponsor. Good housing is just as legitimate for the independent as for the more dependent. Conversely, the sponsor who decides to provide extensive services must realize that he is obligating himself to keeping tenants for a longer time if they should decline in competence. In this case, more of the administrator's time will be taken in dealing with personal problems. It will certainly be more expensive to run such a housing environment. Yet, the need for such supportive environments is tremendous, and the number of reasonably priced projects offering services is still very small. A sponsor devoted to service or a housing authority with above-average local resources would be doing a great favor to older people of his community to build in services to meet the needs of an in-between population who might otherwise become institutionalized.

Some people argue that having such services available on the site increases the risk of inducing premature dependence and reducing the motivation of relatively competent older people to do things for themselves. One cannot dismiss this assertion lightly. Unquestionably, one way for an older person to keep busy is to cook for herself, care for her own apartment, dress up to go see her doctor, and so on. Some of our research seems to give some slight support to this point of view. We do definitely need to be able to identify which individuals may risk a decline in independence by virtue of being placed in an over-supportive environment. If we can identify whether such factors as recent bereavement, passive personality traits, or a radical involuntary change of environment are associated with susceptibility to decline after a move into a too-provident environment, we can then develop screening and counseling procedures to match the person better with her environment.

Having too many services available within the confines of the housing can also risk the establishment of a wall between the "inside" and the "outside." That is, an active in-house life may be established at the expense of tenants' maintaining normal contacts outside of the project. The casual encounters involved in shopping, going to a post office, or traveling to a movie are of inestimable value in maintaining an older person's practice in social and self-maintaining skills. The alternative to becoming ingrown is increased administrative vigilance in stimulating interchange between community and housing, rather than simply deciding not to have on-site services. The problems of maintaining this interchange will be addressed at greater length later.

Thus far, services have been discussed in general, as if they were all in the same category. Obviously they are not. First, it is worthwhile examining how older people themselves feel about these services. In our interviews with nearly 1000 older people who were tenants in senior housing without services, different types of service are viewed in very different fashion. Meals, medical services, transportation, housekeeping, and social services will be discussed.

Meal Services   Less than a quarter of the tenants studied by the Philadelphia Geriatric Center said that they would want to have regular full meal services in a common dining room, given the condition that it would cost them more to live there. Looked at from a somewhat different perspective, only a little over one-third of another large group of tenants said they would spend some money for meal services if they had an extra $20 per month. Given a chance to buy an inexpensive hot lunch when desired, however, about half of them would make use of this service. Among another group of 600 tenants living in housing projects where some form of meal service was provided, four out of five indicated that they would have moved to the project whether or not the meal service had been offered. Finally, while almost one-third of a group of older people waiting to move into housing without services said they would like meal services, when asked the same question after living there a year, only half as many would want them. Our thought is that living in the environment for that first year had given them ample opportunity to test their adequacy in providing for themselves, and that they felt reassured, therefore no longer feeling that they needed

Fig. 1. Full dining-room service provides for some people's social needs and helps extend the period of noninstitutional living for the marginally competent. (Photo by Sam Nocella.)

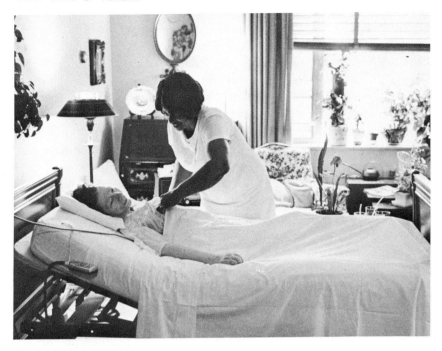

Fig. 2. Bedside medical services are not desired by most tenants, but for marginally independent tenants this option may afford a sense of security. (Photo by Richard Mowrey.)

the service. Thus, at least on a consumer-survey level, it seems clear that an on-site meal service is not the most important quality of a housing environment. However, there is a minority for whom the opportunity to have meals prepared for them is extremely important, and a much larger number who would like to have a small-scale communal eating opportunity. In addition, research has indicated that not all of those who utilize on-site meal services are the marginally competent for whom the service is genuinely supportive. There is also a tendency for people with strong social needs to utilize the communal-style meal as a social opportunity. These people may be quite independent and capable of preparing their own meals, but they find the ritual of eating with others, seeing others, being seen by others, or varying their environment, as being intrinsically satisfying.

Medical Services   These facts about meal services may be contrasted with a similar inquiry about on-site medical services. *More than half* of those surveyed would like some kind of clinic with regular hours of service by physician and nurse. Interestingly enough, unlike the decline in wish for meal services following occupancy, a year later the wish for medical services actually increased. In the trade-off situation, where they could choose to spend $20 per month extra on extra facilities of several different kinds, the strongest-voiced need was again for on-site medical facilities. *Less than 10 percent* of people presently living in facilities with such services would prefer not to have them in their building. When they where given a choice of type of medical facility, the clinic format was the most acceptable, although of those who wished any kind, almost a third thought some kind of infirmary for short-term care would also be desirable.

The meaning of this strong approval of medical services is very clear: elderly tenants gain a major sense of security from knowing that care is nearby if needed. Running counter to this conclusion, however, is the frequently observed opposite attitude that "this place isn't for sick people; it's for healthy independent people like me" (no matter that the speaker may be very feeble herself). Unquestionably, there is such a thing as a "sick" atmosphere that is depressing to the average tenant. Our research has inquired as deeply as possible into such attitudes. While the majority of tenants whose housing had some form of on-site medical services were tolerant of the presence of sick people, more than a quarter thought there were already too many living there. In our York House (a component of the Philadelphia Geriatric Center) many tenants could at one and the same time complain that they did not like having a special medical-care floor in their building while saying that they wouldn't want to get rid of it in case they should ever have to use it. Thus, we are left with considerable ambiguity regarding the real feelings of tenants about this very important issue.

Transportation   Dr. Frances Carp has referred to transportation as "the sleeper issue" of the 1971 White House Conference on Aging, noting that it attracted the attention of delegates to an extent far beyond its earlier presumed importance among the various possible services for older people. In our own work we began relatively recently to inquire about this service, and also found this need to be surprisingly strong among our national sample of older people already living in planned housing for the elderly. Transportation ranked second only to medical services among those for which our respondents would pay some of the hypothetical extra $20 per month.

Housekeeping We also inquired about housekeeping services and found up to half of some subject groups wishing this service. If one already lived in such an environment, he was *very* firm about wishing it to continue. However, as one would expect, such a service was much more likely to be desired by older people of middle-class background than by public housing tenants or applicants—no doubt partly a simple acceptance of the reality that their incomes could not pay for such a service.

Social Services Similarly, more social services than currently present were desired by about one out of five public housing tenants and one out of three 202 tenants. "Social service" no doubt has a negative connotation to many people from low socioeconomic levels, as well as being a more intelligible concept to the better-educated tenant in the average 202 project. Thus, we have no dependable estimate of the amount of tenant-perceived need for this type of service.

To recapitulate, the clear descending order of preference by older people is for medical services, transportation, hot lunches (followed by more complete meal service), housekeeping, and social-personal services (assuming that every environment will have some sort of activity program, we did not include this kind of service in our inquiry). In favor of more services are the supports they offer for failing competence and the greater social solidarity that comes from tenants' doing these things together rather than separately. Against the piling on of services are the psychological threat they offer against continued independence, the risk of creating a "sick" environment, the insulation their presence puts between the housing and the community, and the extra cost that someone must pay.

In planning a service package, the first task is to identify the competence level of the tenants one wishes to serve. The most independent prospective tenants will be discouraged from applying to a project where all meals in a common dining room are mandatory and where there is a substantial atmosphere of poor health (an infirmary area, nurses in uniform, or many visibly ill tenants).

Conversely, the sponsor who wishes to serve marginally independent people who are still not sick enough for a nursing home cannot do without many of these services. The economic and cultural background of intended tenants may have a moderating effect on these two generalizations, however. That is, an earlier middle-class life style makes one somewhat more likely to enjoy the comfort of being served a meal or of having household chores performed for oneself, rather than doing these things alone. It is of interest to note that most of the really successful housing environments for wealthy older people include almost all of these services. It seems to us that in this way these upper-class projects recruit tenant populations that are more heterogeneous with respect to their general level of competence than other more modest projects with similar services. That is, their many services attract people with the financial capacity to pay for services either because they need basic supports or because they wish the comfort of being served. It may well be that environments such as these provide the model toward which all housing might aspire, since not only can people take their choice, but they can also move from independence to relative dependence within the same larger environment without undergoing the trauma of moving.

The financial "if" is a huge one, however. An infinitesimal proportion of the aged population is able to afford the fees that are charged by these multi-service retirement centers. Therefore, it is necessary to come up with some suggestions that stay within the realistic limitations of what the usual public or nonprofit sponsor can hope to provide. We shall suggest three levels of service that differ not only in price but also in the level of tenant independence to which they are best tailored.

  1. *Bare minimum service level*—at a minimum cost—for the most independent tenants.
  a. Activity program. With help from the administrator in starting the program and casual assistance thereafter, tenants should be able to conduct the activities satisfactorily and pay for them with "freebies" and minimum dues.
  b. Medical office. Regularly scheduled weekly hours by physician, and more frequent hours by a nurse who would carry out minor procedures under the direction of the physician.

c. Transportation service. This must be tailor-made for the site in question and might consist of a service as modest as an on-call volunteer emergency driver or as much as a regular multi-stop bus or jitney route.

d. Social and personal counseling services. The administrator should have some training in giving such services for everyday minor problems, and in recognizing when a referral is needed. (See Chapter 12.)

2. *Moderate level of services*—at moderate cost—for marginally competent tenants.

a. Activity program. Direction of activities by a designated individual, whether paid by the sponsor or by a community organization separate from sponsor or authority.

b. Medical office. Daily scheduled clinic hours by a physician and 24-hour telephone access to a nurse employed by the housing project or a local group with specific commitment to the housing.

c. Transportation. Similar to the minimal-service level.

d. Social and personal counseling services. Part-time on-site social worker or other trained helping professional desirable, or a staff member from another local agency who is detailed for a specified amount of on-site time and responsibility.

e. Meal services. An optional hot-lunch program, preferably one whose work is partially the responsibility of tenants.

3. *Maximum services*—highest cost—relatively dependent tenants.

a. Activity program. Directed by a professional with some training in designing activities for the handicapped.

b. Medical service. In addition to daily physician and nursing hours, an infirmary for short-term treatment or a special care area for permanent semi-invalid treatment would be built on the site.

c. Transportation. A more highly organized set of transportation options, offering special assistance to those whose ambulation is limited.

d. Social and personal counseling services. A program similar to that suggested for moderate-service level, but in some cases a full-time counselor or ombudsman might be employed.

e. Meal services. A large space explicitly designated as a

dining room where one, two, or three meals per day are served, with tenants being required to subscribe for some minimum number of meals. Some individualized service in the tenant's dwelling unit might be necessary.

f. Personal care. Assistance in housekeeping, personal grooming, or laundry would normally be required only by those who also need assistance with meals and proximity to medical care, though some lesser forms of personal service may be purchased simply for convenience.

Obviously, the foregoing three levels are suggestive only and not to be taken as rigidly corresponding to any three particular tenant populations. Clearly, one level merges into other, and at a given time, any housing environment will undoubtedly have some tenants in need of each level. One of the major demands on the administrator is, within a given framework of standard services, to be able to find individualized ways of outfitting a less competent tenant with a form of service that does not require a complete reshuffling of the housing environment. He needs to know which community services can come to the assistance of the few least independent tenants, and when to call on the tenant's family for such help.

Chapter 13 considers some specifics of the actual organization of the different types of services. At this point, we want to emphasize the importance of having at the earliest possible point in the planning process a very clear vision of how much service will be offered. These decisions will affect every later decision about the design of the environment, the type of management to be sought, the staffing pattern, and the housing's relationship to the wider community.

WHAT AGES?

Since this book is about housing for the elderly it may seem self-evident that the housing in question should be limited to older people. By far the majority of specially built housing thus far has excluded younger people. It is far from a settled issue, however. The weight of the evidence to date seems to favor age-segregated housing. Those who live in these environments seem contented and explicitly approve of the exclusion of children and teenagers. They have more frequent social contact with friends than older people who live in settings with high proportions of younger people. These research findings run counter to the wishes of many who find something distasteful in the thought of shutting off contact between young and old.

On the other side of the issue, my research suggests that only about 30 percent of older people now living in ordinary nonplanned neighborhoods feel that if they were to move they would like to live in housing limited to older people. This is a lot of people of course, and we can confidently say that the housing demand of this large minority will not be met for a long time. However, the great majority wish otherwise and do not apply for such housing. Many of these people live in undesirable neighborhoods or dwelling units. Yet they do not have the option of moving into low- or moderate-rent housing for all ages except under the worst of conditions; that is, in public housing where age integration means of mixture of vulnerable old people and problem children and teenagers. These latter environments are the only instances where planned housing has deliberately attempted age integration. The consequences for the elderly are very negative, and I have no hesitation in opposing further projects of this kind.

However, have we had enough of a chance to determine whether there are conditions where young and old can live together with mutual enrichment? A national policy that makes age separation mandatory by not providing other options will most surely feed the hostility of the generation gap, deny important role models for children, helping roles for older adults, and increase further our society's aversion to the thought of growing old.

Thus, it would seem that creative experimentation is necessary to determine under what conditions the generations can be housed together. The first requirement is that a sponsor or housing authority have a strongly positive wish to make age integration work. Second, there must be full-time management and other staff with the same zeal, and with the good judgment to know what occasions, activities, and building locations should foster the mixing of old and young and which of these should allow their separation. Third, the architect has an important place in this picture, in using his ingenuity to determine how separate sitting or play areas for different age groups may be constructed, how controlled (but not unlimited) access between such areas can be provided, and how the old can be protected from victimization through the design of plantings, outdoor areas, circulation routes, common spaces, and entrances to dwelling units.

The old 236 program and the 1974 Section 23 program allow such age mixing. Thus, a sponsor who has met the requirements outlined in the last paragraph may wish to be adventurous and try age mixing (figures are not now available about how many, if any, 236 projects have truly integrated age mixes). It is impossible to suggest an optimum proportion of different ages at this point. However, in view of the positive advantages to be gained from social interaction with one's age peers, at least 50 percent of the dwelling units might be designated for the elderly. Some within-project segregation might be desirable, also; placing a family apartment directly above an elderly household should be avoided, for example. Structures whose proportion of elderly goes much lower than 30 to 35 percent will risk isolating the elderly.

Until more experience is at hand on how to integrate successfully, most sponsors will undoubtedly build for the elderly alone. This is their right, and there are many advantages in such an arrangement for the older person who does not mind living with only age peers. People of the same generation are likely to share attitudes, values, and the common experiences of living through the same historical events. Even more important, the social standards of what is right and proper are apt to be appropriate for the elderly when everyone in a given environment is elderly. In age-mixed environments, there is always a tendency for the standards of youth and middle life to predominate, to the inevitable disadvantage of all but the most active and "youthful" elderly.

WHAT COLOR?

Despite gains for blacks in some areas during the past decade, residential racial segregation has clearly become more marked. Once confined to threatened block busting of young black families, zoning fights have begun to erupt over proposed housing limited to older people, undoubtedly representing a fear that any kind of federally aided housing will mean a foot in the door for full racial mixing.

The prospective sponsor of housing for the elderly will be increasingly forced to face this issue. Federal assistance of any kind requires a sponsor at least to go through the motions of saying how he will actively recruit minority tenants (HUD's "affirmative marketing plan"). There is every reason to feel that the national leadership of churches, unions, and some fraternal organizations will exert more moral pressure on local sponsors to try harder for equal treatment.

What is the situation now? As of 1971, about 28 percent of elderly public housing tenants were black, a proportion far greater than the 7.8 percent of all elderly in the country who are black. Since the black elderly suffer from the triple jeopardy of skin color, age, and poverty, it is no wonder that their need is shown in this overrepresentation. Public housing does seem to be doing its duty in this area. The situation is totally different in privately sponsored housing. The Philadelphia Geriatric Center's 1971 housing survey showed that about 3 percent of 202 program tenants were black. Many of this 3 percent lived in housing sponsored by a black organization. *Less than one percent of tenants in white-sponsored 202 projects are black.* Church groups especially, whose purposes are frequently stated in terms of service to needy groups, have clearly not been performing at the ethical level of their statements of goals. Although there are no data on nonfederally aided housing, this situation is probably even worse.

How do dissimilar people get along in housing for the elderly? Our research shows only positive conclusions. That is, hostility or dissatisfaction based on color differences is rare. The Philadelphia Geriatric Center's research made a study of the friendships of older people in five different racially integrated public housing sites in different cities. When tenants were asked to name their three best friends, 31 percent of all choices in these projects were made to people of a different color—a certain sign of a positive group-living situation.

While the situation is wholly positive in an ongoing housing environment, it may not be so easy to convince prospective tenants of this. Unfortunately, people, including younger relatives of prospective tenants, sometimes make decisions based on fantasies about what *might* happen if one lived close to a black. It seems that this impulsive, irrational thinking can sometimes be sufficient to kill a project that is to be located in an area where there is any threat to tenants' physical security. However, given a crime-free location to begin with it should be possible to allay people's anxieties with information like that from our research: During old age, at least, there is a 100 percent chance that members of different races can live together with great mutuality of experience. Now is the time for sponsoring organizations to try out different kinds of affirmative marketing appeals to minorities and anxiety-reducing publicity to majority group tenants. There may be no choice later and it would be far better to develop experience in how to do both most unobtrusively before the compulsion to do so removes the opportunity to go about recruitment in one's own way.

chapter 7

Designing the building

The author is not competent to tell architects how to construct a building, nor does he think that planners and administrators should assume this role. Why, then, such a long section on design? This chapter is written by default because there are so few people presently trained and active in both social gerontology and architecture. Both perspectives are necessary to produce the best environments for older people. The designer cannot conceive a living environment in the absence of knowledge about his ultimate client population. Furthermore, some of this knowledge runs counter to many of the expectations and wishes that he is likely to entertain about what older people want. Conversely, sponsors, planners, and potential administrators need confidence in their ideas in order to work effectively with the architect.

Frequent reference has been made to the architect who refuses to take seriously the wishes of the client and goes ahead with a design that is pleasing to him but nonfunctional for the user. With occasional exceptions, however, this stereotype is not borne out by reality. What does happen all too frequently is that both architect and client work in the dark. The architect, the one who must produce ultimately, may do so unilaterally because knowledgeable assistance is not offered by the client.

The designer of a building for older people has two clients—the sponsor or housing authority and the older person himself. We can assume that most housing for the elderly is being built by sponsors who have the genuine best interest of the older person in mind. In subsidized housing we are less likely to have the developer-consumer conflict of economic interest that characterizes much open-market housing. However, the communication gap is at least as bad when we consider that for open-market building, consumer behavior provides reasonably adequate feedback to the designers as to what kinds of dwellings sell easily and are thus assumed to be satisfying the user's needs. In the case of the elderly, only the very well-to-do have the freedom to choose among many alternative forms of living situations. There is a long waiting list for just about every kind of housing for the elderly, and there is very little opportunity for the consumer to do anything but grab fast for the first available living quarters that he is lucky enough to encounter, and never mind the luxury of being able to choose what he really wants.

Thus, the sponsoring organization must be the advocate for the consumer whether the older person wishes it to be or not, and whether anyone in the organization knows anything about building for the elderly or not. The housing consultant may fill a most important need, because he has been associated with many previous housing efforts and presumably has had the benefit of some feedback from other consumers. On the other hand, he adds another "in-betweener" to the chain between designer and consumer. His expertise is likely to be in the economic and political area, rather than the social, ecological, or architectural. Some of the most vital decisions about housing are thus likely to be made by individual staff or board members of the sponsoring organization, whose knowledge of either design or behavioral science may be meager.

The older person is thus, except under very unusual circumstances, completely bypassed in the decisions regarding the kind of building he will have to use. Understandably, asking the potential consumer what he would like is a difficult task. Consumer psychology has for years asked people about their preferences for one product over another. A later stage of consumer psychology, with Freud in the saddle, thought it could discover what kind of cigarette you might buy by asking whether you loved your mother. Our feeling is that a careful, updated watch on what people actually do is a better guide to planning than either the consumer preference or the depth psychology approach. Some of the information to be presented in this chapter has come from formal research that directly observed what older people do, as well as from asking them what they prefer. Other information was gained from more informal observation and consultation with all types of users.

The easiest guide to design may ultimately be presented in cookbook form: to achieve this specified goal, you should proceed as follows. Even now it would be possible to present some of what is currently known in this fashion; to a certain extent we shall ultimately do this. However, we are so far from having an exact science of designing for the elderly that to write in cookbook fashion would run the risk of making the solutions look too simple.

The cookbook can be useful at some levels. Many unkind words have been said about the major cookbook, HUD's Minimum Property Standards for Housing for the Elderly. It is unquestionably true that minimum standards very quickly become maximum standards. Sponsors and developers with cost-cutting considerations in mind will have a natural tendency to tailor sizes and qualities to meet the bare requirements, knowing that this will probably assure HUD approval, but have no incentive to better the minimum. An alternative to this procedure would be to draw up an *optimal-standard* statement. In this case, one would take it for granted that few buildings would meet all standards. The HUD evaluation of a proposed plan would be based on a complex judgement as to how well multiple goals were being realized. There would still be a few rock-bottom minimums, but the number and type of minimums would have to be balanced by equally important more-than-minimums in other areas.

The tendency of minimum standards to become maximum standards is only one of the problems with the minimum property standard, however. The far greater problem is the physical orientation of most of the material contained in the standards. Although some of the standards have a rationale based on the social and psychological needs of older people, the rationale is rarely explained. Frequently maintenance and economic considerations dictate standards counter to those more desirable from the human point of view.

What is particularly disturbing is that designers and social scientists have been communicating for a number of years. By now, some of this cross-disciplinary thinking should have worked its way into bureaucratic productions such as the Minimum Property Standards. Sadly, there seems to be not only neglect, but active rejection of such input.

Still, everyone planning a building has to know the Minimum Property Standards intimately. A first step should be for sponsors and planners to familiarize themselves with what is actually required. They should then let themselves think very freely about how the standards may be stretched upward. What follows in this chapter will rarely repeat material covered in the Minimum Property Standards, but will go beyond it.

The discussion will be oriented around the idea that some basic needs of older people may be assisted in their fulfillment by the design of the physical environment. As we know only too well, however, the satisfaction of one human need often involves the frustration of another. All too frequently a gain in need satisfaction has to be balanced against the financial burden the satisfaction will bestow on the sponsor. Above all, "the older person" is as varied as man himself, and diversity must be built into the bricks and mortar. As structural aids to need satisfaction are discussed it will be essential to keep in mind these qualifications. As in choosing a site, trade-off will be the usual thing and one will always have to be thinking of ways to compensate for the concession made in the trade-off.

The discussion will be organized around the major needs for security, self-maintenance, knowing the outside world, enrichment of life, social interaction, and privacy. We have no separate category for such purely psychological concepts as happiness, self-confidence, satisfaction, or self-respect. These positive emotions may be associated with the fulfillment of any of the needs already mentioned. Conversely, unhappiness, alienation, and self-hatred may result from the frustration of any of them.

SECURITY NEEDS

Safety Features   A fair amount of attention has been devoted to small engineering details that are designed to prevent accidents. Once in a while one hears complaints from an elderly tenant that the omnipresent grab bars make him fell incompetent. No doubt this happens, but we must look at the question in this way: grab bars give crucial protection to a few elderly, and those that dislike the psychological implication of the grab bar are no doubt strong enough to tolerate those negative feelings. Most such safety features are specified in the Minimum Property Standards.

Safety features that are pretty much taken for granted by now include:

- Nonskid tub and shower surfaces.
- Controlled water temperature in tub or shower so that accidental scalding is eliminated.
- Flush door entrances (i.e., no thresholds).
- Safety shutoffs for gas burners.
- Stove burner controls in front of burners, rather than at the back of the stove, so that reaching over a hot burner is not required to adjust them.

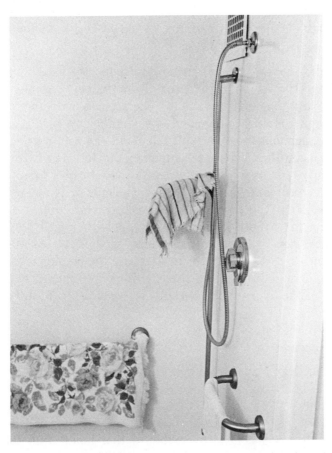

Fig. 1. A flexible shower hose gives more options to the person whose mobility is restricted. The more well-positioned grab bars the better. (Photo by Richard Mowrey.)

- Protective screens or covers for hot water or steam radiators.
- A wall light fixture in each room to avoid tempting the tenant to stand high on a chair while changing a light bulb.
- Requiring the application of nonskid backing to any small rug used in a apartment.
- Every table used in a public place constructed so that it cannot tip on occasions when a reason puts all his weight on one side to help him get up.
- Doors that do not swing shut with enough force to put an unsteady person off balance.
- Slow-closing elevator doors with sensitive reopening mechanisms.
- Handrails for steps and for sloped walks, both indoors and outdoors.

Emergency Signals By far the most frequently used, though not necessarily the most satisfactory, emergency signals are the telephone and pounding on a wall. The security-inducing quality of the telephone could be increased considerably by wiring in several plug-in connections for a portable telephone (an action project might be to persuade the telephone companies not to exact extra charges from elderly tenants in connection with these flexible facilities). The most convenient daytime location for a telephone is not necessarily by the bed. On the other hand, this latter location is extremely comforting for people with anxiety about obtaining help at night. Sometimes there will be only one ideal or possible location for a bed; in this case, it is no problem to locate the phone jack. In other instances, it might be desirable to provide one standard living-room location for the telephone and a choice of two jacks for different bed locations.

Successively more effective, and more expensive, signaling mechanisms are:

- A one-way signal from bedside or bathroom (or both) to summon help from the office or the apartment of a live-in staff member.
- Two-way communication from the dwelling unit, most efficiently via a central switchboard that handles all telephones for the project.
- Electronic portable one-or two-way signaling devices.

The switchboard is definitely a luxury item, but one that financially comfortable tenants are willing to pay for. The one-way light or buzzer signal provides a less expensive security-inducing measure. Every sponsor should obtain comparative cost information and seriously consider this alternative. Since health problems will tend to increase over time, if the sponsor decides to make no provision for emergency signaling at first, he might consider the possibility of building so that such a system may relatively easily be added later. Where no easy access to building wiring systems is provided initially, the cost of adding it later can be prohibitive. The ultimate in a security signal is a portable electronic device being developed by HUD that registers the tenant's location to a central monitoring area if the tenant presses a button. The control office may, in turn, signal back to the tenant, to police, to a hospital, or elsewhere.

Fig. 2. An overhang to give protection from the weather to people getting out of cars at the main entrance is essential (Demchik & Supowitz, Philadelphia, architects. Photo by Sam Nocella.)

Other Health-Related Structural Features   An absolute necessity is a building entrance with an overhang for passengers entering and leaving automobiles in bad weather. Some urban locations may be unable to provide a drive-in separate from the main street, but the overhang is always possible.

If necessity has dictated the use of a slope for access to the building, a hand rail is required. A built-in thawing mechanism for ice might be considered if resources permit.

The design of health services will be discussed at length in Chapter 14. Assuming that some such services are to be included, a major goal is to keep them unobstrusive so as to preserve the atmosphere of an environment for living rather than that of a hospital. In general, this means simulating the community physician's office, rather than the clinic or dispensary. A waiting room should be provided so people are not observable from the hall or lobby. It should

Fig. 3.   Physician services given in a comfortable location that looks like an ordinary doctor's office help counteract the "sick" atmosphere. A waiting room like this also enhances social behavior. (Photo by Sam Nocella.)

be furnished warmly and equipped with reading material and a radio. Although all public facilities gain something by being centrally located, use of the medical facilities is likely to be relatively unaffected by this type of physical accessibility. Thus, where other facilities compete for centrality of location, the medical facilities might be considered for the end of a ground-floor hall, a small wing, or possibly an upper floor. The basement is best avoided, because such locations frequently have an air of gloom.

If a more substantial medical facility such as an infirmary, nursing area, rehabilitation suite, or multiservice clinic is to be included, many would recommend a separate building. This device is most clearly desirable when a full nursing facility serving a population of lower competence than the housing is built on the same property. Separate buildings, possibly connected to the same maintenance center, (heating plant, kitchen, etc.) have the advantage of providing housing tenants with the security of knowing that the facility is nearby, and at the same time not exposing them to the too-frequent of view of physical illness. If the facility is small, or must for other reasons be in the same building as apartments for the well-elderly, a separate floor is a desirable location. There are, of course, social costs of any such segregation by competence. If there is physical separation, management should encourage crossing of the barriers by providing incentives to the medical-care tenants to mingle with tenants in other areas of the housing, and to encourage and organize means by which some healthier tenants might volunteer for services, including friendly visiting, in the medical care area.

It is possible to minimize the "sick" atmosphere even in special care areas. It is a worthwhile investment to provide some kind of apartment kitchen arrangement for these tenants, even if most of their meals are taken centrally or served to them. The more similar their apartments are to the others in the building the better. The nurses station can be an ordinary office, rather than the forbidding glass cage that looks out on all hallway areas. If at all possible, it is best that special-care tenants use the regular physician's office rather than being treated as hospital patients, as in medical rounds. The fewer obvious hospital trappings the better. If oxygen tanks, litters, wheelchairs, intravenous feeding apparatus or other such props are needed, they should be stored out of sight, transferred to rooms

Fig. 4 (*a*) and (*b*)   The independent apartments of Wesley Woods, Atlanta, are at the top and the health-care facility at the bottom. This represents ideal siting of the two structures: close together for a feeling of security, but separated enough to avoid the constant reminder of the possibility of more intensive care. (Charles Edward Stade and Associates, Park Ridge, Illinois, architects. Photo by Hedrich-Blessing.)

unobstrusively, and if possible, used with a screen, curtain, or other device keeping them out of the view of patient and other tenants. Needless to say, typical hospital paint colors and gloss can be avoided and an effort made to emphasize homelike decor. Washable hallway carpeting should be feasible anywhere except where grossly impaired patients live.

Security from Personal Attack   The following story appeared recently in the Philadelphia *Evening Bulletin:*

Four boys ranging in age from 10 to 13 have been charged with the rape, robbery, beating and torture of an 84-year-old widow in a North Philadelphia housing project earlier this week.

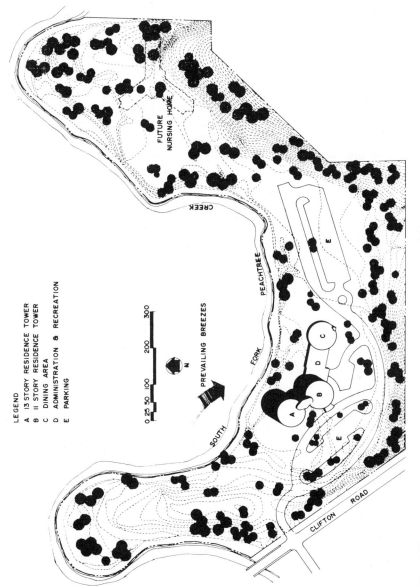

LEGEND
A 13 STORY RESIDENCE TOWER
B 11 STORY RESIDENCE TOWER
C DINING AREA
D ADMINISTRATION & RECREATION
E PARKING

PREVAILING BREEZES

0 25 50 100   200   300

N

SOUTH FORK PEACHTREE CREEK

FUTURE NURSING HOME

CLIFTON ROAD

Fig. 4 (b)

129

According to Det. Capt. Keith Keller, the youths invaded the woman's apartment for several successive days, raped her repeatedly and used matches and a heated steel comb to burn her breast and stomach.

Keller said the four also cut her long hair, beat her with a broom and scrawled obscenities on the apartment walls after taking $200 from a bureau drawer.

An increasingly salient aspect of the urban housing environment, unfortunately, is the older person's safety from muggers, purse snatchers, and milder forms of harassment, such as teasing by neighborhood children. The personal safety problem is a symptom of our whole society's cluster of illnesses that include poverty, racism, alienation, and withdrawal from communal responsibility. Therefore, we should have no illusions about being able to accomplish anything more than first-aid-level improvement in personal safety through specific structural designs for the elderly. On the one hand, protection is an absolute need; where people feel unsafe their outlook on life as a whole is infected. Thus, desperate measures are sometimes required. On the other hand, every desperate measure has a social cost that may compound the problem for the whole neighborhood or small society. We therefore need to consider a whole variety of measures that will keep tenants safe on the one hand while not, on the other, locking them completely into a self-contained fortress. Anyone searching for structural deterrents to crime should read a recent book on this subject by the architect Oscar Newman, *Defensible Space* (1972).

One housing-authority executive has stated emphatically that the only thing that would satisfy his anxious crime-ridden neighborhood tenants would be an unscalable wall with guards at the entrance. Already we have hundreds of unfortunately located housing projects where this kind of fear is at the top of everyone's consciousness. Planners are more cautious in the placement of new buildings, perhaps even too cautious. The ideal of locating all new housing in middle-class neighborhoods is both unattainable and undesirable. Already, many such zoning proposals are being fought by the middle-class populace in the same way that racial integration and busing have been fought. Even more importantly, the need for good housing is very great among elderly people who wish to remain in their own neighborhoods in spite of their security problem. Many minority groups are adamant in their goal of building decent communities for their own members within their own neighborhoods. Thus, while cer-

Fig. 5. Too much central-city housing is located in nonretail commercial or industrial areas. The low density of pedestrian traffic, especially after working hours, constitutes a security risk to the elderly tenant.

tainly granting the desirability of opening up "good" neighborhoods, we are faced with the necessity for creative thinking about structural and administrative measures that can maximize security for tenants who must live in neighborhoods that are less than ideally secure.

A first principle for designing for safety is to maximize the extent to which others can monitor all behavior in public places, especially around entrances and exits. There are a number of advantages to locating a sitting area in the entrance lobby with a full view of the main outdoor entrance. Surveillance of strangers is one such advantage. Such an area is likely to have some inhabitants at most hours of the day. They will be extremely curious about who enters. Even without any power to stop a "suspicious character," their presence can be a strong deterrent to anyone who has no business in the area. The structural principle is thus to design, if possible, a lobby with space and furniture for sitting and with glass giving a good view of the entrance walk. A community room separate from the lobby can also be used for this surveillance function provided it has a large opening, or glass partitions looking out into the interior entranceway, and windows affording a good view of the grounds and exterior entrance.

It is doubly helpful if the offices or reception area also look out on the entranceway. If the administrator's desk is placed so that he faces the outdoors, or can see the outside within a 90-degree angle, a major increment in security is added. For the most part, people do not spend a great deal of time looking out the windows of high-rise apartments. Balconies will increase the number of tenants able to observe the outside areas, but they may require instruction in performing their surveillance role.

An L-shaped building with an entrance near the intersection point of the two wings is particularly good for security, both with regard to people entering the building and outdoor seating areas. The two sides of the L themselves furnish barriers, and also give the opportunity for people to look out toward the entrance and outdoor seating from two different interior perspectives.

In general, visibility from the street into the lobby is more of an advantage than a liability, provided there is some minimum level of non-threatening foot traffic on the public sidewalk. It is especially desirable to have the elevator waiting area visible from outside the building. It is extremely important to locate plantings properly where there is concern about personal safety. They should be planted far away from the public sidewalk and footpaths or clustered in relatively unused areas of the grounds. Trees of the right kind (that is, those whose branches do not form a thick layer at low heights) are more satisfactory as plantings, though one will still need to consider whether a full-grown tree will interfere with one of the necessary surveillance vistas.

Sometimes a high-rise project will, in effect, need to deny the existence of its rear aspect, that is, to provide only an emergency exit always locked to the outside and a wall or fence shutting it off from adjoining properties on one or even two sides. Since the rear of a building is the usual place for parking and clothesline areas, other arrangements would have to be made for these, such as placing them to the sides of the building. It is not unheard of to have a clothesline area visible from the street. A spot an the roof is another possibility. Certainly no outdoor seating should be provided in a low-security area.

Everyone will be alert to outdoor lighting needs. We have not

Fig. 6. The housing pictured in Fig. 5 has compensated in its building and site design for its poor neighborhood location by placing its outdoor seating within the angle formed by two building faces. The seating is also within view of many apartments and the offices of the community center.

studied tenants' reactions to strong outdoor lights near their windows. It is probable that room drapes of sufficient opacity could keep the light from interfering with sleep, if sufficient ventilation were available. For tenants of low-rise projects, a series of outdoor spotlights controlled in the apartment would give a sense of security.

Control of pathways and pedestrian traffic is an essential element in security. A shortcut from external streets through the grounds of the housing site is a menace to older people, at the very least bringing children too close in their play, and at worst allowing the antisocial person easy access to await the right condition for striking. No corner property should have a diagonal walkway freely accessible from the two right-angled streets. The building for elderly embedded in a larger project for families should have low fences controlling access.

A major fence is the point at which we draw the line. A fence that genuinely attempts to keep out all except occupants and visitors has an irrevocable quality that is very different from the token low fence that discourages short cuts but which is obviously penetrable by anyone who really wishes to do so. The asylum of old derived some of its fearsome connotation of isolation from the walls that surrounded it and from the presence of guards at the gates. There is, of course, a mounting tendency for new housing on the commercial

Fig. 7. Another view of the housing shown in Figs. 5 and 6. The relatively unobtrusive fence keeps neighborhood pedestrian traffic out of the seating area, yet allows two-way visual access.

market to provide these medieval fortifications. The objection to these radical measures comes not only from the cost that these arrangements add, but also because of the contribution such measures make to mutual hostility and suspicion in already disturbed neighborhoods.

It goes without saying that most buildings will need a locked front-door arrangement with buzzer, operated from the apartment. It is even within range of moderate-priced housing to have closed-circuit television monitoring of the entrance, if there is a staff member living on the premises in whose apartment the image can appear during the evening.

The locked front door can be dispensed with only at times when the entrance lobby is overseen by a responsible person. Sometimes it is convenient to build office space for a clerical worker with a full view of the doorway. She must double as receptionist, but as long as the required clerical work gets performed this is a very desirable arrangement. Although the administrator may have to perform many

Fig. 8. In the most crime-ridden neighborhoods, a friendly security guard gives the greatest peace of mind to the tenant. (Photo by Sam Nocella.)

Fig. 9. The worst possible main entrance to a high-rise building for the elderly. The photograph was taken from the sidewalk. Full access to the elevators at rear is available to anyone from the street, and tenants must take checks from their mailboxes in view of anyone passing by.

of his activities "offstage," he might do well to do some of his work in such a location. It is also possible to cover the lobby at critical times of day, such as from late afternoon until 10 PM or midnight, with a person hired explicitly for the purpose—a retired person, a college student, or possibly a security guard hired from an agency. In the last instance, part of his job would consist of patrolling the grounds. Unquestionably, such a person contributes a feeling of security. If public transportation works on a dependable schedule, the guard could perform the duty of meeting several runs each evening and accompanying any tenant who happened to be traveling at that time.

In public housing there has been a constant question of the responsibility of local police as compared to housing authority security personnel. Many authorities have considered it impossible to spend money to hire their own security people, yet have been unable to exact adequate protection from local police. We cannot advise clearly one way or the other on this issue, except to urge every authority to stretch its budget to the very limit in the matter of personal security. Even with reasonably good local police protection, supplementary private service can add something extra to the general feeling of ease.

Within the building, especially in projects unfortunate enough to have been built to house both elderly and younger families, there may be risks. In general, the basement is better reserved for utilities and maintenance activities, with its access to the outside strictly controlled.

Upper floors in buildings built in high-crime areas should be designed with no alcoves or other areas where a person might hide.

Fig. 10. A view of the entranceway shown in Fig. 9 after it was closed off in the interest of security. The trash is a problem not yet solved! (Photo by Sam Nocella.)

Fig. 11. This hallway has four blind corners as its wraps around the utility core. The width of the hallway and the raw cinderblock walls confirm immediately the negative stereotypes of "public housing." (Photo by Sam Nocella.)

This consideration may have a strong influence on the basic floor plan. For example, a hallway that wraps around a central utility core in a rectangular shape will have to have fire doors at each corner, which is unthinkable from the point of view of security. This is the locus of a disconcerting number of crimes in one project that we have studied. Fire exits pose a major problem in any such building. One simply cannot build exterior stairs in a high rise for the elderly, yet interior stairwells are a favorite place for crime.

Locking the doors so that one may enter the stairwell from the floor but not from the stair side causes as many problems as it solves. One solution is to build the stairwell on the front side of the building with full visual access (i.e., windows) to people from the outside as they look up. Beyond taking obvious measures such as keeping good lights always in working order, design of the building so as to allow personal surveillance of both elevator and stair of both elevator and stair entrances seems to be the best that we can suggest at this point. As Oscar Newman (1972) has demonstrated, the fewer tenants who live on a single floor, the more responsible the tenants will be in questioning or reporting strangers.

Elevators are another problem for which many solutions have been suggested, such as alarm bells, audio monitoring, closed-circuit television, and automatic signalling to the office if the stop button is pushed. The best protection here is to make certain that only authorized personnel have access to the basement, and that the apartment entrances are protected in the ways described.

Many of the points made here will apply to the low-rise project as well as the high-rise, although there seems to be a general tendency for low-rise housing to be built in lower risk areas. Personal surveillance by staff will be more difficult, but there is considerable compensation for this lack in the fact that tenants do a considerable amount of looking from first and second-floor windows. If they are given some motivating assistance from management in the value of being their neighbor's keeper, this can constitute excellent protection. Newman reports that among the family housing projects in New York City the crime rate is lowest in low-rise projects. He presents much convincing evidence that responsibility for those entering an area is taken much more personally when relatively few people share a common entrance.

Project layout is of the utmost importance in the low-rise project. If the main entrance is controllable, a courtyard arrangement where the units are laid out in a rectangular, U-shaped, circular or elliptical pattern may be acceptable (a "sociopetal" plan). There is a tendency here for people to look out windows to the entire entranceway area, heightening the project's self-monitoring capacity. The rear entrances, if any, as well as ground floor windows, will need especially good security measures. Detached or duplex units

Fig. 12. Small units that cluster around a central space increase the possibility of surveillance of the entrance space by people inside the units, as well as offering many opportunities for social encounters. In spite of the fact that the walkways are public space, each unit has an outdoor area that is clearly "owned" by the unit's occupant (William Kessler & Associates, Grosse Point, Michigan, architects. Photo by Balthazar Korab.)

will be somewhat less secure than row houses or low-rise buildings with an inside hallway. Whenever possible, outdoor areas should be demarcated to indicate that they belong to particular dwelling units. Newman shows that where outdoor space "belongs" to everyone, in actuality it belongs to no one, and intruders have much freer access.

High-Rise or Low-Rise? One of the most frequently asked questions is whether a proposed building should be high or low-rise. One of the issues involved in this decision relates to security, both physical and psychological. The decision must necessarily be based on a complex set of positive and negative consequences. In an age-integrated project, it seems clear that the worst of the many evils is the high-rise structure, where it is almost impossible to control ac-

Fig. 13. Another grouping of socially oriented units. This design would be improved by running the public walk on the far side of the units from the individually "owned" planting areas. (Hirshen, Gammill, Trumbo & Cook, Berkeley, California, architects. Photo by Ronald Gammill.)

cess to building and grounds, and where there are so many within-building opportunities for crime. Newman's research also suggests that parental control of youngsters is better in low-rise projects.

If we assume that a project will serve only the elderly, so far as we know there is no clear evidence to favor one or the other type of structure for security purposes. If a single individual, such as a security guard, is assigned the job of monitoring access to the project, he will probably be more effective in a high rise than patrolling the wider expenses of a low-rise project.

What about the psychological security of the high rise as compared to the low rise? We have interviewed some older people who have a strong aversion to high-rise living, some who are genuinely phobic about living above the ground level, and some who cannot bring themselves to ride an elevator. These people are excluded if the sponsor decides on a high rise. In percentage terms their number is small, however. It is difficult to recommend basing this decision to any extent on the issue of psychological security.

We do have information on the preferences of older people in various situations. Our research with community residents, applicants, and tenants has shown that:

- A significant minority of people have some question as to whether they will be comfortable in a high-rise building.
- Another larger minority (or even perhaps a majority?) of people would not actively choose high-rise living if they had completely free choice.
- People with earlier high-rise living experience strongly prefer to live in high-rise projects for the elderly.
- The very great majority of people who move into a high-rise building end up strongly liking this arrangement.
- Similarly, the great majority who move into low-rise projects prefer that kind of living.
- Anecdotal evidence from some administrators who have responsibility for both types of projects suggests that it is the healthier and more independent people who choose the low-rise garden or detached dwelling units.
- There seems to be greater participation in on-site activity programs in high-rise buildings.
- Other things being equal, tenants in low-rise buildings seem to be more likely to leave the premises and engage in more outwardly-directed activity.

We have found that planners, sponsors, administrators, and behavior scientists are all very likely to assess the wishes of the elderly in terms of their own values, especially in the assertion that "older people like to have their own piece of land and are afraid to live on upper floors." There is no evidence to support either of these generalizations if stated so baldly. Therefore, it does not seem to be such a tragedy that land costs preclude low-rise buildings in many urban areas.

It still may be that there is positive value in the low-rise structure, especially in facilitating continued neighborhood mobility of the tenant. Since the sponsor frequently must build a high-rise structure, he will not be helped by this knowledge. Perhaps the best advice is for the sponsor, when he has a choice, to consider the advantages of building a low-rise structure. If he does decide on a high-rise building, he should recognize the possibility that his tenants will require administrative encouragement to increase their mobility off the housing site.

SELF-MAINTAINING NEEDS

Even if security needs come first, an environment that makes it easy to care for one's own daily needs comes a close second. For a fair number of people, moving into bright shiny public housing dwellings is a first experience with the ease of living possible in modern America. Some of the most satisfied tenants in our research were those who for the first time could heat their dwellings without building their own fire or go to the bathroom without freezing in winter. Let us take these basic basics for granted. However, we still have to recognize that environments with these modern facilities differ considerably in the extent to which they support competent functioning, or make it easy for the person to have a feeling of success about his skill in using them.

If we wish any facility to induce the feeling of competence, we will want it work easily while still not making the tenant feel like a disabled person. Knobs that respond easily, flush handles requiring little pressure, and a toilet paper holder placed to the side rather than to the rear of the toilet will encourage this positive self-evaluation. On the other hand, too many grab bars or a toilet that wipes, dries, and flushes without any initiative by the person will only remind him that the environment considers him incompetent. It is a fine line to tread.

The Dwelling Unit

In some way or another, the dwelling unit is a center for all tenant activities. It is his haven of safety, the place where he conducts some of his most life-enriching activities, a retreat at private times, a place to which friends and relatives come, and a place where the basic tasks necessary to living are conducted. The design of the domicile will be discussed in connection with each of these behaviors. However, the most important behavior in the dwelling unit by far is self-maintaining behavior. Toileting, bathing, grooming, cooking, housekeeping, maintaining sensory contact with the environment, comfort, and sleeping are the basic activities demanded of everyone, all of them performed primarily within the dwelling unit. As we noted earlier, a person's sense of satisfaction with himself as a competent doer can be maintained only when he sees himself performing well what he considers the relevant tasks of living. Therefore, anything that design can add to the quality of task performance will be added to the tenant's feeling of satisfaction with himself.

Dwelling Unit Size   There is no magic formula for size, nor any reliable research data yet on tenant satisfaction as a function of domicile size. HUD's property standards will allow an efficiency (kitchenette, with combination dining-living-sleeping area)

Fig. 14.   Even though tenants themselves do not express major dissatisfaction with the sizes of their apartments, a roomy efficiency like this gives greater ease of ambulation. (Photo by Sam Nocella.)

Fig. 15. There are advantages to a compact kitchen design, but this space would give difficulty to the wheelchair occupant. (Photo by Richard Mowrey.)

apartment with as little as 255 square feet, and a one-bedroom unit 350 square feet in size (plus closets and bathroom). British standards suggest, but do not require, 320 and 480 square feet, respectively.

There seems to be general agreement among advocates for the elderly that new specially built housing for the elderly provides too little living space. Most people who move into such housing are, if anything, oversupplied with furniture. Moving too much into a small area will make living difficult and even unsafe, but the alternative is to part with personally meaningful possessions. Professionals in service to the elderly become irate at the imposition of such low minimum-space requirements on federally assisted housing. Our data are not yet complete in this area. However, very few tenants spontaneously complain of their units being too small. When asked directly, only 17 percent said their apartments were too small. Furthermore, there was no difference between 202 tenants and

public housing tenants in this respect, even though public housing
dwelling units are substantially larger, on the average, than 202
units.

It is difficult to know what this information means in terms of
design. Our answers to the question on apartment size unquestionably reflect partly the reluctance of tenants to appear ungrateful
for what they have, or fearful of reprisal if they express dissatisfaction. On the other hand, when asked, they do express greater
degrees of dissatisfaction with aspects of their environment other
than apartment size. Small size is clearly not as important a deficit
as poor windows, undependable heat, or bad television reception.
But we may have a tendency to project our own middle-life space
standards a little too strongly onto the older tenant. He, in turn, is
taking into account the added ease of housecleaning, ambulation,
and efficiency of storage that comes from having a smaller domicile
than he had during earlier life. What is still needed to provide a final
answer, however, is a direct study of how older people actually use
their space. Do people regretfully part with many pieces of furniture
when they move into an efficiency apartment? Do they bump into
things or have trouble maneuvering inside overly-compact kitchens,
bathrooms, or bedrooms?

Toileting   If the bathroom itself is not to be a barrier, enough space
must be provided to allow a turning radius for a wheelchair, even
though there may be a small minority in a project who will require a
wheelchair. The door should always open into the space adjoining
the bathroom. For several reasons a corner location for the toilet
bowl is preferable: the side wall allows convenient placement of
toilet paper, grab bar, and emergency signal.

An important consideration is the pathway from the bed to the
bathroom, primarily because the trip may be made at night and with
poor illumination. Therefore, the fewer barriers the better, and the
more options there are for turning on lights to show the path the
better. Many are concerned that the bathroom door not be immediately visible to a visitor sitting on the sofa or at the dining
table. These considerations must be balanced with each other by the
architect in relation to the specific layout of each domicile.

Bathing   A great deal has been written about the merits of tub,
shower, and other variations. The important considerations here are

Fig. 16 Some people need bars on either side of the toilet, or at least a wall on one side. The shower is easy to walk in and out of; one hopes that the floor is sloped enough to avoid water outside the shower stall, but not sloped so much that the user feels unsteady on the surface. (Photo by Richard Mowrey.)

those of personal preference, safety, and convenience. Older people are like everybody else, in that some prefer showers, some tubs, and some are ambidextrous. It would be quite impossible to resolve the issue by trying to please the majority by building only one or the other. In terms of safety, both a bathtub and shower entail some risk. The tub is perhaps less safe, since in addition to the risk of slipping in either shower or tub, the latter compels one to step in and out with the body precariously balanced. Some improvement is gained by making the tub height lower, and providing low and shoulder-height grab bars, plus a nonskid surface. The excessively smooth pressed-steel tubs should be avoided, and water temperature controls are mandatory. Many designers recommend strongly that the shower be made with flexible tubing so that it may be used either in a high fixed position as an ordinary shower or as a shower applied locally to the body by hand. In this latter arrangement it may be used either while sitting in the tub, while standing, or while sitting on a shelf with one's legs in the tub. The sitting-position shower has much to recommend it, but requires expert human engineering to make the shelf accessible, not slippery, and near enough to the water controls to allow adjustment from the seated position. There is still considerable hazard involved in getting in and out of such a seat. The safest arrangement is probably a shower stall with seat and flexible shower head, but this will frustrate the bath-lover. Housing planned for people of limited competence might make this sacrifice, but the usual housing will no doubt prefer to allow the option of bath and flexible shower.

Grooming, Dressing, and Personal Care   The important requirements for these tasks are proper illumination, convenient clothing and small-article storage, and mirrors. Many older people become alienated from themselves, being susceptible to the same negative attitudes that younger people have about the looks of the elderly. Psychologically it seems far healthier to encourage the older person to "remember" what he looks like, complete with wrinkles, gray hair and paunch. Beyond enabling him to maintain touch with his real self, mirrors encourage him to monitor his own appearance. We suggest that in addition to an ample-sized bathroom medicine cabinet mirror there be a permanent full-length mirror in the bedroom or on an unexposed wall of the living-bedroom, with a spot or other dependably illuminating light installed permanently so as to make this self-monitoring easy when one stands before the mirror. The full-length mirror ideally should be near the closet and have space for an easily-movable chair near it, in case the person wishes to sit before the mirror for grooming care.

Ironing boards are cumbersome to fold and unfold; the housing with a little extra money to spare might consider installing fold-up self-storing ironing boards in the dwelling unit in order to save space. The project laundry room should have one for general use. On-site dry cleaning is generally not feasible, though a tenants' organization might want to organize a periodic collection and transport service to a do-it-yourself dry cleaning establishment. A communal sewing room with a sewing machine, or a corner of a community room with a lockable closet, will enable some tenants to maintain themselves while deriving enjoyment from creating and from the social interaction of working alongside others.

Most housing environments cannot maintain a barber shop, since male tenants constitute a small minority. It may be relatively expensive to equip a shop and maintain the space necessary, even if a barber can be found who will come regularly enough. The beauty shop is more familiar in some urban sites, though it is primarily the relatively well-off tenants with middle-class backgrounds who can afford this service. Thus, giving up scarce space to a beauty shop may be something one decides to do in two instances: when one is building for a population used to comfort and able to pay for it, or in the less usual situations when the housing is very far from a commercial hairdresser or the neighborhood is considered unsafe. Otherwise, encouraging people to take care of their hair is a managerial, rather than structural, problem. Self-care will be the most usual mode, which will be facilitated by the lighting and mirrors described above. Some sponsors may wish to consider a built-in dressing table with sitting-height mirror, though in general, builtins remove some of the very desirable ability of tenants to construct their own furniture arrangements.

Housekeeping and Cooking   In general, housekeeping constitutes a major meaningful use of time for the female tenant—meaningful in that it is a role that gives continuity to her life, a way of exercising her competence, a source of personal pride, a means of filling the day, and a way of setting off one time of day from another. The labor-saving device or structure is undoubtedly as attractive to the older person as to younger people. As improvements are made in materials and hardware, elderly tenants will generally be willing consumers, unless the amount of new learning required to use them is inordinately great. The no-dust corner, the eye-level oven, washable kitchen wallpaper, and so on, are generally welcome. The more storage space the better, unless it begins to encroach greatly on living space.

It is well to be aware of where some particular difficulties lie. Reaching high places is particularly hazardous. Thus, it helps to have some wall lighting fixtures, as compared to ceiling fixtures, and enough storage space for frequently used articles to be stored at a height that does not require a stool to reach. The compulsive house-cleaner will always have trouble reaching the cabinet tops. However, a stove hood and exhaust fan will cut down on the frequency of cleaning the grease from high kitchen places. Very low storage

Fig. 17. A major error in design for the elderly is this drawer-type refrigerator that forces the user to stoop. (Photo by Sam Nocella.)

Fig. 18. Even though the kitchen is in full view of the living room, a comfortable dining space is perfectly located with respect to the kitchen and natural lighting. (Photo by Sam Nocella.)

places also represent a problem, though these are necessary and have to be lived with. Once in a while a particularly bad idea comes along which must be resisted, such as a refrigerator in a pull-out drawer just above floor level—a real deterrent to kitchen competence.

Many tenants express the wish for a way to close off a dirty kitchen from view. On the other hand, there is great convenience in being able to put food directly on a table close to where the food is prepared. One might try for a solution that would allow room for a table very close to the food preparation area with a sliding door or divider that could close off the area once the table is served. Of course, many people will prefer to carry their food, perhaps to a table on the distant side from the kitchen near a window. Our research has told us that elderly tenants prepare and serve meals to others relatively infrequently. However, this occasion is an extremely important one for those who do so. If a space is designated for dining, it should have seating for a minimum of four

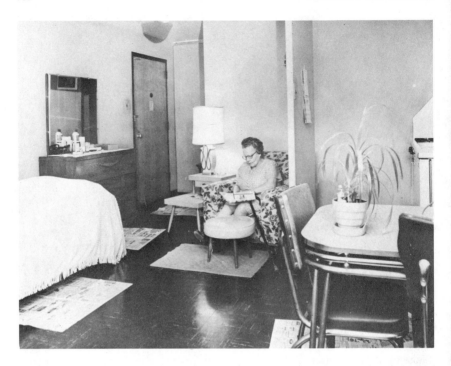

Fig. 19. Penny pinching has resulted in a tiny efficiency apartment with the bed greeting a visitor as she enters. Th token wall separating part of the kitchen from the living space communicates the idea of second-class citizenship. (Photo by Sam Nocella.)

people, substantial illumination, and electrical outlets for table appliances. Although daylight is desirable for kitchen areas, this should not be provided at the expense of daylight to cheer up a living area.

Sleeping Most of the dissatisfaction with apartment size that we have found revolves around the lack of a separate bedroom. About one quarter of the tenants studied in the Philadelphia Geriatric Center's research who lived in an efficiency apartment would spend some of a hypothetical income increase on an apartment with a separate bedroom. A number prefer the coziness of a separate, small sleeping area, while many simply like the idea of being able to keep intimate possessions—bed clothes, dressing-table objects, and so on—out of the sight of visitors. Because of the humanizing aspects of the separate bedroom (rather than for the extra space *per se*) it seems that every effort should be made to provide a separate bedroom for every apartment.

Since people frequently do not think of ways to display pictures and objects, and since walls are considered sacrosanct to nails, we suggest the provision of a wall panel and shelf for this purpose. A corkboard or bulletin board, with a shelf or set of shelves below it may be utilized for pinup photographs, framed pictures, memorabilia, newspaper clippings, and so on. A low-height horizontal molding to support picture hooks might also be considered.

If the unit must be an efficiency, a frequent solution is to build the main room in an L-shape, (with the bathroom forming the inner angle) so the bed can be placed around the corner. The housing might consider providing a divider, with shelves on the bottom part, that the tenant could use either to divide and shield the bed from view or to place against the wall as a piece of furniture.

Fig. 20. A good piece of furniture and location for maintaining a satisfying activity. (Photo by Richard Mowrey.)

Flooring Floor material seems to be one of the less important aspects of the dwelling unit. Older people's lifelong housekeeping practices seem to be adaptable to new surfaces. Adhesive tiles may not be everyone's favorite, but they are easily cleanable and do not rule out other coverings. New hard, permanently shined finishes should be considered if financially feasible, and if they represent no slipping hazard. Wall-to-wall carpet is preferred by many people. Management might obtain a favorable price from a supplier in return for the hope of continuous business from tenants in the housing development. On the other hand, providing wall-to-wall carpeting as a standard dwelling-unit feature removes the desirable opportunity for a person to choose and to match the carpeting with his taste in other aspects of room decor. It also makes it more difficult for rugs to be used if the tenant desires.

Windows Windows represent one of the most frequent of all dwelling-unit problems. Since the author knows nothing about the mechanics of window design, the task is simply to remind every sponsor and designer that he cannot assume that just any window that happens to fit esthetically or conform to the required module will do. What we really need is a great deal of human engineering research in how the aged can best exert their energies to open and close windows. In general, complaints are most frequent in this area—one has to reach too high, pressure must be exerted at an awkward angle, the window sticks, and so on. Especially frequently is frustration voiced at the aluminum sliding window that loses its easy sliding capacity over time or goes off its track. Sometimes, of course, the windows that close and open more easily are unsatisfactory in keeping wind out. In some locations, the direction of prevailing winds or typical storms may have to be taken into account. Wind whistle, window frame banging, and moisture leaks may frequently be prevented by matching the right kind of window to local conditions. If storm windows are used, management must handle the changing of panels and out-of-season storage.

We have also had many complaints about windows that are too high to look out of comfortably. Unless there are very strong indications for clerestory windows, no window should be so high that one cannot look out while sitting down in front of it. This is desirable not only from the point of view of getting light and being able to watch interesting scenes, but the surveillance capacity offered by a window is also a strong element in augmenting a site's personal security. Wherever possible, windowsills should be provided that are wide enough for knickknacks or small flower pots. We have had no particularly good or bad reports about sliding glass doors, except for complaints that they take too much potential furniture space from small efficiency apartments. Needless to say, they should be provided with substantial locks and with some adhesive device to indicate clearly to the walker when they are open and when they are shut.

Air Circulation and Heat   Domiciles are still being built without air conditioning using the reasoning, "Old people don't care about it the way young people do." If anything, the effects of extreme heat and cold are greater on older people than on younger. We feel that it should be mandatory to have individually controllable heat in every apartment, and when air conditioning is included, that it be individually controlled as well. An elderly tenant's entire outlook on life may be adversely affected by heat or cold that goes beyond his individually preferred limits.

Lighting   Some older people do not have enough lamps, or if a lamp does go bad, they may tend not to fix or replace it. Therefore, we recommend having more than the usual number of built-in lights and also night lights at the corner leading to the bathroom and inside the bathroom. Every room should have one switch-controlled light in each room, preferably located on a wall rather than on the ceiling. A manager should himself notice and alert his staff to notice the lighting in tenants' apartments and be prepared to give advice on changes if he sees potential hazards in inadequate lighting, exposed cords, or limitations to constructive activity imposed by improper light placement. Glare from a window can sometimes be a problem; some consideration should be given to controlling it through exterior window sunshades or recessing windows.

Walking   Most buildings are now constructed so that there are no architectural barriers to mobility throughout the common spaces and into the dwelling units. Any domicile with stairs in it automatically puts a limit on its usability by someone with problems in ambulation. If a project decides to build some walk-up or two-story

Fig. 21. Even though air conditioning was prohibited as a matter of policy in most public housing, architect Louis Sauer of Philadelphia was able to provide this kind of cross ventilation in almost every unit. (Louis Sauer Associates, Philadelphia, architects. Photo by David Hirsh.)

units, it should also maintain a flexible policy about allowing changes to ground-floor units for tenants of these units whose ease of mobility deteriorates.

Hand rails along corridors are most helpful to the unsteady older person, but they do convey something of an institutional quality. Any project that begins with the idea of serving marginally competent tenants should begin by having hand rails, while others might decide to add them later if some of its tenants appear to grow less able.

Projects with long halls might consider that totally confident ambulation depends on the tenant's always being aware of just where he is. Totally symmetrical or mirror-image structures may be disorienting. It is not difficult to make two wings look different with paint, wallpaper, lighting, or floor covering. Different-colored doors or door frames not only counteract the antiseptic high-rise quality

Fig. 22. The long hallway is intrinsically dehumanizing. This effect is potentiated by the lack of outside light, the bareness of walls, and the glare from regularly spaced ceiling lights on a glossy floor surface.

but also make it easier for a person to distinguish his own apartment. The apartment doors might be designed with offsets that vary as one looks down the hall. Even within a single hall, any change in flooring, lighting, or decor will give orienting cues.

Frequently halls have light glaring in from a window at the end that may hurt sensitive eyes and make it difficult for the tenant to orient himself. If a windowless corridor end is chosen, a special attempt at making the lighting both adequate and cheery must be made. Sometimes a projecting canopy can both keep the natural light and reduce the glare.

Many determinants of the ideal design of outdoor pathways involve safety considerations, especially where crime is a risk. Wherever there is a grade to be traversed a handrail is necessary. The paths that are necessary for a tenant to travel to go from one building to another, or to street and public transportation should be uniformly concrete paved. This type of pavement will constitute the least problem to the marginally mobile. Where esthetic or financial considerations make some other surface more desirable, those pathways should be optional—circuitous routes, strolling paths, and so on may be made of gravel, dirt, flagstone, or rough asphalt.

There are also many personal safety reasons for locating an urban building very close to the street, where pathways will be relatively short. In these cases, there may have to be a second main-building entrance adjacent to the parking lot, though in true crime-risk areas, it is better to have a very well-lit parking area and walk leading to the single main entrance.

In some fortunate suburban, rural or small-town locations there may be enough land and enough security to allow an extensive layout of paths, outdoor corners, garden and woodsy walks, and so on. These luxuries unquestionably give something special to the total effect of an environment. One should not be surprised to learn, however, that use of these areas is never as great as the sponsor would like. It will always be the ablest and the nature-loving few who fully utilize such resources. Justification for the expense of extensive grounds with walkways must be sought in the enrichment they give to a relative minority, rather than in their mass appeal.

Walking is both a means to an end and a form of enrichment. Surveys show that the most frequent form of transportation for the older person is his own feet. Thus, the paths to bus stop and local

Fig. 23. Continuing engagement with the outside world is discouraged by transportation barriers like this.

shopping are particularly important. The housing environment may
have some influence on the maintenance of sidewalk repairs, the
enforcement of snow-cleaning regulations, and possibly on the
development of undesirable teenage or criminal hangouts and
loitering places along these important routes. A real service may be
done for the new tenant by including information on interesting and
safe places to walk in the information brochure or bulletin board
notice.

Shopping   We have discussed shopping in relation to site selection, planning of services, and walking. The frequency of consideration of this activity underlines its importance in the lives of older people. An on-site store should be centrally located, certainly not far from the entrance lobby and elevator areas. We have seen some commissaries tucked away in the basement or a far corner. They are invariably dreary and have a much harder time attracting customers.

Fig. 24.   A small commissary provides for tenant needs and gives meaningful roles to those who operate it. (Photo by Richard Mowrey.)

Work Varying percentages of older tenants continue in paid employment. For the most part, the design of the environment is irrelevant to this behavior, except as it affords easy access to the place of employment, such as negotiable pathways, transportation aids, safe passage, and so on. Once in a while a person may come into a housing environment with a skill that could be practiced if space were available, such as cabinetmaking, watch repairing, or hand tailoring. In these relatively rare instances, the administrator may be able to find a corner of a basement where a work surface and a light might be installed, or he might allow the tenant to keep a locked cabinet or a workbench in a communal hobby or workshop area. A much bigger operation is the sheltered workshop, for which there may be a relatively limited demand. Among less competent populations, such as those who may populate congregate housing, the appeal of a workshop might be greater than in ordinary housing. The sponsor should decide early whether or not to go into this area, because specifically designed space is necessary. There is considerable information on sheltered workshops in the rehabilitation literature which we recommend to the interested, though we shall not cover it here.

KNOWING THE WORLD

To live a satisfying life one must be able to comprehend the world around him. "Successful adjustment" is, in fact, defined by some people as the ability to manipulate the objects and the social environment in which one lives. Therefore, anything we can do to add clarity to the housing environment, without destroying its esthetic or human quality, will no doubt aid some individuals to live more happily there.

Orientation We have spoken already of the importance of lighting and lack of total symmetry in keeping a tenant aware of where he is in the hallway. Similar considerations apply to site entrance walks, exterior building entrances, and ground-floor entryways. The first look at a building may color the prospective tenant's longterm attitude toward it, and his first look is likely to be taken when he is anxious for other reasons, such as the need to move. Ambiguity as to how he should enter will compound his anxiety.

Fig. 25. There is no doubt about the name of this housing and its street number. Their graphic quality conveys a sense of status. It would have been even better to include the street name.

We suggest several approaches to clarity:

1.   A definite street address (i.e., not just "York House South, Philadelphia, 19141," but always including "5325 Old York Road" when an address is printed on any material like a brochure or stationery). It is helpful to include the nearest cross street.

2.   A street number *and* a name sign visible from the sidewalk at the main approach. Such signs can look very institutional, especially when additional specifications like "Zenith Housing Authority" or "Associated Church Charities" are included. The task is clearly to design a highly visible and high-status denoting sign.

Fig. 26. The pillar at the entrance aids in orientation. In a more urban area, the street address should also be included. (Photo by Richard Mowrey.)

3. Making certain that city street signs are provided at nearby intersections. Some cities, for example, do not put up signs denoting main arteries except at major intersections. Corners near the housing site should have every street clearly marked.

4. The main walk to the main entrance should be clearly denoted, whether by locating the sign there, building an imposing gateway or pillars, or paving with a different material from other paths. For entrance walks of any substantial length, an "Entrance" sign with arrow might be provided.

5. If the office is anywhere other than near the building entrance, it, too, should be clearly marked by signs and arrows.

6. If the front door is locked and must be opened from within, instructions should be provided in large type at the doorway.

Fig. 27. Bulletin boards help in maintaining one's orientation to the world within and without the housing, especially when notices are made as legible as these.

7. A listing of tenants' names and their apartment numbers at the entrance should be maintained and clearly legible. If there are only a few dwelling units that use the entry, additional directions (i.e., "2nd floor," "rear," etc.) might be in order.

8. Immediately inside the building, aesthetically pleasing signs should direct the person to the office, elevator, or other important spaces if their location is not immediately apparent.

9. People expect elevators to be visible on entering a building. Since it is also safer to be able to see the waiting area from outside, there is almost no justification for making the user walk around a corner or behind a wall.

10. A large-scale simplified map of the neighborhood with transportation route numbers to more distant locations can be very helpful.

LIFE ENRICHMENT

A very wide range of possibilities exists for building in opportunities for growth and meaningful activity in ways that go beyond the basic life-sustaining activities. Existing housing provides radical contrasts in this area, from the resource-poor public housing with no common space other than the outdoors to the riches of the retirement village with golf course, archery range, pool, and sauna. Lest this structure-oriented section seem naive in ascribing too prominent an enriching role to physical factors, let us state once and for all that the major factor in a vital activities program is management and staff. Our concern here is with the physical features that can potentiate the effect of creative staff.

Every housing environment can provide enrichment through organized activities, individual activities, the esthetic enjoyment of beautiful and warm surroundings, effective use of the outdoors, and the opportunity to watch interesting things. As we consider each of these categories separately, it will be obvious that the greater the financial resources of the project, the more varied will be the enrichment. However, no project is so poor that it cannot become more enriched by thinking carefully about the best utilization of whatever resources it may have.

Organized Activities As far as we know, every high-rise or large single-entrance building has at least one room designated as common space, whether it be called a community room, all-purpose room, activity room, or merely a lobby. Smaller garden, row, duplex, or detached-unit projects may not have even this much. Since we are talking primarily to people planning new projects, let us say very strongly that a project simply should not be built unless it can include such space, or unless the site is chosen explicitly because it is within one block of an existing activity center. We have spoken repeatedly of the importance of locating any resource whose utilization we wish to maximize as close as possible to the potential user. There is a direct inverse relationship between distance and utilization, whether the scale be in miles or footsteps.

Even the within-project location of a center may affect participation noticeably. The excellent activity program of the Cleveland Metropolitan Housing Authority operates in a number of locations. Its staff feel strongly that maximum participation comes when the activity center is within the high-rise building, as compared to the situation where the tenant must walk 60 feet from his residential building to a separate activity building. The latter, in turn, attracts more tenants than the center located in one building attracts from

Fig. 28. Warm and beautiful surroundings make people of any age feel good. The clock is attractive, but should always have numerals as an aid to time orientation. One hopes that there is an alternative to the step barrier at lower right. (Photo by Richard Mowrey.)

another building located two blocks away. Even within a single building, recreation activities held on an upper floor suffer from a slight disadvantage as compared to those held on the ground or second floors.

The moral, thus, is as usual, to choose a central location for organized activities. The all-purpose room has relatively little competition for this central space, as it can connect directly with the lobby. However, where spaces are more differentiated in use, the lobby, the elevators, the staff offices and a store or snack bar may pre-empt these prime locations. It is reasonable to think of activity space as second in priority for centrality of location, since the activities themselves have intrinsic drawing power and depend a little less than do these other spaces on natural traffic for recruiting of participants. Thus, a group activity room might be at one end of a ground-floor wing, or in a wing of its own connected directly to the

Fig. 29. Staff have obviously tried hard to humanize a sterile space, but the poverty of materials and structure is against them. (Photo by Sam Nocella.)

main building. Slightly less desirable would be a second floor location, and even less so a basement or top-floor location.

The all-purpose room may use up the budget of a sponsor. If other spaces can be built, what priorities should be put on other types of space? No answer will fit all situations, to be sure. However, there does appear to be a purpose served by smaller rooms equipped with tables and chairs. Such rooms cannot usually be justified on the basis of high density of use. However, every project has tenants who may be drawn to specialized, smaller-group activities if they are held in a room of smaller scale than the community room (such rooms also have great utility for unprogrammed social use, as we shall discuss later in this chapter). These rooms may be designated as game rooms, card rooms, parlors, and so on— even as small a room as 10 feet by 10 feet will justify its presence in diversifying a project's activity possibilities.

An auditorium with a stage is definitely a luxury. Where resources

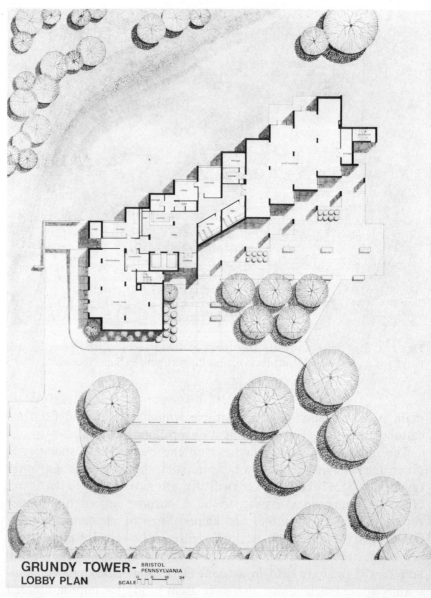

GRUNDY TOWER- BRISTOL
PENNSYLVANIA
LOBBY PLAN SCALE ⌐┬⌐┬⌐━━━┐
0 9 16 24

Fig. 30. An ideal solution to the competition for centrality of location among various spaces. The lobby is large enough for seating and affords a view of the entranceway, the elevators, and mail areas. The manager's office and receptionist are located close to all important areas. The multipurpose room can afford to be further from the center because of the intrinsic drawing power of its activities. (Louis Sauer Associates Philadelphia, Architects.)

168

Fig. 31. One or two small social rooms may encourage small-group activities. (Photo by Richard Mowrey.)

Fig. 32. A function room large enough to accomodate all tenants is a desirable luxury. (Photo by Sonny Gottlieb.)

are limited a community room with folding chairs can usually serve the purpose, although it ought to be large enough to seat at least 75 percent of the project's tenant population at one time. Where a project serves a particularly independent and active tenant population, and there is ample budget for activity personnel to facilitate the program, an auditorium with stage, level floor, and portable seats and tables might be considered third in order of priority to a medium-sized community room and a couple of small rooms. Activity centers planned to serve both housing environment and the surrounding community might also find a use for this type of space. Only the genuine luxury establishment where money is no object will even consider a fixed-seating sloped-floor auditorium.

There is considerable question as to whether specialized spaces for a number of activities are desirable. Unquestionably, options are extended and sometimes a gracious look imparted to a housing environment by the presence of purpose-built spaces whose uses are designated by permanent and semifixed props: music room, library, art gallery, weaving room, pottery shop, pool room, and so on. Our impression is that the law of diminishing returns applies as spaces are added beyond the first couple of special-purpose rooms. Systematic observation reveals a very low density of use of such spaces.

Let us momentarily leave this issue unresolved and consider the possible consequences of having only a single multipurpose activity space. Our observations reveal their use to be approximately as follows, in decreasing order of frequency:

1. Unprogrammed sitting and socializing
2. Scheduled activity participation (meetings, lectures, movies, concerts, parties)—infrequent, but of high density when they do occur
3. Lunch, where applicable
4. Television watching

Specialized activities such as listening to music or hobbies and crafts almost never occur there unless explicitly and aggressively organized. On the other hand, these activities also will not usually take place unless there is a staff member assigned to organize and lead them. Thus a decision must be made very early in the planning as to whether there is enough operational money or community resources to insure adequate staffing for the full utilization of the space.

Our own suggestion would be to put a craft and hobby room fourth in the priority line, provided it could be equipped (loom, sewing machine, jig saw, kiln, pottery wheel) reasonably well to

Fig. 33. (*a, b, c,* and *d*) Specialized spaces such as a separate library, pool room, art room, or card room may have a low volume of use, but increase opportunities for the enrichment of some tenant's lives. [(*a*) Photo by Richard Mowrey. (*b*) Photo by Richard Mowrey. (*c*) Photo by Richard Mowrey. (*d*) Photo by Sam Nocella.]

Fig. 33 (*b*)

Fig. 33 (*c*)

Fig. 33 (*d*)

begin with and there was assurance of adequate leadership. Public housing authorities will not be able to do this, but a senior center organization can. While there are an unfortunate number of little-used spaces of this kind in existing housing environments, coming generations of older people should find such activities more and more consistent with their accustomed life styles.

We have observed very few craft-like activities going on in a project's single community room. This does not, of course, mean that such behavior is inconsistent with the purpose of these rooms. It may be that the basic reason is that housing with only a community room as common space is also likely to be poor in resources for leadership in craft activities. It could also be that people feel uncomfortable engaging in such self-expressive behavior in a location where traffic is dense and onlookers many. Actually, much can be done to experiment with ways of delineating parts of community rooms so that they temporarily become specific-activity spaces. For small-group singing, for instance, an upright piano can be set at a right angle to the wall near a corner, and pianist and singers can be

Fig. 34. A corner location for a piano allows its use by people who might feel diffident about playing in a more conspicuous place. This electronic organ has the advantage of being easily changed in location.

partially shielded from the full scrutiny of casual traffic. It is also worthwhile to experiment with 4 or 5-foot high storage cabinets on casters, which may stay locked and placed against a wall most of the time, but moved out as a partial room divider during scheduled activities. The back of such a piece should be attractively designed so that an ugly functional exterior is not presented to other room occupants. People can always work behind the divider at movable tables, or fold-down counter space may be designed. The important point is that some people need moderate privacy to make them feel comfortable while painting or making objects. Yet, complete privacy is neither attainable nor desirable. The partially divided space limits the audience to a usually more tolerable few, and to some extent encourages watching by those who are really interested.

Just behind the hobby room in priority for the right tenant group is a library. "The right tenant group" means one deemed particularly likely to value such a resource—housing beamed toward retired teachers, professionals, or members of any group who were particularly oriented toward learning as a way of life. Our experience has been that while libraries get very low density of use, their symbolic meaning is very positive for these groups.

Individual Activities We have spoken of the special concessions that can be made to individual activity interest within the dwelling unit or related to the maintenance of the housing plant. Some organized activities basically involve creative effort, such as printing, pottery, weaving, and so on. Beyond these already-discussed subjects, one can think of the dilemma of how to deal with the instrumental musician. Does one allow a piano in a small apartment? Hopefully the walls constructed to afford adequate auditory privacy in general will allow the continued exercise of musical talent.

Pet ownership is a touchy issue. We have found no high-rise projects that allow pets; the problems here seem insurmountable. However, very few other building types allow them either, and this is harder to understand. Knowing the proverbial importance of the pet dog or cat to an occasional older person, it seems incumbent on a sponsor to think of a way to allow this all-important life enricher to the few who care that much. A person who can handle the independent life style required by garden, duplex, or detached-unit living can probably handle the extra jobs of cleaning, feeding, and walking the pet. Some special requirements may be imposed on the pet owner: no wall-to-wall carpeting, or a special crack-filling coating for the floor. He may have to agree to certain conditions, such as use of an approved cat box, regular sanitary inspection, willingness to guarantee payment to a dog-walker if unable to do it himself, and of course, realizing that if the pet constitutes a genuine nuisance to others he may have to get rid of it.

Esthetic Enjoyment   It seems necessary to assure people repeatedly that older persons appreciate beautiful things too. Mental patients and public housing tenants have frequently been told, by implication, that the beautiful things of life are not for them, and older people have come in for the same sort of disrespect. Stark exteriors, tile or cinderblock interior walls, unadorned entryways, and drab

Fig. 35.   It is hard to prevent a high rise from having the stigma of public housing. Oscar Newman feels that the low-rise structure is worth its additional land cost in its better ability to blend in with other neighborhood structures.

colors are likely to be justified in terms of both cost and their lesser degree of inappropriateness for members of these deprived statuses. In his study of crime in New York City public housing, Oscar Newman (1972) attributes some of the crime risk to the unmistakable stigma of physical construction that sets the typical public housing project apart from its neighbors. Shady neighbors see buildings of this type as fair game for their shady activities. While Newman's complaint is directed toward the high-rise building located amid low-rise structures, it seems clear that the stigma of ugly design is just as effective in contributing to the lowered livability of the cheap-looking project for the elderly.

It is of interest to note that a HUD study has shown that per-unit construction costs of 202 projects were at the very least no more expensive than public housing, yet these latter are much more likely

Fig. 36. Not every high-rise public housing building is stigmatized. This building also allows a view of the river from almost every unit. (Louis Sauer Associates, Philadelphia, architects. Photo by David Hirsh.)

to bear the stigma of depersonalized design. Noninstitutional paint colors cost little more than the drab greens of the asylum. Especially if one considers the lack of vandalism in housing limited to the elderly, there would seem to be no reason for wall surfaces whose only virtue is ease of maintenance.

Some things do cost more. To nondesigners like the author it seems inconceivable that any architect could produce a box-like structure unadorned with window mouldings, exterior accents, or breaks in the surface. Sometimes small things may contribute a great deal to the perceived beauty of even the least expensive building. An entrance overhang frequently contributes status to a building, especially when built in an identifiable colonial or "modern" style. Panels of color on a building's exterior give identity and beauty, as do admittedly more expensive tile patterns or mosaics. Large building scale risks conveying the institutional stigma,

Fig. 37. An unusual-looking entrance facade can give status to an ordinary high-rise building. (Demchik & Supowitz, Philadelphia, architects. Photo by Sam Nocella.)

although some of the above personalized touches may "elevate" them to the class of the luxury institution rather than the poor-man's institution.

Balconies can give a something-special look to a building, although they do add to its cost. Whether or not to provide balconies is a question that has preoccupied many planners. Facts relevant to this question have emerged from our research. In a couple of high-rise buildings we have studied, we have observed directly and counted whether people are on their balconies or not. Our estimates

Fig. 38. Balconies lend status to a building, in addition to their other functions. (Photo by Richard Mowrey.)

Fig. 39. An aesthetically pleasing structure motivates more visiting by children and grandchildren. (Photo by Sam Nocella.)

run less than 5 percent—however, it is important to note that this is the number counted at a *single time*. We also have asked people how frequently they use their balconies—in several different research projects, people with balconies tell us that on the average they use them once or twice a week in good weather, although about one third of our tenants use them almost every day. About one fourth of our tenants without balconies tell us they would spend some of their hypothetical $20 extra per month for this purpose. It does seem that this information adds up to the idea that it is difficult to justify balcony costs on the basis of large demand and density of use: by every standard, a majority of tenants express little interest in having balconies and use them infrequently if they have them. On the other hand, to a substantial minority they do seem to be important. The balcony would seem to be a good example of a feature that could be provided as an option, with about 20 percent to 25 percent of apartments being built with private balconies, this percentage being derived from a conservative interpretation of the above figures.

Fig. 40. This balcony with a beautiful view was built in a project also housing families. The grillwork spoils the view, has the connotation of a prison or asylum, and is totally unfunctional for the elderly. (Photo by Sam Nocella.)

Naturally, local conditions such as sun, rain, wind, and temperature might dictate the locations of the balconies and the proportion of apartments built with them: hopefully a combination of good weather and an exceptional view might constitute adequate justification for building all units with balcony. In privately built housing, an extra rental of $10 per month for units with balcony probably would be feasible. This rent differential does build in a mechanism for undesirable status grouping. However, our feeling is that even in the absence of a rent differential for special features, people will find other ways to denote their peers' status; therefore it seems like a minor problem. In public housing, it might be more difficult to convince an authority that tenants deserve such a "frill" when they cannot charge more rent. What we would anticipate happening here is that there would be a minority of tenants who would wish such apartments badly enough to ask to be on a waiting list for the next opening and be willing to move from their balconyless apartment when one becomes available. Because of the less elastic nature of this demand, the proportion for public housing might be reduced to 15 percent or 20 percent.

The shared balcony may be a more feasible feature where the budget is low. In one building that we studied there was relatively high density of use—about 10 percent to 15 percent of the tenants— of such balconies in summer evenings as the sun went down. They do, of course, serve a social as well as a purely personal-enjoyment function. The location of such one-per-floor balconies may be determined by many considerations. However, they will get more use if shaded from the afternoon sun (in general, if resources are limited, in moderate climates the gain seems to be greater from facilitating shaded afternoon sitting in hot weather than sun-exposed sitting in cool weather). As with all other facilities, central locations encourage greater use. An ideal location would be directly opposite the elevator exit on each floor, preferably with ample windows or a glass door through which a balcony sitter could see people getting off the elevator and be seen.

The balcony has a use beyond the enrichment of the balcony sitter's life. Balconies give interest to buildings by breaking the monotony of the alternating windows and exterior panels, plus giving all tenants another increment in perceived status.

Fig. 41. The shared balcony is a good compromise with cost. (Louis Sauer Associates, Philadelphia, architects. Photo by David Hirsh.)

We shall discuss the combination common balcony-hallway (single-loaded outside corridor) in the next section, since this kind of balcony is more relevant to social behavior than to esthetic enrichment.

Halls are difficult to beautify. Colorful, patterned wallpaper can reduce the institutional quality, as can heavy-duty carpeting whose pattern will mask stains. Lighting is extremely important. Some overhead lights may be necessary, but there should be wall lights also to break the monotony with patterns of relative lightness and

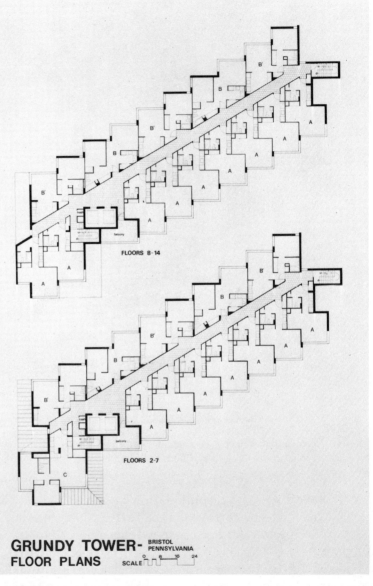

FLOORS 8-14

FLOORS 2-7

GRUNDY TOWER- BRISTOL PENNSYLVANIA
FLOOR PLANS SCALE 0 8 16 24

Fig. 42. The living-floor plan of the building in Fig. 41 shows the proximity of the shared balcony to the elevator. If other demands allowed it, it would be even better for balcony occupants to be able to look at people leaving the elevator. Some space for seating is available in the widened hall by the elevator. The offset angle of apartment doors helps greatly to break up the monotony of the hallway. (Louis Sauer Associates, Philadelphia, architects.)

darkness along the walls. A shallow alcove for a light adds still further to a comfortable appearance. Different colored doors and door frames are very easy ways to make the hallway more attractive. Setting doorways in by only 6 or 8 inches adds to the interest of a hallway.

By far the best way to build a hall is to make it as short as possible. A cylindrically shaped building, whose floor sections are round and whose apartments are wedge-shaped, minimizes hall length. In most such cases, the elevators, stairs, and service core will be in the center, with the apartment entrances on the outer periphery as one exits from the elevator. From the point of view of esthetics, this arrangement seems much preferable to the long hall. Our feeling is that this arrangement should be reserved for situations of high physical security, since there is some hazard in the possibility of a mugger's concealment around the bend. This situation is more pronounced when the building is built with the hall wrapped around

Fig. 43 (a). The exciting cylindrical-shaped towers of Wesley Woods, Atlanta, Georgia. (Charles Edward Stade & Associates Park Ridge, Illinois, Architects. Photo by Hedrich-Blessing.)

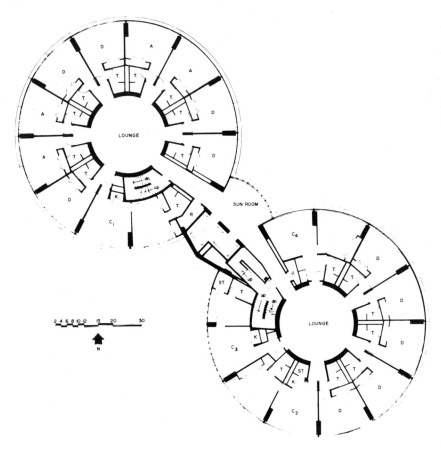

Fig. 43 (b).   The floor layout of Wesley Woods allows a social-behavior-inducing central area with no pillar or obstruction. Each lounge is individually decorated with contributed furnishings. The sun room is ideally located across from the elevator.

a square elevator-service core. The corners make it even easier for someone to hide out of sight from the elevator exit. One situation we have seen (Wesley Woods, Atlanta, Georgia) has the service-elevator shaft in a small connecting wing between two cylindrical towers. The entire center space of each tower is open, so that one walks a few paces from the elevator and into an open circular area about 30 feet in diameter, off which the apartment doors open. The

Fig. 43 (c).   Traditional, modern, or mixed decor can all be pleasing, and older people adapt to new styles as well as anyone else. (Louis Sauer Associates, architects. Photo by David Hirsh.)

effect is extremely pleasant, and tenants take considerable pride in this unusual design.

We have found little to support the idea that any particular style of decor is preferable to another. A warm feeling may be conveyed by a colonial or Victorian decor, but this frequently is the result of the greater allowable clutter, or informality, in these styles, as compared to "modern" decor. Current fashions sometimes are jarring to the new tenant as he first experiences a new building. Adaptation is (sometimes mercifully) swift, however, and one cannot argue convincingly that "modern" is less acceptable. All too frequently contemporary furniture and fixtures border on the institutional. Metal-bordered tables, imitation wood-grain surfaces, ceiling lighting, starkly four-square chairs, and shiny plastic upholstery material may be preferred by some because of their greater durability and ease of maintenance. These features detract greatly from livability. It would be preferable to equip common spaces sparsely with purchased furniture and supplement it with gifts that can be retired and replaced with other gifts when worn out than to fully equip the area with indestructible institutional furniture. Some environments succeed quite well in encouraging tenants and their families to put their own pieces of furniture in hallways or common spaces near their dwelling units. The esthetic results of such collections are, to be sure, mixed, but seem preferable to a carefully decorator-selected grouping.

Our clearest information on the behavioral effects of the physical environment comes in the area of social interaction. In general, the closer one is to other people, the greater the likelihood that he will interact with them. In the institution where privacy is greatly limited, of course, interchange is deliberately and self-protectively turned off in the midst of physical proximity to other patients. In a more normal living situation, however, easy accessibility to people with whom one has something in common is the key to rewarding social behavior. The "something in common" is frequently a matter of age—people who are roughly the same age are more likely to share values, to have experienced the same historial events, and to have similar associations to names, songs, and so on than are people of different generations.

We do not yet have adequate information on which to base an opinion as to whether the greater clustering of older people afforded by high-rise structures leads to more friendly visiting or casual contacts than does living in more dispersed units. We suspect that where people have a choice, the more active and independent will choose the dispersed style of project; their better state of health might well enable them to maintain at least as high a level of social interaction as those in poorer health, whose visiting behavior in turn is facilitated by living in a high-rise building.

What are the factors that produce social interaction more easily in a high-rise building? The existence of halls, elevators, and a front entranceway force people to use the same physical spaces, and these forced encounters obviously lead to social behavior. Research shows very clearly that people who live next door or across the hall from one another are more likely to be friends than people who live several doors apart. People who live on the same floor are more likely to be friends than people who live on different floors. People who live in the same building are more likely to be friends than people who live in neighboring buildings.

Furthermore, this "local dependence," as the sociologist Dr. Irving Rosow calls the proximity effect, is likely to be greater for people who are limited physically, or restricted in their freedom of movement by social norms or personality disposition. Thus, women, the foreign-born, the sick, and the poor are more likely than people of contrasting statuses to choose their friends from among close neighbors. The high-rise building, then, has many advantages for people whose ability to move freely through space in search of friends with common interests is limited.

Since many elderly tenants come into planned housing with the explicit aim of curing their loneliness or adding to their social opportunities, we can accept social interaction as a positive goal of housing and explore how structure can amplify these opportunities.

THE SIZE OF THE PROJECT

One of the first decisions to be made about housing is how many people should it serve. We have delayed discussion of this important matter so long because it seems to us that one of the really important considerations in determining size is whether the size of the project really has anything to do with the chances of an older tenant's living a fulfilling life. Psychological research on high schools has been quite clear in demonstrating the following facts:

- There are more varied activities in the large school.
- A greater *proportion* of students in the small school engage in school activities, however.
- The small school is more likely to encourage the marginally endowed student to participate in its activities.
- The large school is more likely to provide an opportunity for the gifted to grow.

- An activity cannot take place at all unless there is a bare minimum number of potential participants from which to recruit.

Since we do not yet have comparable information on housing for the elderly, we must argue from what *seems* reasonable. The British Ministry of Housing decided at one point that 75 units was the maximum number that should be built in one project. We inquired extensively among English authorities as to the origin of this standard. It was traced to a minister who thought people "looked happier" in small projects!

Evidence is at hand to show that both very small (5 to 30 units) and very large (200 or more) projects exist where people are extremely satisfied. Our informal observation is that there are more activities performed by tenants on the site in large projects: tenants in small projects seem to be better integrated into the outside community, but get little help from within the project in amplifying their social lives unless there happens to be some resource like a senior center located on or very near the project. The last point made by Barker and Gump relating to the minimum number of people required for an activity to take place is almost certainly true in housing for the elderly. A very small project cannot have an active social life of its own, unless people are sharing the basic activities of daily living, such as cooking, housekeeping, or shopping. No one activity is likely to appeal to more than a small proportion of the tenants. Thus, tenants in very small projects may be better off if they are very independent and if they remain part of a nearby social network outside the housing.

It is almost impossible for a tenant in a small project to become "lost," however. Administrator, other tenants, and even nontenant neighbors will be very alert to an individual's needs or signs of distress. In a large project such disappearances would seem to be easier. We have looked very carefully at many large projects, however, and have been constantly surprised at how vigilant neighbors are with respect to one another's welfare. The right not to visit or be visited is greatly respected, but one another's goings and comings are still of great interest. As we have indicated elsewhere, casual encounters in a hallway can be satisfying social occasions for some; the sudden absence of such heretofore expected encounters with a neighbor is likely to bring a knock on the door from even the most reserved next-door neighbor.

There may be a threshold effect, a size beyond which problems begin to develop. We have seen a couple of buildings where the number of elevators was inadequate for the population or where the length of the hallway from the remote apartments to the elevator strained the limits of comfortable walking. Certainly, no manager can hope to know personally more than a couple of hundred tenants—but hopefully he might have the compensation of a larger staff among whom to spread the work. A large single-story building, or a very large number of garden apartments or detached units may be unable to avoid having people so dispersed that they cannot make full use of a central activity area. In this case, as with small projects, it is probably better for such projects to serve very independent people, especially people with their own cars.

There is no strong evidence to suggest that there are social deficits that are intrinsic either to large or small projects (provided that the latter can work out their finances properly). It does seem that small projects should not accept people of marginal competence unless they provide some special means to oversee their welfare. It would also be desirable for sponsors of high-rise projects of 200 tenants or more, or scattered projects of 100 tenants or more to look very carefully to see that their physical arrangements are consistent with the needs of tenants. The very large project should also have help for the manager in personal-social tenant relationships—an assistant, a social worker, or group worker—so that the shy, sick, or seclusive tenant does not become forgotten.

The desirability of maximizing the number of people using a single building entrance and of putting the high-action locations (community room, activity space and management offices) near the entrance has been mentioned previously. The more seating space in and near these areas the better. While some people go to these central locations to watch others, plenty of others go to pick up a conversation. Every lobby or community room has its steady clientele, even clique, for whom the area becomes a second home. Others move slowly and deliberately through the area long enough to say hello to a few people, to meet a friend, or to survey whether there is someone there whom he might wish to cultivate. Some such contacts lead to deeper relationships, and to visiting in one another's

Fig. 44. The lounge space is small and sometimes overcrowded, but is ideally located to allow its occupants to observe the highly interesting traffic at the main entrance. (Photo by Sam Nocella.)

dwelling unit. Many others stay on the casual-contact level. The latter can be extremely meaningful, and the environment provided in the central entrance area can be the critical element in affording social fulfillment to such people.

The entrance lobby itself should ideally be large enough for at least a dozen people to sit in comfortably. Not only should the seats be comfortable (*not* decorative cast-iron chairs, for example!) but also they should be relatively movable for conversational grouping or solitary placement. They should also be placeable against a wall surface, since people prefer the physical and psychological security that comes from a solid backing and the knowledge that nobody will approach them from the rear. Many administrators intensely dislike the look of older people sitting in a lobby. Their views are frequently shared by families, board members, community residents, and some tenants, all of whom are made very anxious by the look of people

Fig. 45. The amount of interesting activity to watch in this entrance lobby is increased by the proximity of the receptionist and the mailboxes. (Photo by Richard Mowrey.)

Fig. 46. All important areas are visible to a person located in any area: reception desk, elevator, entrance lobby, and sitting room. In addition, an on-site store is located to left of picture. (Demchik & Supowitz, Philadelphia, architects. Photo by Sam Nocella.)

Fig. 47. Nothing could be less comfortable and discouraging to lobby watching than these cast-iron seats.

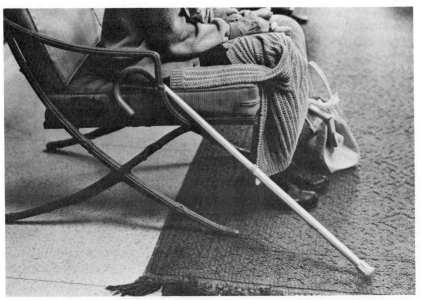

Fig. 48. A chair should have stably balanced arms extended forward as far as possible for ease in getting out of the chair. The designer of this chair understood the direction in an exactly opposite fashion.

who seem to be inactive. Their fantasies sometimes lead them to think that the "sitters-and-watchers" are grimly awaiting death. Actually, for many, this sitting by the front door is a highly active social event, and for others, the watching aspect is a highly participating event, though "passive" by our middle-life standards. If one is unable to move about as one was once accustomed, what better substitute can there be than to watch the behavior of those who do move about easily? Thus, we advise designers and administrators alike to encourage, rather than discourage, lobby sitting.

The lobby, as we have spoken of it throughout this chapter, has a number of demands made of it. In addition to being the entranceway, it is a social room, a point from which interaction between tenants and management can be encouraged, a gateway to the community room and possibly activity spaces, a place from which to monitor the admission of outsiders, and a space for the very visible location of elevators in a high-rise building. Thus, the lobby is likely to be cut up with many doors and entranceways. If it is also to have wall space for sitting, its size becomes fairly large. Cost limits will frequently keep down its size, but there is no excuse ever to build a tiny vestibule with no seating and no visible elevator.

The community room will always be separate from the lobby. No matter how large and warm the lobby, its high level of traffic makes it unsuitable for the protected leisurely sitting and planned activities that go on in the community room. On the other hand, there are many virtues in giving some of the inhabitants of the community room a good wide view of the lobby, whether with a very wide opening, a double door, or a glass partition. The last frequently acts as a means of attracting people entering the building to the ongoing activity in the community room while still affording auditory separation of the two areas. The advantages of giving the community room occupants a good view of the outdoor entrance walk outweigh the disadvantages. The uneasy, seclusive, or suspicious tenant will undoubtedly dislike the scrutiny given to his goings and comings. However, traffic is intensely interesting to many people; the more chances given to the sitter-and-watcher, the more enriched his life will be. Just as importantly, such a situation allows the community room occupant to monitor the behavior that goes on near the building entrance—a definite plus for safety.

The same considerations apply to the one-story motel-like structure. Having a single main entrance will enhance both social behavior and security, although there would have to be other ground-floor exits.

Where the number of units sharing a single entrance is very small, say eight or fewer, it is unlikely that an entrance lobby will get much use as a social space. In this case, functional utility and physical safety are the primary considerations.

On the living floors of elevator buildings, chairs or benches placed by the elevator may encourage some degree of interaction. Much has been speculated about the use of small common rooms on each floor to enhance social behavior. Our research evidence discourages this notion. When the social room is at the far end of the corridor from the elevator, even with a beautiful view it goes virtually unused for anything other than staff lunches or naps. The sitting room by the elevator has a better chance, especially if it is completely open to the hall on one side, but even here, use is very low. One exception was in an urban high rise in Puerto Rico, where the designated small social space by the elevator on each floor, as well as the space at the ends of hallways, were furnished by tenants and plainly used. This is probably much more likely to happen in a society where interaction is normally freer than in our suspicious mainland cities.

Living-floor social spaces also get somewhat more use when they are outdoor balconies, as we have mentioned earlier. The single-loaded outdoor deck serving as corridor is another relatively high-use small social space, with the disadvantages both of displaying the traveler and of allowing him to look into other people's apartments as he walks along the deck. The tenants of Victoria Plaza in San Antonio, reported on by Dr. Frances Carp, complained some about this lack of privacy. However, we have found that such decks encourage very high use on hot evenings, much of the use being for social purposes. In one building studied in our research, half of the building featured a double-loaded enclosed corridor and the other half an outdoor single-loaded deck; the total amount of social behavior was several times higher in the wing with decks.

Except in these unusual instances, however, the number of people residing on a floor is seldom large enough to result in very frequent unplanned conversational groups. For such contact, people seem to prefer either their apartments or the really central ground-floor spaces. One reason for this preference is that living floors have so much less traffic to watch than ground-level spaces.

Fig. 49. Traffic past the more central living units aids in providing social encounters. However, the necessity for walking outdoors to other site facilities may limit occupancy to the most independent older tenant. (Photo by Richard Mowrey.)

Therefore, the expense of building small social spaces on every floor is difficult to justify. Dr. Sandra Howell of Massachusetts Institute of Technology has made the very valid point that while space alone cannot generate social activity, the lack of such small social spaces will most certainly prevent it. It is very true that special effort by the manager might succeed in getting the tenants on a floor to use these spaces to form cohesive small groups. Such effort is very demanding; our empirical observations show that apparently managers do not foster this kind of small-group activity very effectively. Our suggestion would be to make any such small amount of space into an outside balcony large enough for at least six people, with large windows or glass doors looking into the hallway to enhance the visual permeability of the space, but to avoid committing any large amount of space for this purpose. Some planners have placed social rooms on the top floor, either to take advantage of a view or deliberately to separate this activity space from competition with ground floor traffic and noise. Such a noncentral location gives the room an extra strike to begin with. Some people simply will avoid an activity that takes them to the top floor.

Floor laundry rooms are also frequently advocated, sometimes on a skip-floor or every third-floor basis, on the theory that they will be used both as laundries and as social centers. Again, our observations do not bear this out; only very rarely have we seen more than one person occupying such a room. Admittedly, most that we have seen have not been designed properly, so someone should really put the social-laundry idea to a fair test by designing a floor laundry with these features:

- At least four machines
- Pleasing decor, comfortable furniture, and a magazine collection
- Sound deadening (most laundry rooms totally prohibit conversations when a machine is operating)
- Good lighting, including large window area if possible
- Central location
- Good ventilation

Otherwise, a larger single ground-floor laundry with all the above features would probably do just as well, especially considering the fact that people might be stimulated to use other ground-floor areas while their laundry is in the machine. Direct access should be provided to a clothesline area, which is much more likely to be used as a social area in good weather with adequate security. The typical dingy basement laundry room should be avoided.

Projects with a dining room will find that the dining occasion is the height of the social day. Full advantage should be taken of this enforced clustering of tenants beyond the actual eating time. The project that can afford a dining room can probably afford a smaller lobby adjoining the dining room, or an end of the dining room with comfortable chairs and no tables. People will anticipate the meal time by coming to such an area half an hour or more before the meal. This is a most socially useful half hour, as is the corresponding post-meal half hour, especially if there are comfortable seats and warm decor where people wait. These highly social occasions also will stimulate tenants to concern themselves with how they appear to others.

Much research has been done on seating patterns. In general, it is most comfortable for people to talk to one another when their shoulders are angled at less than 180° to each other. The side-by-side position makes both eye contact and hearing difficult, and the face-to-face position, by enforcing eye contact, makes some people uncomfortable, perhaps because it symbolizes an adversary situation. A four-person table will put adjoining pairs at right angles to one another, a hexagonal six-person table will increase the group size in a desirable way, keep the angled orientation, and separate the face-to-face oriented people by a greater distance, which might relieve anxiety. The problems of interpersonal compatibility grow with the number of people to be seated, however. Four is probably a better number for a majority of tables, but there should be some six-person tables for larger self-chosen groups. The rectangular six-person table with two or three people sitting side-by-side should be avoided.

Fig. 50 (a).   Mealtime is the high social occasion of the day.

Fig. 50 (b).   Six-person dining tables are enjoyed by gregarious tenants. There should be two-person and four-person alternatives also. (Photo by Richard Mowrey.)

Fig. 51.   This area and its adjoining lounge is thick with people and conversation for half an hour before and after each meal. (Photo by Sam Nocella.)

More than the average amount of space should be provided between tables for people who walk with a wide gait, a shuffle, or with wheelchairs. Tables should be heavy and balanced so as to be able to take the full weight of a person's arms as he uses the table top for leverage in getting out of his seat. Some tables should be available that are high enough for a person in a wheelchair to come comfortably close while eating.

Special attention should be paid to the decor of the dining room, and frequent upkeep applied to prevent it from looking grimy and depressing. Textured table cloths or floors will inevitably develop the odor of spoiled spilled food, while smooth plastic table surfaces look institutional. Much can be done to produce a friendly atmosphere for eating by wood paneling, low lighting, graphics, plantings, and possibly room subdividers—ceiling hangings, screens, poles, or half walls.

The coffee bar, snack bar, or grill has been mentioned previously. Their social usefulness is probably enhanced by being located near enough to some regular activity or traffic to allow people to watch while sitting down. On the other hand, it should be clearly demarcated from other areas. Therefore, a half wall low enough for the sitter to look over, a large lattice, or widely spaced pole dividers might be used to shut off the bar from the rest of the community room, the lobby, or activity area.

Outdoor Spaces   Outdoor sitting is definitely as much a function of the weather as of the amount of interesting activity to watch. Expert advice should be sought so as to take advantage of every desirable sitting location under every possible condition: sun in winter, shade in summer, wind protection in winter, breezes in summer, outdoor sitting under a roof, and so on.

Some of these weather-determined locations will also be able to take advantage of interesting scenes to watch, such as the building entrance, a parking lot, a city sidewalk, a schoolyard, moving water, a cityscape, or a distant view. Where physical safety is good, seats near the clothes-drying area will attract small groups. If there is a much-used path leading from the sidewalk to the entrance, seats beside the path will serve the same function as indoor lobby seats.

The design of the outdoor seating is a major problem. The tradition has been to use very heavy fixed-location concrete or wood

Fig. 52 (a). If natural shade is not available, umbrellas may help. (Photo by Sam Nocella.)

Fig. 52 (b). Outdoor seating by the main entrance is a highly prized location. (Photo by Richard Mowrey.)

two-person benches. These have the disadvantages of being impossible to reposition in accordance with weather conditions, of frequently being uncomfortable and difficult to get out of, and of being impossible to rearrange for various social needs. In some locations, there is no choice but to make benches immovable to prevent

Fig. 53.   This outdoor seating has some shade and is oriented toward pedestrian traffic. This conversation group would have a better social orientation if some benches placed at right angles to one another were available. (Hirshen, Gammill, Trumbo & Cook, Berkeley, California, Architects. Photo by A. Youngmeister.)

Fig. 54. A great deal of pedestrian traffic comes through this wide circle between two buildings. It is popular for the usual social reasons and also because of its easy provision of people movement to watch. (Photo by Sam Nocella.)

stealing. However, any housing may provide relatively inexpensive folding aluminum chairs that can be stored in the building, taken out by a tenant, and returned when he is finished. Better-designed outdoor seating is definitely required, however. Planning and architecture students at the University of Southern California's Gerontology Center have designed such benches, which have been installed in MacArthur Park, a major gathering place for the elderly.

Aesthetic and functional considerations both require some fixed seats, and their arrangement can do much to provide options for tenants. To make a two-person bench private a tenant needs only to sit in the middle of it: therefore, all benches may be this size (benches long enough for three are wasted because of the difficulty of conversing down a straight row). Care should be taken to isolate a few benches from other benches for the person who likes to sit alone. There should be a number of bench pairs at right angles to one another, the preferred orientation for social interaction. A couple of U-shaped sets of three benches might be set up to accomodate larger groups. Where there is a natural center of activity such as a fountain or flower bed, benches might be set in a wide circle facing inward. This arrangement is more for watching than for social interaction. Therefore, a path should go through, not around the outside of the circle, so pedestrian traffic can be watched. If the option of looking outward from the circle is desired, back-to-back benches may be used.

There is no excuse at any time (except possibly in a narrow circle bench around a fountain) for any bench to be without a back, nor should the seat be made of concrete. The seat should not slope per-

Fig. 55. These living units have porches in close proximity that allow enough privacy while still stimulating social behavior. (Hirschen, Gammill, Trumbo & Cook, Berkeley, California, architects. Photo by A. Youngmeister.)

ceptibly from front to back, and it should be relatively shallow. Most ordinary park benches are too low for older people. Permanently placed tables get relatively little use, although a couple of concrete tables with built-in chess boards may get occasional use. Four-person square redwood tables would be portable enough to be taken out and inside again each day for occasional use. Larger picnic tables with fixed plank benches are dysfunctional for stiff-limbed people, young or old.

If there is a bus stop adjacent to the site, benches with a roof overhang will encourage social behavior in addition to providing comfort.

In the case of detached, duplex, row-house, or garden apartments, a front-porch equivalent is well worth the effort, whether it be an extension of an entrance overhang under which a chair can be placed or a full screened porch. Being seen on one's front porch constitutes

Fig. 56. Outdoor seating in a pleasant courtyard. It is totally unused because it looks out onto nothing and because objects are thrown from windows above by children who live in the same building. (Photo by Sam Nocella.)

an effective social invitation, while at the same time offering the person the chance to watch automobile and pedestrian traffic.

Social Behavior within the Dwelling Unit Little evidence is at hand now to suggest any compelling effect of design on social behavior. It seems to be more a matter of personal preference than structure that determines whether a person will have neighbors visit within the dwelling unit. For a few people, visiting may seem less of a strain if there is a way to screen off the kitchen or one's bed from the view of company. Space for several seating choices and a dining table is a bare minimum requirement for visiting. We have found that where security is good, many people will leave their apartment doors open so they can be seen from the hall in case someone wishes to visit. Some thought might be given to making it possible for the tenant to sit where he may observe the door and also be seen by a person in the hall. Some tenants leave doors open for ventilation, others to gain a sense of security that someone may hear them call in an emergency. For these nonsocial door-opening reasons, tenants should have chain locks on the doors (and administrators should have available a chain-cutter for emergencies).

PRIVACY, TERRITORIALITY, AND PERSONAL PROPERTY

Housing normally does not have the same problems that institutions have in providing adequate opportunity for a tenant to be alone when he wishes. The dwelling unit is the tenant's private refuge, always available, and for the many who have moved from a shared household it seems like heaven on earth to have a place of one's own. There are other situations, however, where staking out one's turf may still be an issue.

In every housing environment there may be an occasional person who prefers sometimes to be in a common space and still reserve his right not to interact. Some do this successfully in the midst of activity or conversation: fellow tenants soon learn to recognize the signs he emits indicating that he wishes not to be bothered. Others will take a position where it is difficult for others to approach him— the center "half" of a park bench, a chair placed in a corner or along a short wall, and so on. This kind of public retreat apparently fulfills some people's needs. Solitary outdoor fixed benches are the

Fig. 57. Some people can, and should be allowed to, maintain privacy in the midst of a social scene.

easiest way to provide for such people. Some corners in community rooms can be fitted with single chairs, others with two-person couches placed at right angles for the social types.

There are occasional housing projects that encourage two unrelated people to share a dwelling unit. There are always major problems in such an arrangement. If it must be done, care should be taken to make it easy for each occupant to define his own territory. The bedroom should be designed so that closet and bureau can be placed adjacent to their owner's bed, with all of these spatially separate from those of the roommate, preferably with the only shared space being the entranceway. If closets must be built in some other location not clearly related to each person's bed, they should be clearly positioned and preferably distinguished in their exterior color or decor.

In low-rise units there is an opportunity to personalize outdoor spaces in a way that is not possible with the high-rise building. Oscar Newman (1972) has made much of the fact that for people to wish to defend an area it must "belong" to an individual or a small group of individuals. Thus, wide expanses of lawn or concrete tend to be seen as everybody's and therefore as nobody's. Even when security is not the issue, people will use the space adjacent to their dwellings much more readily when there is something marking it as belonging

Fig. 58.   Even a very small amount of personalized outdoor land enhances the feeling that one has a home.

to them rather than to everyone. Thus, we suggest that there be some space at both the front and back of each ground-floor unit with a boundary denoting the change from one tenant's to another tenant's property. A small flower bed, a low hedge, stepwise terracing, a walkway, or even a small (six to twelve-inch) fence would do it.

Some projects have a walkway running parallel to and connecting the units. There is usually an option as to how close such a path will come to the structures. Such a path should come no closer than about 20 feet from the unit entrance. Both the path connecting this main path to the dwelling and the lawn beside it thus become personal property, and therefore more likely to be sat in or planted. Management, frequently responsible for grass cutting and snow shoveling, will naturally favor the arrangement giving long uninterruped expanses of lawn and a minimum total length of paths. These understandable impulses should be resisted in favor of the humanization of territory. In the back, vegetable gardening, charcoal broiling, or sunbathing are more likely when the plot is clearly one's own.

We have perhaps sometimes stretched a point in suggesting that desirable behaviors may be evoked by the proper physical design. The designers and planners are now free to ignore it all. Hopefully, however, they will be more likely to think in terms of social and personal needs of the consumer, rather than purely in terms of maintenance ease, cost, durability, or the administrator's comfort.

Design Considerations

Desirable Feature	Comment

A. Safety

Nonskid tub or shower-floor surface

Water temperature controls

Emergency signals	Two-way audio; dwelling unit to office, located in both bedroom and bathroom.
No thresholds on doors	Door-bottom strip for air and sound insulation.

Safety shutoffs for gas

Stove controls at front of stove	Back-panel controls risk getting burned

Burn shields for steam radiators

Some switch-controlled lights on walls	Less temptation for tenant to try to replace ceiling bulbs.
Nonskid rugs	Management should require treatment of small rugs.

Nontipping tables and chairs

Main doors balanced for easy opening

Pneumatic closers for main doors

Handrails in halls, on stairs, sloping walks	Necessary except for most healthy groups.
Phone jacks in living area and bedroom	Tenant may feel safer if phone near him.

Slow-closing elevator doors

Two-way audio communication between elevator and office

B. Health

Windbreaks and sunshades

Entrance overhang	Also may add to symbolic value of facade.

Covered transportation waiting area

Unobtrusive health-care area	
Warm decor for physician's office	Should look as much like living areas as possible.

Design Considerations (Continued—1)

Desirable Feature	Comment

C. Personal Security

Fence	High, protective fence inappropriate except in most crime-exposed location. Low fence or shrubs discourage ordinary pedestrian cross traffic.
Fenced-in clothesline area	Since two-way access to building required, fence may be necessary.
Security guard	24-hour protection necessary in some high-risk locations.
Outdoor, front entry, hallway, or elevator TV monitor	As above.
Front door lock operated by buzzer from dwelling unit	Instruction and continuous effort necessary to make tenants use properly.
Outside walk and entrance visible to both pedestrians, staff, and tenants	Monitoring by other people is most effective security.
Inside entryway visible to tenants and staff	Lobby seats, community room, receptionist's desk, staff offices effective locations.
Outside seating located near main entrance in view of pedestrians, tenants, and staff	
Outside seating nested in front building angle	
Entry from outside limited to single front door	
Vegetation limited to flowers, trees, or low, sparse shrubs	Thick shrubs give cover for criminals.
High outdoor illumination	Especially front walk, parking area, route to transportation stop.
No on-site pedestrian shortcuts for non-tenants	In high-crime areas, limited access is desirable.
No upper-floor alcoves or other hiding places	Right-angled hall turns should have convex mirrors.
Stairwells visible from outside building	
Low-rise unit front entrances facing inward	Crescent, L, or U-shaped configuration

Design Considerations (Continued—2)

Desirable Feature	Comment
Clear "ownership" of front and back-yard ground-level areas	Personalizing of space enhances people's responsibility for what occurs there.
Minimum number sharing a single entrance	Same principle as above.
Dwelling-unit peephole	No more than 60" high!

D. Size

Small (less than 50 units)	Less efficient to manage, and less opportunity for complete activity and service development; but opportunity for closer tenant and management relations, also integration with community.
Large (100 units or more)	Managers consider 100 units the minimum for efficient management. Some risk of depersonalization, site boundedness, and withdrawal of marginal tenants.
Dwelling-unit size	The larger the better, but little evidence that relatively small units are widely disliked. HUD MPS 255 sq. ft. for efficiency, 350 for 1-BR

E. Self-Maintenance Skills

1. Toileting

Full turning radius for wheelchair	
Outward-opening bathroom door	
Toilet in corner, lifting bar on right (or left) wall	
Toilet paper on side, not behind toilet	
Bathtub *plus* flexible shower and seat	The issue of tub or shower will never be settled.
Low tub height	
Clear, night-lit path from bedroom to bathroom	

Design Considerations (Continued—3)

Desirable Feature	Comment

2. Grooming

| Housing-provided full-length lighted mirror | Self-respect is aided by knowing how one looks. |
| Fold-up self-storing ironing board | |

3. Housekeeping

Much storage space	Where possible, maximum height 60".
Permanent-gloss, non-skid floors	Wall-to-wall carpet a desirable luxury.
Windows that work easily	
Window height allowing view while sitting	
Windowsills wide enough for flowers, etc.	

4. Eating

Dining-table space for 4	
Choice of dining-table location	Near kitchen or by window.
Movable screen or divider to shut off view of kitchen	

5. Sleeping

Separate bedroom desirable	
L-shaped room or shelf divider to hide bed	If efficiency units must be built.
Display mechanism for pictures	Pegboard, bulletin board, picture-hanging rail.

6. Body comfort

Individual unit heat control	
Air conditioning in most climates	
One wall-switch-controlled light for every room	

7. Walking

| Hand rails in corridors | |

Design Considerations (Continued—4)

Desirable Feature	Comment
Minimize steps	Any steps will limit occupancy to most healthy.
Clear contrast between step treads and risers	
Short hallways	
Smooth-paved main walks	Optional paths (e.g., garden walks) may be gravel or other pavement.

8. Work

Space for craftsmen to work	Workbenches, hand tools, etc.
Sheltered workshop	Requires professional direction.

9. Orientation

Denote location through color, graphics, asymmetry	Different hall colors, contrasting door colors.
Definite street address	
Noninstitutional exterior sign	
Street name signs near site	
Signs for main entrance, office, important interior spaces	
Instructions for gaining entry to locked front door	Continuous instruction to tenants on selective access to building.
Entryway directory of tenants	
Elevators visible from front entrance	
Large map with local resources marked	Also brochure for tenants with addresses and phone numbers.

10. Life-Enriching Activity

At least one centrally located community room	View of outer entrance and lobby desirable for occupants of room.
Community kitchen near community room	
Entrance lobby with many seats	Tenants love to watch entrance activity.
Small-group activity room	Card playing, small meetings, visiting.
Designated-activity rooms	Library, crafts, sewing, pool table.
Separate auditorium with stage	A luxury item.

Design Considerations (Continued—5)

Desirable Feature	Comment

11. Aesthetics

Aesthetic decor for all common space	Resist institutional furnishings—some clutter is desirable.
Warm exterior materials	Color accents and breaks in surface help.
Consistency of building structure with other structures in neighborhood	
High-status-connoting building facade	
Long hallways broken by variations in light, color, and surface	
Balconies desirable	Shared balconies near elevators desirable.

12. Social Behavior

Concentration of pathways and important areas near entrance and lobby	The more necessity for encounters, the more likely is social interaction.
Small on-floor social spaces	Relatively *low* usage.
Single-loaded outdoor corridor deck	Good for security and social interaction; bad for poor climate or those with strong privacy need.
Aesthetically pleasing, climate-controlled laundry room	Ground floor, with outside light and immediate access to clothesline area.
Comfortable lobby with chairs adjacent to dining room	The high social occasion is half hour before and after meals.
4-person and 6-person dining tables	A few 2-person tables for the less gregarious.
Wide dining-room table spacing	Some tables built for wheelchair use.
Snack bar, coffee shop	View of high-traffic areas desirable.

13. Outdoor Activity

Seating to suit all climatic conditions	Sun, shade, wind protection, shelter from rain.
Seating with maximum view of people activity, traffic, distant vistas	
Two-person benches	All with backs.

Design Considerations (Continued—6)

Desirable Feature	Comment
Right-angled, U-shaped, and solitary placements Some portable seats desirable Benches at transportation stop Front porch for low-rise units	Personal choice maximized.

14. Privacy

Individual dwelling units are the main means for gaining privacy	The needs for building security and for facilitation of social behavior do sometimes collide with wish for privacy. Where security is no problem, side entrance for those not wishing to be observed is desirable.

PART THREE

Management, Tenants, and Programs

chapter 8

The manager

The aspect of housing for the elderly that is most important, but about which least is known, is management. The reason we know so little about it is that there has been no technology of housing management developed through the early years of development of senior-citizen housing as a national phenomenon. In fact, as this is written, there are an infinitesimal number of people doing this all-important job who have had training specific to that job. To this writer's knowledge, the only university-based training programs that give instruction in both gerontology and housing management are the masters-level programs at North Texas State University and the University of Arizona, and the nondegree program at the Institute of Gerontology, University of Michigan. The National Center for Housing Management, spawned by HUD, promises to rectify this situation. It is now engaged in the instruction of people currently managing housing for the elderly.

What this means, of course, is that a professional role for the administrator is still in its early process of formation. We are all most vulnerable to experience when we are in the process of developing, so the present time may be the very best from the point of view of influencing the shape of this role for the years to come. In this section, we shall look at what is known about administration as a science and an art and consider very carefully the kinds of managerial preparation, selection, attitudes and behavior that we may wish to foster in order to make the housing environment a success.

THE HOUSING ADMINISTRATOR, 1971

In order to get some basic information about the situation as it existed going into the 1970s, the Philadelphia Geriatric Center surveyed the nation's two major housing programs for the elderly (the low-rent public housing and the Section 202 direct-loan program) by mail. The response was excellent, by the usual standards for this type of survey: about 60 percent of the 800 administrators of public housing projects and 70 percent of the 200 administrators for 202 projects responded to our request to complete a questionnaire about themselves, their attitudes toward their jobs, and their housing environments. Since a substantial proportion did not reply, we cannot, of course, be absolutely certain that those who did respond are typical of all administrators. However, this study provides the only information we have on the subject, and here is how the administrator looks:

1. He is typically middle-aged or older. Relatively few are under 40. More than a third (37 percent) of all our public housing administrators were 55 and over, and a very surprising 58 percent of 202 administrators were in this age range.

One factor in the tendency of the 202 administrator to be relatively old is that many of the sponsoring organizations have deliberately recruited a retired person to take on this job. We do not know whether the average age of the public-housing administrator in sites with housing built especially for the elderly differs from that of the administrator of family housing. However, it seems likely that there is some tendency for housing authorities to assign its middle-aged and older managerial personnel to senior-citizen housing, since less than 20 percent were under age 40. At the very least, we may say that recruitment for these positions from the ranks of younger people has not been very successfully pursued.

2. The administrator is likely to be male. The public-housing manager is just slightly more likely to be male, where the proportion of males to females among the 202 housing is a little less than two to one. Sexism? Probably so, but it is of interest to note how the public housing ratio is approaching equality; perhaps this form of housing may constitute the vanguard in demonstrating that effective management is not a sex-linked characteristic.

3. The administrator is typically a person with some college training but not a college graduate. About one-quarter of the people performing these jobs in public housing, and about 40 percent of those administering 202 projects are college graduates.

4.   The housing administrator will not become wealthy from his job, as now constituted. The median salary of the public-housing administrator was around $8000, the 202 administrator around $8800 in 1970. Many factors, of course, condition these figures. Some executive directors of small housing authorities are included in the public-housing totals, since they may perform all administrative functions; thus, the public housing figures may be inflated, and the actual administrator's salary even smaller than indicated. Among the 202 administrators, the higher end of the age range is partly composed of retired people who are paid much lower salaries than would otherwise be paid. (Dare we say they are being exploited?) In any case, salaries are likely to change very rapidly and upward, as the move toward professionalization continues.

5.   The administrator comes to his job from a variety of earlier occupational backgrounds. Public-housing managers are notable for having had to learn on their present jobs: only about 15 percent had previous experience in housing, half that many in welfare-related jobs, and less than 1 percent had worked with the elderly before. Among 202 managers, while the percentages with previous relevant experience are higher, still only one-fourth to one-third had the benefit of any of these types of experience.

One is forced to conclude that the management of housing for the elderly is an occupation into which most incumbents have fallen; they have not arrived there with a sense of accomplishing a long-standing occupational goal after following an obstacle-ridden path toward their occupation of choice. But how else does a new occupation establish itself? Precisely with the active effort of the most gifted of those who began by "falling into" it. In a way, this path toward housing management is similar to the paths taken by many people who do other types of work with the aged. The aged are a low-priority, negatively valued group, and it takes something special to attract a social worker, a physician, a research worker, or a psychiatric aide to work with older people. Let us then be thankful that a large number of dedicated people have found themselves in jobs requiring them to administer housing environments for older people.

Actually, while the paths toward this occupation are many and not always self-chosen, as a group, administrators seem reasonably satisfied with what they are doing. Four out of five find their work "very satisfying," and slightly over two thirds hope still to be working in housing for the elderly five years hence. Even if we discount a certain amount of this positive thinking as being conditioned by the need to give a socially desirable answer to our questions, we still did not produce any compelling evidence that housing managers are dissatisfied, on the whole, with the exception of their salaries. Only a third of the public-housing administrators and half of the 202 administrators felt that they were adequately paid.

According to their reports, administrators spend large and approximately equal amounts of time in direct contact with tenants and in various forms of record keeping. Next in order of time demands are the tasks of supervising other employees and dealing with the sponsor or the housing authority, while relatively little time is spent in talking to relatives of tenants.

Managers enjoy most their various means of communicating directly with tenants, whether it be in their offices, in the hall, or in the tenant's apartment. Other activities are less satisfying, although the only one actively disliked by any significant number is the inevitable paperwork (25 percent). Managers see the area in greatest need of more attention as that of visiting tenants in their apartments. While they do not avoid this type of interaction now, almost half feel that more of it would be desirable if there were time.

Within the context of general satisfaction, there are a number of problem areas where satisfaction is not complete. The following list shows the percentages of administrators who expressed some degree of dissatisfaction with each aspect of their jobs:

	202 Managers	Public Housing Managers
Not enough pay	41%	56%
Relatives of tenants who are demanding or uncooperative	51	50
Tenants who are impolite	42	49
Too much pressure	38	45
Too much work	25	35
Management policies and practices	20	32
Not enough recognition or prestige	10	21

Clearly, aside from the everpresent salary issue, it is the interpersonal aspect of their jobs that causes most tension. Knowing that managers are dissatisfied with the way many tenants and families of tenants relate to them should lead to the development of training procedures that stress human-service problem solving. A local or regional housing group in search of in-service training devices should strongly consider a group discussion method that would allow managers to ventilate their own frustrations while working mutually toward a technology of human service delivery within the housing environment.

Conversely, the following aspects of their jobs gave much satisfaction to managers:

	202	*Public Housing*
Helping older people	92%	96%
The gratitude expressed by tenants	82	75
Being in on policy formation	62	55
Trying out new programs	72	51

Thus, human relations are also the really satisfying, as well as the most tension-evoking aspect of the job. The creative, but less person-oriented aspects are less essential components of satisfaction—the average administrator has fewer occasions on which to exercise his innovative talents, as shown by the lower percentages of enjoyment of policy and program planning. In addition, a fair number could not rate these activities because they did not even apply to their situations.

The youth of the housing-manager profession is reflected in the relatively few signs of professionalization the average manager shows. Only half of the managers had *ever* attended a training course or training conference devoted to problems of managing housing for the elderly. Very few were members of any national organization even remotely related to the jobs they do, such as the American Association of Homes for the Aged (less than 1 percent), Gerontological Society (less than 1 percent), National Association of Housing and Redevelopment Officials (13 percent, most of them being executive directors, rather than housing managers), or National Association of Nonprofit Retirement Housing (16 percent of the 202 managers). Only 10 percent were members of any related state or local organization. While these managers recognize that professional meetings, management conferences, and periodicals ought to be the source of much good information on housing management, what they learn on the job is apt to be their only available source of information.

In summary, the typical manager appears to be a person who finds many more satisfactions than frustrations in his job. He has had little opportunity to learn formally about how to do his job, but has had to learn by doing. He is just beginning the process of professionalization. In order to do his best, he needs to be able to discuss appropriate job attitudes and attitudes toward older people with others who are doing what he is doing. He also needs to compare his experience with that of others in order to improve his skill in the technical aspects of housing management. We shall speak at greater length in succeeding chapters about attitudes and managerial roles.

chapter 9

The role of attitudes in the management of housing for the elderly

There has been a long history of investigation of attitudes and their relationship to behavior. An attitude has been defined as a psychological readiness to act in a particular way. Thus, a prejudiced attitude toward blacks may be seen as the internal readiness to act toward a specific black person as if he were a nonperson, exclude him from an invitation, laugh at him, and so on. This definition presumes that attitudes are at least consistent with behavior, if not direct causes of behavior. On the other hand, both everyday experience and research have made it clear that behavior is frequently at variance with the attitude one expresses. We may all be guilty of expressing more favorable attitudes toward a minority group than we actually show in our behavior. It is far easier to express an attitude of respect to older people than it is to speak kindly to a tenant making a loud and unreasonable complaint at the same time that two phone calls are coming in, the hot water heater has failed, and a board member is waiting to talk.

Nonetheless, there is a *general*, though imperfect, tendency for attitudes to be correlated with behavior, and under some conditions, behavior can be changed by an educational process directed toward attitudes. Thus, it is very important to examine the attitudes that may affect the behavior of the manager. The housing administrator, by being aware of his own attitudes, can not only alter them if necessary, but also redirect his behavior on the changed attitude.

The administrator's attitudes toward older people are inevitably conditioned by various stereotypes regarding older people that are shared by the larger society. An example is the stereotype about sexual aging, which tells us, in joke form, how old folks cannot perform any more. To be sure, when we look at any data on sexual activity, there is a decline with age—thus, the stereotype has spoken a truth. What the stereotype does not tell us, however, is when the "decline" sets in—about the age of 20, to be exact, in the case of males. Neither does it tell us a thing about the individual elderly person—the 33 percent of men whom Kinsey found to be sexually active after the age of 70 amounts to more than one and one-half million in absolute numbers—any one of whom might be your elderly tenant. Still, if you operated under the influence of the stereotype, you might be so unbelieving of the possibility of such behavior by your sweet seventy-sixers that you could let all kinds of things go on in your housing. Or, you might be so convinced that it should not happen that it would seem disgusting if it did.

In both of these instances, the problem is not that a stereotype necessarily lies about the statistical probability of an older person's differing from a younger person. The problem is one of believing it so much that one applies the statistical norm to every individual. Or there may be the reverse kind of problem where one wishes very strongly that a generalization such as the decline of sexual activity was *not* true, and denies the reality of an unpleasant fact. For example, we know a geriatric worker who entertains himself with elaborate fantasies about all the sex that goes on in his old age home.

Does this type of denial do any harm to the older person himself? Probably not, in the case of the caretaker who enjoys thinking about all the sex behind the scenes. But there are more malignant forms of denial. Some unpleasant facts about aging are: the older a person gets, the greater the probability that he will die this year; the older a person gets, the more likely he is to suffer from a chronic disease; the older a person gets, the less likely he is to be able to do a novel task quickly. Careless denial of these facts may mean that we program inadequately for the health care of the aged person, or that we build our housing in a place where there are too many choices to be made too quickly, as one tries to cross a boulevard to a shopping center.

Thus, we must acknowledge, first, that the thinking of all of us is subject to stereotypes. Second, some stereotypes are dead wrong, but many contain at least a germ of truth. Third, we can do damage either by accepting the stereotype and applying it uncritically to every individual, or by denying that the unpleasant generalization can apply to *any* older person. Many attitudes are based on stereotypes about older people, about people in general, and about ourselves. Let us consider some such attitudes and try to determine when they lead to good outcomes and when to poor ones. These particularly important attitudes deal with dependence, detachment, deviance, and disengagement.

DEPENDENCE

Many of the unpleasant facts about aging have to do with physical health. It is a short step from physical health to the larger question of dependence and independence. The attitude that varies most widely among housing managers is one that expresses the degree to which the manager sees older people as dependent or independent. Looking at the matter rationally, it is plain that there should be no such attitude. If we were rational human beings, we would assess each older person as an individual and perceive realistically the ways in which that particular person is independent and the ways in which he is dependent. However, we do tend to form much broader conceptions like stereotypes, which are ready to supply pseudoinformation when we are lacking real information. The dimension of independence-dependence seems to be particularly liable to this impression formation.

People who are intent on perceiving the independence in older people may be characterized as "Marine Sergeants": they outrageously berate the manner in which the average, tough oldster who copes doggedly with adversity is sabotaged by those who want to infantilize him. In the opposite camp are the "Bleeding Hearts," who feel exquisitely for the poor, frail, helpless older people, and see their need for many services. What possible consequences might arise from these admittedly overdrawn, contrasting attitudes? The Sergeant manager may well bring out the greatest independence in the tenants. His personal manner could be the closest thing to being treated like an ordinary human being the older tenant has experienced in a long time. In a generally healthy group, tenant activities may flourish under the necessity of being organized by tenants themselves.

If the group is, in reality, not genuinely healthy, the Sergeant may find that his enlisted men fall on their noses. Even if he has a generally healthy tenant group, we know that there will be some tenants who cannot respond to his call for independence. Thus, on the negative side, such an administrator may define his own role totally outside the area of tenant activities—no consultation on programming, no interest in attending scheduled activities, no linking to outside social agencies. The tenant in turn might interpret the Sergeant's personal breeziness as insensitivity, or his lack of interest in aches and pains as rejection.

The Bleeders, on the other hand, are apt to be there when there is a weakness requiring support. Poor health, slowing of psychomotor speed, increased difficulty with decision making, and other common deficits of old age do occur in any group of older people, and the support of a "Bloody" manager may be just what such people need. One such manager brings something from her own kitchen several times a week to a proud lady who refuses to apply for welfare. It is hardly necessary, on the other hand, to spell out the negative side of proceeding on the assumption that most older people are marginally competent. One of our managers, a lady with great good feeling and ability to reach out to elderly tenants, expressed surprise that the tenants of one of her two identical buildings were obviously more independent than those of the other, despite the fact that assignment by the housing authority was random. She did not spontaneously mention the fact that her own headquarters, and the locus of three quarters of her activity, was in the "less independent" building.

These attitudes may be evidenced on an even larger scale than in the management of a building. Planners themselves are very subject to judgments based on the logic of a Sergeant or a Bleeder. As mentioned previously, over the years federal policy made it extremely difficult for a housing authority or a nonprofit sponsor to build housing offering services other than housing alone. Sponsors themselves may fall into the trap of taking an official position against poor health. They are frequently preoccupied with the question of screening applicants: how can we keep this place full of self-sufficient people who won't look sick and dependent? And all get very nervous when an erstwhile well-aged tenant begins to decline, sometimes to the point of initiating a premature transfer to a nursing home so the other tenants won't have to look at him. On the other side, it may be the Bleeder in us that plans a community totally encapsulated from the stream of normal life, thinking this the best way for several hundred older people to live—company store, resident physician and social director in a retirement village located 20 miles out of town. It would be difficult to decide who is more self-righteous—the one who confidently says "*Our* people are the healthy cream of the crop," or the one who says, "We offer *everything* these poor folk need."

Planners, policymakers, and administrators of communities for the elderly should be able to identify such attitudes in themselves; their task is to disentangle the aspects of the attitude that are firmly based on the real needs of the older people and the aspects that are irrational and expressive of a cultural or personal stereotype.

It may be instructive to consider some of the possible psychodynamic aspects of the Bleeder and the Sergeant attitudes. The Bleeder wishes to help. Let us accept a large proportion of the wish to help as a realistic, socially useful need; thank God that we have people who wish to help. How strongly does he need to help? This may be a critical issue. If he is driven by inner needs not admitted, or understood, his actions may backfire. It is a very short distance from the wish to help to the compulsion to dominate. Worse yet, is to feel inadequate in the normal power seeking in which we all engage, and thus to seek an object whose weakness allows him to be an easy target for an administrator's power need. Too many Bleeders experience a "good feeling" by the great contrast between their own competence and the slowness, the perplexity, or the physical disability of the older person. Frequently, the same person may be reacting to guilt over his own failure to be a "good child" to his own parents. The person who felt inadequate compared to his own parents and was angry at this invidious comparison, but guilty over his anger, is likely to betray a hostile undertone in his need to help. The hostility may involve unconscious, but deliberate, manipulations to keep the older tenant dependent on him. Many authoritarian procedures, such as apartment inspections, may be rationalized as helping, but done in an intrusive way that denies the right of the individual to self-determination. Unfortunately, whole staffs can be organized around the idea that the tenants' needs should always be anticipated.

The Sergeant, on the other hand, may also be authoritarian, under the assumption that the maximum should be demanded of his people who, after all, are no different from young recruits. Or, he may adopt a *laissez-faire* attitude, trusting that all will find their way without support. Underlying both types of behavior is difficulty in accepting weakness in oneself. To strive to elicit the maximum degree of independent behavior in each individual tenant is laudable. To insist that each tenant *must* be that way, or, "by George he doesn't belong in my place," is a pretty effective way of covering over my anxiety that I may not be self-sufficient myself. Very frequently, people whose personal anxieties take this turn have built a life style around denying any softness or need for warmth in themselves. To be a party to anyone else's need for nurture reminds them too much of the human need they have desperately rejected. One could probably trace early experiences that led our overdone Sergeant to conclude that life never could offer him much dependable support; therefore, he had better live as if he did not need it.

Most administrators, of course, are neither extreme Sergeants nor extreme Bleeders. We all have a bit of the neurotic in us, however, and the sooner we try to recognize the warning signs the better. A feeling of contempt for a clinging or dependently demanding tenant should lead one immediately to say to himself "There is something wrong with such an intense feeling. Am I really responding to the person and the situation, or am I responding to my own anxiety?" Likewise, the impulse to protect should be the occasion for a manager to suspect himself and his motives, unless he has carefully considered the individual status of the potential protectee and concluded that he is realistically unable to meet a challenge.

DETACHMENT

Where the administrator stands in his feeling about his own and his tenants' dependence is central to many other attitudes, but this is not the only attitudinal dimension of importance. Managers differ widely in their amount of personal detachment or involvement with tenants. How personally he becomes involved is, of course, partly a matter of his personality and temperament. It takes all kinds to rule even a small world, and we have some people going into management who are detached, and other who simply cannot keep out of tenants' affairs. On the other hand, it is not only a matter of personality. Social work and psychiatry have evolved an ideology of human service that emphasizes the dichotomy between professional detachment and personal involvement. The dangers of the latter have been written about extensively, as evidenced by all the writing about the phenomenon of "countertransference" (becoming involved with the patient in such a way as to use him to help work out the therapist's problems) in psychoanalysis. This ideology has been passed on to many professional areas, with the result that practitioners may feel guilty when they interact as human beings with the people they serve. A housing manager confided in me that he was tantalized to the point of psychosis by the delicious aromas of cooking from the apartments of his multinational tenant population; his convictions about professional detachment made it impossible for him to accept any of the invitations he got to sample this international cuisine.

Many managers are understandably vigilant lest their behavior betray favoritism or give a tenant some special claim on him. These dangers may be overemphasized, however, and are frequently used as a rationalization for either an ideological or temperamental disposition to retreat from personal closeness. Thus, where we ended up in the middle of the dependence-independence attitude, we suggest that the best managing is done somewhat on the involved side of the detachment-involvement continuum. Our housing studies show that many people move into housing communities for social reasons, and many more live a great proportion of their social lives within the community. It is very significant that when we have done sociometric surveys of housing sites, tenants frequently give the manager's name as one of their three best friends.

It would seem that no matter how aloof a person is by nature, he can still ask himself on a specific occasion whether he is ducking an issue by pleading professional distance. He might even do a bit of self-analysis by asking himself whether closeness frightens him. People who expect rejection are likely to feel anxious if they deviate from the prescribed transactions of the manager-tenant relationship. Telling oneself that the older person is probably more vulnerable than he is might help let down the bars. The manager might do some of his routine business with tenants in their apartments, rather than only in the office; locate his office directly adjoining a tenant area, rather than being buffered by a secretary; accept invitations and small gifts without guilt; and feel free to talk about his own family, interests, and so on with tenants.

DEVIANCE

Another basic attitude may be called "tolerance for deviance." Old age has its share of people who are alcoholic, faddist, sexually deviant, neurotic, bigoted, and so on. The aging process itself, or the physical disorders that come during old age, may compound these traits or may result in the various symptoms that have been labeled "senility." Theoretically it is possible to screen applicants thoroughly enough to eliminate such socially undesirable tenants; one can also get rid of a tenant who exhibits antisocial behavior after admission. The degree of tolerance of the manager may have a strong influence on the characteristics of the tenant population. Some administrators are very quick to preserve the smoothness of functioning of the community by removing the deviant personality. Most often, this is done with the good of the group in mind; older tenants do seem quick to reject those whose social behavior is questionable. The manager who is intolerant of deviance accepts as a fact that anything that bothers the majority of tenants is bad for them.

There are two things wrong with this attitude. The first is the question of the rights of the deviant individual. Our communities at large may not banish those who are peculiar unless they constitute a danger to themselves or to others. The courts in some localities have denied the right of the housing authority to move families with behavior problems out of public housing. The manager might well ask himself the question, "Is this tenant suitable for a mental hospital?" If the answer is "No," and the tenant pays his bill and is not a danger to others, then he probably has the right to stay.

The second thing wrong with exercising too strict control over population homogeneity is that it implies that the older people have no resources with which to deal with the deviance. Do they really need that much protection? The first major deviant act in a new housing site that we studied involved a lady's using the community's esthetic pride and joy, a marble fountain in front of the building, to wash the sand off her feet as she came home from the beach. It turned out that at least 50 tenants were looking from their windows and saw her climb into the fountain. She was greeted by an immediate chorus of angry voices protecting the social norms of the community, and she never did it again. Looked at in one way, the necessity for dealing with peculiar neighbors keeps normal people's social skills exercised. Very frequently, action like this is far healthier than removing all possibility for self-determined norm maintenance.

The manager who is made anxious by such departures from the commonplace is likely to have an overly rigid set of personal standards. This is particularly likely to be true when the manager has successfully risen above his parents' educational or economic level through dedication to the American ethic of hard work and determined purpose. Some of the harshest words said about unconventional people have come from managers who are unable to allow themselves a little pleasure or freedom to be unconventional at times.

In short, the elderly deviant personality has a right to remain integrated into special communities unless it is extremely clear that he is a hazard to himself or to others. The ability of the manager to maintain a sense of humor, compassion, and a conviction that his tenants can deal constructively with deviance is essential in making this right a reality.

DISENGAGEMENT

"Disengagement," referred to in Chapter 1, has been defined as a process where the aging individual relinquishes his ties to society and society in turn "releases" him. Whether or not he knows disengagement by name, every administrator is likely to have some convictions that can be classified as espousing engagement or disengagement. We all believe in activity to the extent that we want to provide older people with a wide variety of things they can do if they wish. A manager is likely to be considered a failure if his housing community does not have a thriving program of regular games, amusements, interest groups, and trips. Although there is relative unanimity about the virtues of "constructive" use of time, managers show wide differences in their reactions to signs of disengagement among tenants. On the one hand, an extreme acceptance of tenants' inactivity may lead the manager to a merely perfunctory concern with fostering recreational or self-maintaining skills. One major trouble with disengagement theory in practice is that it has allowed an easy rationalization for *laissez-faire* behavior. The manager whose own needs for passivity, or whose fears of assertive behavior are strong, may fall right in with the erroneous view of disengagement which says that *all* older people are happier if they don't continue to strive as they did during middle life.

On the other hand, rejection of disengagement as an often constructive phenomenon can also be a problem. We are very indebted to the disengagement theorists for calling several points to our attention:

1.   People are too quick to judge old age in terms of cultural values that glorify activity and involvement.

2.   There are psychological gains to be had from such mechanisms as enjoying one's inner world rather than only the outer world, or of savoring the thought of one who *has been*, as contrasted with one who *is*.

3.   Relinquishment of emotional ties with the world may be actively sought by some older people.

Research has, as mentioned earlier, indicated that the great majority of older people continue to respond to and be rewarded by the pleasures of earlier life—whenever society allows them. However, we do know that there are some people who fit the pattern of disengagement, and who will never respond, except under great pressure, to the appeals of activity organizers. Most people do not naturally understand the positive side of disengagement, and find themselves becoming very emotional in persuading older people to participate. This attitude may result in a manager's badgering a nonparticipating tenant to join social activities. He may actually thus increase the anxiety of a person who is trying to conserve his energy by remaining on the periphery of community social life. One of the most frequent managerial sins is the refusal to allow chairs in the entrance lobby for fear that the place will have the look of an "old folks home." Such a manager may well be concerned about the public image his community may acquire in the eyes of the neighborhood, families of tenants, and his board of directors. Even more probable is his own anxiety over a life that is different from his own. As a society we glorify involvement, hard work, even frenetic activity. Old age connotes poor health, social rejection, failing faculties, and death. An older person who does not exhibit these signs of decline helps us deny the fact that we, too, will age. Therefore, we are likely to insist on engagement beyond the point where it is appropriate to the particular older person.

In order to give a maximum degree of choice, the administrator needs to provide for those who wish to remain active and those who do not. The provision of space and staff time for activity are obvious necessities, usually limited only by budgetary consideration. How does one provide for disengagement, though? One way is to tolerate or even facilitate lobby sitting. It is plain that the "sitting and watching syndrome" is not inactivity at all—it is a vicarious, inner-directed substitute for motoric participation in the stream of life. Our experience has been that people who have the energy to participate will do so; the provision of comfortable seats in the lobby or in outdoor areas will in no way make active people passive.

Our research with managers has confirmed the existence of attitudes such as those discussed here. Less often, however, can we predict actual managerial behavior from knowing these attitudes. One possible explanation for the fact that relatively few administrator characteristics and behaviors seem related to attitudes is that the profession itself is new. That is, the more established the profession and the more clearly articulated its technology, the more likely is a coherent belief system to exist which can, in turn, influence behavior. While our research has, in fact, demonstrated that such attitudes do now exist, there are few institutionalized supports to help the administrator amalgamate his knowledge, beliefs, and actions into a consistent managerial style. We predict that the future development of housing management as a profession will see the articulation of attitudes that are increasingly relevant to the determinants of practice.

A second possibility is that we may have overestimated the extent to which the manager's attitude counts, not only in the manager's own behavior but also in the lives of his elderly tenants.

It does make psychological sense to feel that the manager's attitude is extremely important to the overall well-being of the tenant. It seems, however, that our enthusiasm should be tempered by the thought of how resilient and adaptable most older people are. Is it realistic to think that they are so sensitive as to have their day made by a pleasant word from any one person even if he is the manager? Child psychologists are still trying to sort out the conditions under which a "bad" parent ruins a child and those under which the child thrives in spite of it all. It is by no means proven that there is a one-to-one relationship between "good" treatment by parents and the adjustment of the child. The manager's degree of influence on the tenant's inner adjustment is probably smaller than factors such as the tenant's lifelong personality and his current environmental situation. The tenant's psychological well-being is extremely dependent on his health, which is relatively immune to managerial intervention. His social behavior and the way he uses his time are also likely to be conditioned by factors outside the housing environment. However, every tenant has a characteristic way of thinking about his everyday environment—a net balance of satisfactions and dissatisfactions which is sometimes called "happiness," or "attitude to life." This attitude may be particularly subject to the influence of the administrator, as the tenant assesses the hundreds of little things in his daily life that indicate whether the world is right or wrong for him.

The manager must show some moderation in his aspirations about how much he can help his older tenants. He cannot blame himself much if his charges become sick, or if they show behavior malajustments; neither can he really take credit for good health! He certainly can, by his planning, active direction, and individualized attention, affect the way people spend their time. He is most critical in creating the kind of total environment that will be experienced as "heaven on earth," or as "something to be endured," as expressed by tenants in two of our research sites.

One can go a step further to suggest that the administrator's influence is probably least where the tenant population is very healthy. He may do his best job as a benevolent business administrator and friend in a housing situation where all tenants have independent lives. But most tenant populations are not that healthy. As the housing environment ages and the average tenant becomes less competent and therefore more vulnerable, the potential effect of the manager is greater. Even where initial screening eliminates all but the most competent, populations do age. Sooner or later every manager will have a situation where his attitudes toward dependency, detachment, deviance, and disengagement do matter with a large number of his tenants.

chapter 10

Initiation into tenanthood

There are several stages involved in an applicant's becoming a tenant: the application, the waiting period, and the day of occupancy.

THE APPLICATION PROCESS

Many contacts begin with a phone call for information. Every administrator will have the prospective tenant come in personally unless he lives in a distant city and it would constitute a hardship for him to travel for an interview. Ideally, it is desirable for the person who answers the phone to be able to provide basic information for such inquiries, so as to avoid encroaching on the administrator's time. There is no reason why basic information on facilities, price, and admission policies cannot be given on the phone by clerical personnel. The administrator may also wish to alert such callers to the size of the waiting list, or estimate the period of time before an opening is likely to occur. He should also consider whether he wishes his secretary to say anything about the advisability of making a formal application substantially in advance of the time when tenancy is actually desired. Usually, the outcome of such a call is the provision of basic information and the making of an appointment for a personal interview.

Some housing environments send application blanks to such people to be filled in prior to interview, while others interview first. The latter seems more efficient since a fair number of those who come for interview will not apply. What should one try to determine at the time of interview? One factor in this decision is that housing with many applicants can afford to be choosier than housing with an undersupply of applicants. Nevertheless, all housing will be

239

interested to varying degrees in the financial, medical, and psychological status of applicants.

Financial Criteria for Admission   Every housing environment must assure itself that a tenant will be able to keep up his rent payments. Public-housing authorities utilize procedures that specify fairly completely how this assurance is obtained. Other sponsors will have to make more decisions about the kinds of assurances they will seek. It is certainly appropriate to ask the tenant his monthly income and its source, and where there is doubt, for his net worth. Some housing sponsors insist on independent verification of this information, meaning that a signed release must be obtained allowing a bank or other institution to furnish the information directly to the sponsor. This is, of course, a touchy area, and such an inquiry may turn some potential applicants away. Other sponsors attempt to obtain a signed guarantee of financial responsibility from a third party, usually an adult child of the applicant. This is perhaps the most completely safe procedure from the point of view of the sponsor, but some tenants will be understandably reluctant to impose so on a relative, while others will have no such guarantor available.

The housing sponsor has the privilege of turning away at this point anyone who cannot meet the financial requirements. However, our conviction is that every sponsor who avails himself of federal assistance for housing, or whose larger organization has any tax-exemption privileges, has the duty to provide a continuous flow of subsidies for some tenants who cannot afford the going rate or whose funds give out during his tenancy. The primary vehicle for offering such help (as of 1974) is the federal Rent Supplement Program, where a sponsor is reimbursed from federal funds for the difference between the locally established public housing rental and the standard rental charged fully paying tenants of the housing. Rent supplement funds are in relatively short supply, but the sponsor must take the initiative in applying to HUD for these funds. Use of rent supplements can be controversial, and it may well be a formidable task for the administrator to convince his board that the idea is worthwhile, and to defend the idea to his tenants who pay the full rate. The thought is frequently expressed that having people from lower current income levels than the majority of tenants introduces tension into the social life at the housing and puts the receiver into an inferior social position. However, the great majority of elderly tenants are perfectly strong enough to tolerate such tension if it does arise. By are the greater part of this objection is a rationalization for exclusionary wishes that are inappropriate to the recipient of federal assistance or to the sponsor who professes a social motivation to its housing efforts. Another mechanism for helping people who are unable to pay the full rent is the Section 23 Leased Housing program administered through a local public-housing authority. In our research we have found no evidence whatsoever of any negative effect of mixing income levels, nationalities, or races in housing limited to older people, and have no hesitation in recommending that a sponsor accept whoever comes its way through the leased-housing channel.

A few sponsors are able to make a slight monthly overcharge and apply these funds to the direct subsidy of current tenants or to a reserve fund for such future use. Private sponsors can do this freely, although those using federal assistance must work out the procedures with HUD. Finally, some sponsors use their own capital for rent supplements as a way of giving direct social service. We feel that every organization should seriously consider doing so. Low-income community groups formed explicitly to provide housing, and small bootstrap sponsors will, of course, be unable to. Large churches, unions, and fraternal organizations, on the other hand, sometimes have existing capital that can be used for this purpose. If not, they can always establish a new fund designated thus, to which both outside contributions and direct contributions from within the organization can be made.

Naturally, each applicant should be informed about the likelihood of future rent increases, and in vulnerable areas, of the large increase that might come if local tax exemption is withdrawn. If the applicant's financial situation looks marginal, the manager should make a realistic estimate of the likelihood of a subsidy's becoming available. The tenant should be fully aware of the possibility that he might have to move away in a real financial crisis.

Medical Criteria for Admission   Decisions about medical criteria for admission have presumably been made early in the planning of the housing. Whatever they are, how can they best be applied during the application process? Everyone knows that the applicant, his family, and sometimes the personal physician will stretch a point to gain admission in reporting current health and medical history. There is no foolproof approach to screening out the less than optimally healthy. Even the most satisfactory approach, an examination by a physician chosen by the sponsor, is bound to err; in addition, this is an expensive procedure. We suggest that all factors considered, the best procedure is to ask both applicant and personal physician questions that are as specific as possible and that are relevant to the future course of the tenant's health:

1. Have you been in a hospital during the past 5 years? Where? Please give dates of each hospitalization. For what illness were you treated?
2. Have you been unable to leave your home because of sickness for a week or more at any time during the past 5 years? Please give approximate dates of each occasion. For what sickness did you have to stay home?
3. Do you have to use glasses? How often? always; for reading only.
4. Do you use a hearing aid?
5. Do you ever use a cane, crutches, wheelchair or walker? When, or how often?
6. The physician should also be asked to provide all current diagnoses and to rate the severity of each.

By asking questions that are phrased fairly objectively, the respondent's attention is focused on facts rather than impressions, although the latter might also be requested from the physician. The York House personal physician's blank is shown in Appendix 3, indicating that it is useful to include both objective and evaluative items. The administrator himself, ideally in consultation with a physician other than the applicant's own, must make the final decision about whether the information reported is consistent with admission policies or not.

There is, of course, an element of protection for the physically ill client in not allowing him to enter a living situation that will make demands greater than he can comfortably meet. The administrator or the application office will be able to make this decision on the basis of the interview and the answers to the above questions in most instances. If they are really in doubt they should definitely insist on an independent physician's opinion.

Psychological Criteria for Admission The administrator's attitudes toward handling deviant individuals once they are admitted as tenants have been discussed at some length in Chapter 9. This section considers policies regarding the admission of people who appear to have psychological problems. Workable criteria that are fair to the individual, the sponsor, and other tenants are even more difficult to establish for psychological health than for physical health. Let us divide the question into two parts: first, can we predict who will exhibit psychological problems as a tenant? Second, should we admit an applicant who has such problems?

It is very difficult to identify psychological disorders other than the most gross types on the basis of an application interview, since the applicant will probably put on his best face for this occasion. Even if one added the opinion of someone trained in psychological observation, or attempted to use a short test to screen out the depressed, the psychotic, or the overanxious, the number of problems correctly identified would go up only a little. The fact is that we know too little about identifying problems in older people to proceed in this screening task with any confidence. We would undoubtedly end up with a number of errors of the type that exclude suitable people—a much worse error, in our judgment, than admitting some people with problems. In addition, requiring applicants to undergo a psychological screening test or a probing interview would create much unnecessary anxiety.

Thus, we suggest simply being alert to any information pointing to major delusions, suicidal thoughts, or antisocial tendencies, and a look at the medical history for hospitalizations or sicknesses that are ambiguous enough to require further inquiry to see whether they are major mental disorders.

Even a past history of mental disorder should not disqualify a person as a tenant. If such a history is uncovered, it is the responsibility of the person handling the application to try to determine from physician, family, or agency whether the condition is likely to interfere with his *present* life. Some housing environments go so far as to welcome former mental patients. The Toledo and Columbus, Ohio, housing authorities have established successful projects jointly sponsored with the state mental hygiene department, deliberately designed to furnish congregate housing for a mixture of former patients and "normal" applicants from the regular housing authority list.

In short, my feeling is that every person has the right to be considered for tenancy. The neurotics, the complainers, the difficult personalities, have to live somewhere. Public housing is probably likely to get more than its share of such people—problem personalities who have been dependent on society much of their lifetimes. Wherever possible, the support that can come with planned housing is preferable to institutionalization.

THE WAITING PERIOD

The applicant should be given a tour of the premises at some time during the application process. Acting as tour guide is a task that ought to be performed by tenants. It is not a good use of his time for the administrator to perform this task. Even more important, being a guide is a task that can give meaning to the lives of a few tenants who enjoy this role.

Assuming that a tenant is judged acceptable for occupancy, what then? In some instances there is little delay before occupancy. Much more likely, the housing authority or sponsor has a discouragingly long waiting list. Many sponsors are fond of quoting the length of their waiting lists as signs of how successful they are. Experience has demonstrated that at least some proportion of any waiting list is composed of people who will actually not move in if offered a place. In some instances, a complete check will reduce the list to 50 percent or less. Both management and the applicants will benefit if the people on the list are periodically contacted and their current status reviewed. The sponsor may find that a time comes when all presumably available applicants evaporate, and he has no tenant to fill a vacancy. Periodic checking before such an emergency arises will allow him to anticipate a shortage and take active measures to recruit people actually ready to move. Even for the project with a long waiting list, it is much more efficient to establish a regular checking procedure that can be done by plan, rather than having episodic binges where it becomes necessary to telephone many people before hitting a "live" applicant.

From the point of view of the applicant, the waiting-list experience is very stressful. Mrs. Marie McGuire Thompson has spoken very eloquently of how the housing management can help allay some of this anxiety. The most important step is simply to give periodic assurance to the long-suffering "waiting-lister" that his application is still alive. With no word month after month, the applicant may become discouraged and cease to think of moving as a realistic possibility.

The least that can be done is to devise a procedure whereby a regular form letter is sent to people on the waiting list stating that they are still candidates. The letter might contain a stamped return postcard asking the applicant to affirm that he still wishes to move. For large housing authorities or sponsors with long lists, this somewhat impersonal procedure may be the only feasible one. There will, of course, be many who do not respond. A telephone call may be necessary for them, but the mail responses will greatly reduce this number.

If there is staff time available, telephone contact is much more satisfying in terms of enabling some psychological assistance to be given. Mrs. Thompson has noted that this kind of contact allows some very specific types of help to be given. As the time for the move approaches, the applicant will have many questions. The housing personnel should volunteer advice about what furniture and belongings should be brought and which not brought. Many will feel very insecure about arranging for moving and will appreciate helpful hints about how to pack, how to plan for the uncertainties of commercial moving operations, and how to shop for a mover. Since moving is a heavy expense that some applicants cannot afford without strain, management may attempt to maintain a list of people willing to do small jobs at low prices, or even volunteers who would be willing to help a particularly needy person.

Many personal crises may arise during the waiting period, giving ample reason for the extension of social and counseling services if the resources of the sponsor allow it. A large housing authority with a social service department or a sponsor that maintains a wide-range care program may itself offer appointments or telephone service for problems uncovered during routine waiting-list checks. Many housing operations will not be able to perform these tasks themselves, but they ought to consider it part of their job to make referrals to appropriate local resources.

An unpleasant aspect of the waiting list is the determination of priorities for occupancy. Some priorities are built in: urban relocatees, for example. All sponsors have considerable latitude in choice of priorities, and ideally, extreme need may give reason to advance an applicant's place ahead of some who applied earlier. HUD has been liberal in allowing a nonprofit sponsor to give precedence to its members, and has made no effort to monitor tenant-income limitations. For the most part, the 202 projects, after ten years' experience, have not been notable in abusing this privilege, though exceptions do come to mind. The nonprofit sponsor that sees its future in a strong relationship to the community will treat date of application most carefully as the major determinant of occupancy. When special privilege is blatantly accorded organization members, political favorites or relatives of board members, the word quickly gets around. The short-term gain of granting a special favor may be undone in the long run by alienating other segments of the community.

OCCUPANCY DAY

When a project opens for the first time, the financial gain of occupying the building as quickly as possible is obvious. There are two limiting factors, however. One is purely physical. A high-rise building with only two or three elevators simply cannot crowd more than 7 to 10 moving operations into a single day. More important, moving day is one of the most stressful any tenant will ever undergo. The administrator should be very aware that research shows an increase in death rate, illness, and psychological difficulties in connection with certain types of relocation. Although voluntarily chosen housing changes by physically and mentally healthy older people has not been shown to constitute a risk, caution is nevertheless indicated. Some of the stressful factors include:

- Leaving a home that had been bought with one's own earnings
- Departure from a neighborhood to which he has emotionally belonged for an extended time
- The loss of feelings and memories evoked by the constant association with home, neighborhood, and neighbors
- Loss of friends and neighbors

- Inability to move some of one's possessions to the new dwelling unit
- A dwelling unit built in an unaccustomed "modern" style
- The necessity of learning how to work new appliances
- The social task of meeting new neighbors and friends
- The necessity of adjusting one's living style to the needs of management and other tenants
- Reorientation to the new pathways, sights, sounds, and physical resources of the new neighborhood
- Increased face-to-face contact with other older people, leading to a cementing of the idea that one is also "old"

Most of these stresses are unavoidable, and the average new tenant will deal with them in a constructive and adequate manner. The more the moving-in process is planned to minimize them, however, the more energy the tenant will have to put into building a new positive life for himself.

Several days prior to the move, the applicant should be phoned to check that all is smoothly scheduled. Family should be encouraged to give personal assistance on moving day. The manager should give the tenant a specific time, usually an early morning or an early afternoon hour. Realistically, a commercial mover usually cannot be scheduled so closely. However, the tenant should be encouraged to come in himself with a few of his basic belongings at a specific hour, so that he may be greeted and shown his apartment while the movers arrive in their own time. Naturally, such arrangements are not always easy to keep to, and the tenant should be assured that it is all right to appear at some other hour if necessary.

Every tenant should have a personal welcome and escort to his apartment. When a number of people move in on the same day and a dozen other pressures associated with a new project demand the administrator's time, other staff, borrowed staff from other agencies, outside volunteers, or tenant volunteers may be utilized. It is, of course, most important to orient the greeters to the basics of what is expected of them. The moving-in occasion might be a good opportunity to launch an organized auxiliary or volunteer group whose work would be expected to continue in other areas once full occupancy is attained. Using tenants as greeters gives an exceptional chance for the exercise of the talents of a few, although this should be reserved until the first tenants themselves are well socialized into the new environment.

If leases are used, the new tenant may be asked to sign on first coming in on moving day. An air of informality may be maintained by pointing out significant features of the environment as the greeter walks with the tenant to his dwelling unit. Restraint is suggested, however, because the tenant's attention will inevitably be trying to assimilate the details of the new environment that are particularly meaningful to him. Thus, much of a long stream of orienting information will be lost on him. If meals or medical services are given on the site, however, these must be described, and their location actually seen by the tenant.

The time spent in the new tenant's dwelling unit by the greeter should be relatively short, since the day is not primarily a social occasion. A brief, concise pointing out of the necessities is vital, however:

- How the key works, and how the door is locked from the inside
- How the stove works, including reassurance about its safety features
- How the refrigerator works (it should be turned on if not working already)
- How the faucets work, if of the single-control type
- How the windows work
- Regulation of heating and ventilation
- Emergency call systems, if any
- Location of fire exits

Part of the manager's work prior to occupancy should include a firm arrangement with the telephone company for the telephone to be installed on the scheduled moving day.

An information booklet for new tenants is extremely helpful. Since some tenants with visual, reading, or language problems will not be able to use the booklet, it cannot do the whole orientation job, but is very reassuring for the majority of tenants. It should be written very simply and sparingly, giving the kind of information that is likely to be relatively stable, with emphasis on helping the tenant, rather than on laying down a set of regulations.

Specific orienting information of some kinds may be best reserved for the bulletin board or for more ephemeral publication, such as mimeographed sheets. Mrs. Thompson has observed several housing sites where the administrator has made large maps locating the project with respect to nearby facilities such as transportation, hospital, supermarket, drug store, and so on. The map will communicate best if it is simplified or schematized, showing the housing, the pathways for walking or public transportation, major landmarks and traffic arteries, and the locations of the facilities. The addresses and telephone numbers of strategic resources should be posted or included on the information sheet. Businesses or facilities that give special rates or attention to the elderly may be identified, and brief summaries of the regulations for their use (i.e., off-peak-hour cheap transit fares) included.

If at all possible, a call back to the new tenant later the same day may be indicated, after he has had time to try out his unit and think of questions that might be answered.

When new tenants move in as replacements for earlier occupants, the pace will of course be much different, and it will be possible to arrange a more relaxed combination of personal attention from the administrator and staff and assistance from "oldtimer" tenant greeters.

During the period of initial occupancy, stress on sponsor and management will also be high. There will inevitably be mechanical difficulties, and adequate provision for off-hours plumbing, heating, and electrical assistance must be made. Many problems may arise during evening hours, and it is extremely desirable to have temporary staff coverage during this time.

In summary, the application process, the waiting period, and the actual moving in are times of special stress where a little extra effort from the housing authority or sponsor can go a long way. Although most tenants will be strong enough to deal with the problems constructively and most will have help from their families, some tasks necessarily fall on the administrator, who can make all the difference to an anxious applicant.

chapter 11

The many roles of
the administrator

The central topic in our consideration of housing management is how the administrator performs his job—what his duties are, the extent to which these duties are consistent with his idea of himself, and his effectiveness in getting the job done. The concept of "role" allows us to talk meaningfully about the administrator. However, we need to define what we mean by "role" and distinguish among several aspects of the concept. The basis of the necessary distinctions arises from the question "From whose point of view are we defining role?" The origin of a role lies in the wishes of significant individuals or groups that a given set of tasks should be performed. Their expectations that a job task be performed in a particular manner may be referred to as a *role prescription*. A role prescription may be formalized, as it is in the "job description" of federal civil-service jobs or those in other bureaucratic organizations. There is always an informal element in the role prescription, however, where the immediate contextual demands of a job, the individual expectations of a supervisor, or the needs of the particular consumer may impose some variation on the standardized job description. In many situations, a relatively small proportion of the tasks of the performer may be spelled out in words; there is a voluminous literature on organizational roles that considers in detail how the expectations of others are transmitted to the performer.

One of the determinants of the strength or firmness of a role prescription is the history of the occupation. In general, the longer jobs of a given type have existed and the more people employed in such jobs, the more people doing the jobs have communicated with each other. And the more jobs are performed within large bureaucratic structures, the more likely are the role prescriptions for the jobs to be clearly specified, formalized, rigidified, and finely differentiated from other related jobs. Managing housing for the elderly is a relatively young profession, and therefore role prescriptions are likely to be relatively diffuse (that is, composed of a variety of specific operations, not always consistent with each other nor clearly definable), variable (requiring different operations in different situations or from different people), and informal. For example, there are administrators who knew almost nothing about housing at the time they were hired, but were given the highly diffuse role prescription, "See if you can locate some federal aid and get housing for our older people started." A highly regarded administrator has been told that his job is to "Keep a roof over the heads of these people and make the accounts right every month." An equally highly regarded administrator has been told to do whatever he needs to do to make the housing environment like a home. In short, room for variation in role prescription is great.

Role prescriptions may be examined in terms of *who* prescribes. Most of us have multiple bosses—that seems to be the way of our complex world today. The housing administrator may be more vulnerable than most to the many-masters effect, however. Like most performers in the human service arena he has two major masters: his employers and his consumers, who almost never are one and the same. The employer's prescription itself may be the net result of input from a variety of sources. A housing manager in a large public-housing authority is likely to have different and sometimes conflicting prescriptions from his management supervisor, the housing authority's director of social services, or the professional who directs a supportive service linked to his housing environment. In housing sponsored by a private nonprofit organization, the administrator frequently is responsible to his board, but even this situation may involve formal and informal expectations from different board members about how he performs his job. In other types of organizations there may be multilevel role prescriptions coming from staff of the parent organization, from governmental regulatory agencies, or from health or social welfare professionals.

From the consumer's direction, role prescriptions will rarely be formalized but they are none the less powerful. A never-ending stream of tenant complaints about the behavior of a few mentally impaired tenants may be translated into a very clear role prescription: one of the administrator's jobs should be the maintenance of "quality control" over the mental competence of the community. Unquestionably, the tenants' power to impose their role prescriptions is less than the employer's power. However, the diffuseness of role expectations in this period of early development of the housing-administrator profession makes it possible for a sensitive administrator to facilitate the input of his tenants in setting his own mangerial directions.

Role prescription, whether from consumer or employer, is thus an essential ingredient of the general concept of role. It is clearly not synonomous with role, however. Since the performer is himself an active participant, he contributes an equally essential element to the definition of a role. He has a unique biological constitution, social background, life experience, current environmental pressure, and personal need. Clearly, what he wants his job to be is going to condition what he actually does. What the administrator considers is right and appropriate for him to do in his job will be called his *role perception*. Role perception will, other things being equal, be a more potent determinant of the job as actually performed in situations where role prescriptions are diffuse, in situations where new approaches and therefore new problem solutions are demanded, in situations where there is a smaller reservoir of past experience to guide present behavior, and in performers with strong personal needs and high abilities.

Even role perception does not refer to a single concept, but, rather, it has a public and private aspect. *Overt role perception* is the way the performer publicly defines his role as he speaks to his board, converses with his tenants, writes his own job prescription, or dutifully responds to research questionnaires. *Covert role perception* refers to the way he defines his own job in terms of his innermost needs, aspirations, and internal responses to pressures from the outside. The overt and covert aspects of role perception are similar or different in different people and different situations. It seems fair to say that an outsider may never know exactly how an individual perceives his own role. The performer himself may not be totally aware of all facets of his own role perception. The gap between overt and covert role perception may be greatest when pressure for social desirability is highest: when the administrator is writing his annual report to his employer, or when he is describing his model program to a meeting of his peers. He is much more likely to reveal his private definition of what he thinks he should be doing to his spouse, to a colleague who is also a good friend, or possibly in an anonymous research inquiry.

One could characterize role prescription and role perception as pressures on the individual to perform his job in a certain manner. This is the final aspect of role, *role performance.* Role performance is behavior, behavior that is overtly observable and has tangible results that can be examined, classified, and evaluated: paperwork, speaking with a tenant, making a policy decision, accepting an applicant, putting a hand on a tenant's shoulder, and so on. The most important aspect of role is the performance itself—the proof of the pudding is in the eating. However, role performance may never be understood without knowing how role prescriptions and role perceptions harmonize, conflict, or interact in determining actual performance. Even more important, if we are to be able to influence role performance so as to produce a better life for older people, the pressure points we must seek are in prescriptions and perceptions.

Theoretically, role performance should be the aspect of the administrator's role that is easiest to analyze, since it occurs as behavior directly observable by others. However, as yet there has been little or no research on how the administrator actually performs on his job.

It may also be difficult to get information about role prescriptions. Even where there is a written job description, the informal expectations of significant individuals in the interpersonal world of the administrator may diverge from the official expectations. An extremely significant area where nothing is known involves the political world of the housing authority or the nonprofit organization's board of directors. It would be most difficult to organize a research project that could gain access to the board members, much less devise an interview that could cut through the distorting elements of political caution and social desirability to learn something about what they really expect their managers to do. Yet, some day this research must be attempted if we are ever to be able to increase the administrator's skill in doing his job for the tenants in addition to maintaining a cooperative and mutually trusting relationship with his employers.

It is easier to obtain information from tenants regarding their role prescriptions for their administrators. In our research we asked tenants how they felt about a number of policies and administrator behaviors. While tenants prefer a manager whose rules are clear and one who exerts himself easily in their behalf, they also want him to maintain an appropriate distance in his everyday relations with tenants. Less than half of our tenant respondents felt that they should have a substantial part in the determination of project policies. Tenants are also ambivalent about what medical standards for admission should be. They would like to see independence emphasized, yet are loathe to see stringent medical requirements being imposed on tenants, probably seeing themselves as being potentially vulnerable to being sent elsewhere.

Certainly, the administrator cannot hope to perform his job solely on the basis of what he is told by his board, the community, or his tenants. His behavior and his own interpretation of what he is doing or why he is doing it will be determined by all of these, but at least as much so by his own convictions, personality, and temperament. Managing is thus a compromise, and how he performs the various tasks will be determined by different combinations of these influences.

The administrator will be called upon to perform an incredible variety of tasks. In a very large and financially privileged project he may have the luxury of a large staff, with a division of labor enabling him to function exclusively as policymaker and coordinator. In most instances his life will be much more varied, however. In this chapter a number of these tasks will be described briefly. Many of these briefly treated topics represent areas to which an entire book might be devoted. There are sciences of personnel administration, organizational management, business administration and procurement, to none of which does this brief treatment do justice. Other sources of information should supplement the discussion of each of these managerial roles.

RELATIONSHIP WITH THE BOARD OF DIRECTORS OR HOUSING AUTHORITY

The administrator of nonprofit housing usually works very closely with a board composed of community leaders. In the case of public housing, the executive director of the local authority has somewhat the same relationship to the politically appointed housing authority members; the administrator of a particular housing site does not usually deal directly with the authority unless he also functions as executive director. The administrator who relates to a board or authority is expected to have the professional expertise to advise the board on national housing policy and programs, housing planning, everyday administration, and local resources. If the administrator does not read new legislation, request guidelines from governmental bureaus, and keep up with current trends in service delivery, the board will frequently miss opportunities to act creatively. Wherever possible, the manager should reserve time at every board meeting for a succinct reporting of new information for possible use by the board. Regular reading of such information sources as *HUD News, HUD Challenge,* and the *Journal of Housing* (published by the National Association of Housing and Redevelopment Officials) is necessary to be able to do this job effectively.

The board or authority will, naturally, be attuned to local situations and especially to the needs of its perceived constituents, whether they be voters, party members, politicians, or church members. Frequently the administrator will have to decide to counter a board's tendency toward parochialism by advocating a broader view of whom the housing should be serving. This freedom to educate the board may be at a maximum when the administrator has a reputation and demonstrated competence that is recognized in the world beyond the housing site. Conversely, the politically appointed executive director who limits his competence to performance in the political rather than the professional arena will not be listened to as he attempts to make policy recommendations. Liberalizing of admission policies may frequently be supported by reference to trends on a national level—"We should move ahead now since it's going to be inevitable in a year or so anyway."

With a sensitive touch, treading the area between condescending school masterism on the one hand and frightened acquiescence on the other, the resourceful administrator will find many board or authority members grateful for his attempts to keep them briefed. He should be alert to suggest that board members participate in conferences on housing sponsored by professional organizations.

There are occasions when the administrator or director may have a hand in influencing the choice of new board appointments. There seems to be a slow trend toward the representation of people with technological expertise on boards, in addition to the usual criterion of weightiness in community affairs. If possible, every board should have on it someone known to be firmly committed to social justice and social welfare, a socially oriented person, and someone from the medical care arena. With a few experts in relevant areas, board committees may function creatively in such ways as the recruitment of minority-group tenants, development of on-site services, community relations, and so on, as well as including the more usual fund raising, personnel, budget, and other committees. There is a growing move toward representing tenants on boards, often by direct election, especially in public-housing authorities. The executive director of an authority should try to sell his authority on the idea of inviting a manager or a tenant to the meeting in order to maintain closer contact with the real problems of housing.

It seems fruitless to speculate at length about the politics of dealing with board members, responding to their pressures for special favors such as early admission of a friend, dealing with threats for noncompliance, and the like. The only effective teacher here is experience.

OTHER LINKS TO THE COMMUNITY

The most potent link to the community is usually through the board or authority; the unimaginative administrator may stop here. We have discussed a number of community service facilities with which the administrator must be familiar.

To some extent, the administrator of public housing suffers from the negative social image accorded its tenants—the "project director" may be rejected in the same way that the "project kid" is. Thus, he will have to try harder to become integrated into the community network of social agencies, nonprofit organizations, service clubs, and so on. The housing-authority executive director is more likely to get calls to speak before such groups than is the manager. It is most desirable for the director to nominate his project managers for such duty, if at all possible. It is good personnel psychology for him to spread the honors around somewhat, and it gives the community a broader look at the scope of the authority's operations to have exposure to the managers.

We have spoken earlier of the various initiatives that the administrator should take in promoting the assistance of other agencies in helping his tenants. He should, in turn, be quick to come to their aid on request, including helping to modify his housing's admission priorities if a particularly needy client is referred by one of these cooperating agencies.

There are many opportunities for the administrator to engage the interest of his suppliers in the work of his program. He should not hesitate to make requests to them for contributions to the tenants' recreation program or other such funds, nor to keep them informed about the uses to which these contributions are put.

The near neighbors of a project are very important to its well-being. It is possible to ignore the surrounding community and then regret this lack of concern when some issue such as a zoning variance request comes up. It is relatively easy to distribute notices to the nearby residents about a holiday party, a carnival, or other activity. Volunteers may be most easily recruited from the population that lives within walking distance. The minister, priest, or rabbi of every congregation should be visited or invited to the housing site for some specific occasion.

Another important link to the community is through the families of tenants. Unfortunately it is usually at times of trouble that contact with family members occurs. Although there may not always be time to cultivate families individually, the manager ought to state verbally at the time of occupancy his readiness to talk to the family whenever they wish. He ought to use his updated file of names and addresses of next-of-kin for periodic communications. It is a good investment to mail the tenant newsletter to these family members. "Family Day" is a useful vehicle to keep interest high. It can be conducted in a variety of ways, such as a bake sale, party, craft show, or musical celebration. Even a very small effort to speak to both the tenant and his visitor when passing in the hall builds good will. Needless to say, the benefits of concerning oneself with family may be enjoyed later in the form of administrative ease in necessary business with families or as increased investment and interest by the relative in the tenant.

THE ARBITRATOR ROLE AND TENANT COMPLAINTS

In our many interviews with a wide variety of people employed in housing for the elderly it was obvious that dealing with tenant complaints is one of their most important roles. When personnel talk freely and honestly about the negative aspects of their job, invariably they have strong feelings about the complainer or the tenant who cannot seem to live without finding fault with his fellow tenants. There is no evidence that older people complain more than anyone else. Every group-living situation seems to require a substantial amount of griping to sustain its existence. Two pieces of advice about handling complaints come to mind. First, take legitimate complaints seriously and provide ways of making corrections if possible. Second, treat other complaints as psychotherapeutic problems rather than revealing either the bad character of the complainer or the vulnerability of the managerial ego.

For maintenance problems, it helps a lot to insist that a complaint be written down and passed along to the maintenance man—written either by the tenant himself or by a staff member. This procedure reduces the possibility of staff's simply forgetting to pass the word along, and it also gives some reassurance to the person making the request that someone will eventually see the request. On the other hand, if the request is one that cannot be complied with, it is far better to say so directly than to make an empty promise. Not following through will quickly make the tenant cynical about the chance of his complaints having any impact.

Every environment has its share of tenants who cannot keep out of other tenants' business, and its share of other tenants who are supersensitive about their privacy. The overinvolved and the detached ways of life are incompatible, yet their path crossing is inevitable. So also are the puritan and the free liver, the joiner and the isolate, and so on. The manager as arbitrator of complaints arising from these basic incompatibilities will function best if he listens sympathetically and offers his counsel primarily to the complainer. Most such conflicts cannot be solved by trying to get the aggressive gossip or busybody to change. Rather, the person who bothers to complain may be reassured about the legitimacy of his discomfort, advised of ways to avoid the scrutiny of the curious, or provided with self-therapeutic phrases to use to talk himself out of his outrage.

No environment is perfect. A sure sign of the overall health of a small society is its ability to criticize and to translate the criticism into change, while still preserving the integrity of both management and members. Even in the simplest environment where all tenants are reasonably well and the services offered are minimal there will be a steady stream of gripes. Room for many more is provided when food and housekeeping services are offered. Experience seems to indicate that the atmosphere is usually more positive when formal channels for criticism are provided.

THE TENANTS' COUNCIL

The tenants' council is perhaps the most satisfactory vehicle by which complaints surface constructively. Our research shows that a surprising number of administrators are either against the existence of such an organization or feel that things work well enough without one. Tenants' councils made up of younger people have, to be sure, challenged traditional ways and sometimes have very painfully forced housing authorities to share power. It may be that these experiences have made some managers wary of being too ready to allow such an opening, even in housing limited to the elderly. There does seem to be some beginning of minority-group awareness among some older people, and the housing project for the elderly is a natural place for an activist group to look for both members and a cause. Our feeling is that even if a tenants' council unearths some disruptive issues, the alternative—managerial discouragement of the formation of such a council—can only produce far worse disruption.

The tenants' council usually has more important business than handling complaints. Many of the activities discussed in Chapter 13 may be planned and conducted by such a group. Services to the temporarily sick, volunteer work on and off the site, and the maintenance of a buddy or telephone security system may be done by a tenants' organization.

Almost every such organization has a complaint committee or a regular meeting with the administrator at which suggestions for change are discussed. Where meals are served, a food committee will elicit interest among tenants and channel complaints into a manageable structure. Among other advantages, tenants are very effective in rebutting inappropriate complaints made by their peers.

The administrator may need to extend himself actively to launch a tenants' organization. It may amount simply to making this suggestion at a public meeting early in the life of a new project, or going to a few natural leaders who identify themselves in the first few weeks after opening. In other instances, the manager may have to call a first meeting, appoint a temporary chairman, organize an election, or otherwise shepherd the beginning of the organization. Needless to say, the less he intrudes the better, but he should not withdraw so much as to let an organization fail to emerge or die after it is formed.

It is desirable for the manager to avoid routine attendance at tenant organization meetings, but he should indicate his willingness to come when invited. He should set up and actively maintain regular meetings with the officers, the council, or committees of the organization. He should also on occasion request a special general meeting, or time at a regular meeting, to bring concerns of his to the group, such as explaining the consequences of a new law, warning them of an impending rent increase, announcing a new service, or asking for help in maintaining a better environment.

Tenant organizations rarely attract a majority of tenants to business meetings, or even to membership. Some have a tendency to become established in concrete, that is, to have a small group of self-perpetuating officers. These problems may bother the administrator, but he should wait to be asked before doing anything about them.

Money is the means by which an organization exists, and the manager may encourage the organization to charge nominal dues and engage in fund-raising activities. He should also do his best to persuade his authority or board to contribute an annual minimum budget.

THE CHIEF'S ROLE: RULES AND REGULATIONS

We have discussed earlier some of the attitudes that a manager brings into his work, such as his own needs for detachment versus involvement, or for control versus democratic permissiveness. Within reasonable limits we feel that there is room for effective management within any of these combinations of attitudes. Our research also indicates that there are relatively few administrative problems around rule enforcement in housing limited to older people. Nonetheless, there will have to be a bare minimum framework of such requirements.

Such rules as there are should above all be stated clearly. Ambiguity represents a particular problem to some older people. The best rule would seem to be to have as few rules as are necessary to insure respect for the rights and property of others, but to state these rules succinctly on admission and in written form, and stick by them. Research done in family housing projects suggests that for the majority of tenants a manager who sticks firmly to the rules that he is supposed to uphold is surprisingly widely appreciated. Given this preference for high structure, the majority of tenants may not perceive an unjust or too-harsh rule or may be reluctant to object to it. One would hope that there would always be an alert tenant critic who could discern the point at which an administrative atmosphere begins to serve itself rather than the needs of the tenants. This is one function served by a tenants' council.

Tenant-established norms may be as effective as those enforced by management in monitoring disturbing behavior. The lack of salience of the disciplinarian's role in the milieu of housing for the elderly has been demonstrated in our research, where most tenants, and even managers, were somewhat at a loss when we asked them what the three most important rules of their housing environment were. Everyone accepts the idea that the rent must be paid on time, cats and dogs are forbidden, minimal standards of personal and dwelling-unit cleanliness maintained, and control over building access exercised. Many other types of rules stand out by virtue of their rarity: any control on leaving the building, any requirement that a tenant perform a maintenance task, any control on short-term visitors, or limitation on the use of alcohol.

Many specific occasions will arise where limitations may have to be placed on behavior. In actuality, we have observed more of this kind of control than managers have been willing to report when interviewed. Most such informal rule enforcement is in the interest of administrative efficiency or of a positive image in the eyes of the community. Administrators are sometimes loathe to allow tenants to be seen sitting in public places, or to allow free use of some social areas during hours when the administrator is not on the premises. Furniture placement is sometimes rigidly controlled. For the most part, managerial behavior in these areas actively interferes with the tenants' efforts to live satisfying lives. A certain amount of un-programmed clutter, both physical and behavioral, is necessary to a livable environment.

Federal policy has tended to oppose the idea of requiring any maintenance tasks from tenants, certainly an admirable antidote to practices earlier in the history of welfare programs when demeaning tasks were indiscriminately required of welfare recipients. However, one of the real deprivations of the world of the elderly is that it may demand too *little* of him. It seems to us that every housing adminis-trator should consider, in concert with his tenants' council, what kinds of mutually beneficial tasks could be performed by tenants. Hall maintenance, flower gardening, or cleaning tasks in common spaces are tasks that might be performed by tenant volunteers with gentle pressure from management or the tenants' council. Considerably easier to sell are prestige jobs like elevator operation at peak hours, receptionist, telephone-message and mail clerk. A resourceful manager can find plenty of other jobs for tenant volunteers. He might be advised especially to learn enough about the occupational background of his tenants to determine whether there is expertise in stenography, teaching, plumbing, electrical work, repairing, or stationary engineering represented among them. Such resources could be a great help both in time of emergency need and even in the absence of emergencies—union and safety regulations permitting.

A special problem in regulation with housing for the elderly is monitoring changes in tenants' incomes and the conditions of tenants' dwelling units.

In public housing there is little freedom. A rent audit must be performed biennially and many authorities specify how frequently apartment inspections must be held. It would seem that the adminis-trator should try to make the apartment check into a friendly per-sonal visit done at least three times a year. If these are spaced randomly (with records being kept by the manager to enable him to know to whom he owes a visit) and handled as friendly visits, the monitoring operation is accomplished as the secondary result of an attempt to maintain close relations with tenants. The manager may not be able to do it all personally. The secretary, bookkeeper, and maintenance man are essential figures in many housing environ-ments, and might be trained to stop in for a five-minute informal chat, during which time any condition of the apartment requiring attention or giving a clue to any tenant problem may be noted.

The rent check is another matter. No attempt has been made to monitor income limits in federally assisted housing other than public housing and rent-supplemented housing. In these instances the matter is loaded with tension, hostility, and perhaps justifiable paranoia, especially among those who resided in public housing before reaching the senior-citizen age. In general, eligibility is likely to continue unchanged for the elderly, since relatively few experience a rise in income. It would be a great help to morale to simply be able to assume this stable-or-downward motion of income and allow the exceptions to fall through the sieve. The cost-benefit net would surely be in the direction of dollars saved by ceasing to police the over-62 (or possibly over-65 or over-70) incomes. If it must be done, we strongly recommend that a housing authority try to get central-office employees to do this hatchet job, rather than adulterating the administrator's pro-tenant role by making him snoop incomes.

INITIATING SEPARATIONS

Probably the most distressing role an administrator is called on to perform is to tell a tenant or a tenant's family that a person can no longer remain in the housing. As we have said before, moving is traumatic for any older person, and the trauma is enhanced by physical or mental impairment and by the move's being forced on him from the outside.

Our experience has been that most administrators wait as long as they feel they can to initiate such a move. For the minority who move too quickly in this direction, however, we wish to emphasize our basic conviction that housing for the elderly must allow its tenants to grow older and less independent without eviction until continued residence becomes a danger to the person, or possibly to others. The implications of this policy are clear: if this dictum is followed, all housing for the elderly will slowly grow to consist of less and less competent people, ending in a stable state of impaired people one step above the institutionalized category. Long-range thinking is required to deal with this dilemma of whether or not to resist change by replacing less competent tenants with healthy ones and transferring those who lose their original independence. We don't really know how this will work, since our oldest housing is only 10 to 15 years old now. One possibility, however, is that the housing now being built will slowly change into institutions and that later cohorts of independent aged will move into new housing built as new tenants require housing. The probable effective life of most buildings now being built is estimated as 50 years. At this point the decision may be made to "retire" the building or to remodel it so as to make it more frankly an institution.

In any case, the point we are making is that it would not be a tragedy to see today's housing change toward the institutional, as the homes for the well aged of the earlier twentieth century have evolved into nursing homes.

Every administrator realizes that the presence of a healthy spouse can usually prolong the time a tenant can remain, although a special effort has to be made to reassure oneself that the spouse is capable and that the declining person is getting adequate attention. If financial resources permit, special paid assistance can perform the same function. Research and experience in housing environments that offer various service packages will help develop guidelines as to what the average needs of projects of different sizes will be for employees to assist in housekeeping, cooking, and personal care. The administrator might consider the possibility of allowing live-in help where apartment space will permit it.

There is some reason to think that a move may be less traumatic when it involves only a change in apartments within the same building, or a change from one unit of a multiservice facility to another. Thus, the administrator who has a special-care area in his building or a nursing home next door will have less reason for anxiety about the effect of the move on the tenant.

Tenants themselves are very sensitive to signs of incompetence among their peers. One of the manager's most difficult tasks will be that of deciding when such pressure to separate a tenant is in the best interests of all concerned, as contrasted with occasions when he must resist the human tendency of better-off tenants to wish to expel deviant members. The administrator's position should be clear about the more obvious disabilities that affect only limited sectors of the individual's life: hearing difficulty, partial vision, physical disfigurement, or the necessity for cane, crutches, or walker look unpleasant to others but do not usually in themselves necessitate removal. Even where forgetfulness becomes obvious, or a decline in personal neatness occurs, extra work by the manager in listening to the complaints of offended tenants, and talking to them about helping the declining tenant may prolong his stay. In these cases however, the manager's vigilance to indicators favoring more dramatic action should be heightened. A visit to the dwelling unit to see whether the condition has produced safety hazards is in order. The tenant's movements should be observed carefully to note whether he shows any tendency toward disorientation or difficulty in traffic negotiation.

If it seems clear that the mental or physical condition requires transfer, a medical opinion is indicated on the specific question as to whether the condition is reversible. In the latter case, tenant and family should be offered the option of the apartment's being held for his return, provided the rent continues to be paid. Many functional mental disorders of old age can be expected to improve following psychiatric treatment. A friendly housing environment to return to is one of the best incentives to recovery for an anxious or depressed patient. Brief acute hospital treatment or psychiatric day hospital care frequently may enable the tenant to return to his original unimpaired state.

Should both administrator and medical opinion agree on the inevitability of permanent transfer, the family should be consulted first, in order to give them time to make inquiries about possible alternatives without keeping the tenant in a state of anxious expectation any longer than necessary. Eventually, the administrator owes the tenant an opportunity for a direct personal conversation about the move. His emphasis during such discussions should be less on justifying his own decision than on allowing the tenant a chance to express his feelings. The manager should do all he can to provide information on the new location, and to reassure the tenant about the capacity of the new environment to satisfy his needs. The administrator should urge the family to take the tenant to see the new location prior to the actual move, and introduce him in advance to key people there.

In the absence of family the administrator himself may have to take primary responsibility for locating a new home and for interpreting the move to the tenant. Wherever possible he is best advised to seek the help of a local family or other service agency, but in rural locations he may have to contact public or private institutions himself.

Nothing can make this process pleasant. The best that can be done is for the administrator to keep in mind always that the tenant is likely to view the move as catastrophic, and to act and speak with appropriate gentleness. Many families are understandably reluctant to take positive action. Every manager will at some time or other come to the point with a procrastinating family when he will have to name an ultimatum date beyond which the tenant will simply have to go to the family's home if no suitable place is found. Fortunately, this final step is rarely necessary.

THE SUPERVISORY ROLE

In some instances the administrator is "it"—he has no one to help him and therefore no supervisory worries. More usually he will have at least a maintenance man and clerical help to supervise. The administrator must be the expert in human relations in relation to these and other employees. He should play this role very strongly, since his employees may well have more direct tenant contact than he. It is helpful to establish a regular time for a tenant discussion meeting, even if as few as three people attend. Hearing about the complaints of a tenant, the peculiarity of another, and the family news of still another will at the very least keep all in touch with what is going on. The administrator will at these times be able to emphasize the importance of taking a social orientation to the way complaints, maintenance problems, and other requests are handled by employees.

In larger environments where there is a finer division of labor, it becomes even more important for each employee to recognize the problems encountered by the others, and how their jobs interlock. Among other benefits, it is very good for employee morale to have their opinions sought regarding housing policy or tenant welfare, and especially for them to see their ideas acted upon and recognition given for their help.

Again, let us say that learning the art of effective supervision is a life's work in and of itself. The manager is urged first of all to practice the art, and if he is interested, to seek out some writings on how to supervise that may help him organize his own ideas and put them better into practice.

We shall be similarly brief about the roles of financial manager, purchasing agent, and maintenance man, any of which the manager may be called upon to perform. They are necessary roles, very demanding, and when there is only one person to do them, all the talk in our book may seem to be an expensive luxury. However, it is also very easy for a manager to escape the very difficult roles of planning for the future, counseling, or stimulating tenant activity by retreating to the ledger or the boiler. The administrator should be very hard on himself if he sees that he is having difficulty finding time for tenants. To put the situation squarely to himself he might make a time log showing what he does over the period of a month:

April 1	8:00–8:30	Open mail
	8:30–10:30	Phone—ordering supplies, dealing with board members
	10:30–11:15	Tracing short circuit

Being honest with oneself will quickly determine whether there are "collectable" pieces of time that could be converted into socially oriented work such as tenant visits or making phone contact with social agencies. If there really is no time for such activities the log will be excellent ammunition to use in persuading his board or executive to provide help for him.

There is, of course, much to be learned about purchasing, economizing, and taking care of the plant. But it is easier to get help for these activities than it is to get help in doing the tenant-relations part of the job. Thus, our lopsided treatment of the social roles of the manager seems very much in order.

chapter 12

Assisting with tenant problems

Whether anyone approves or not, the administrator will inevitably be called upon to perform the role of counselor. Caution might lead one to recommend that the administrator avoid this role, considering that most of them have had little or no training in psychology, social work, or counseling. Theoretically he may risk doing great damage if he attempts to meddle with human feelings.

Our own viewpoint, however, would be that since the administrator will inevitably be called on for personal help by tenants, or be forced into this role by emergency situations, he should be educated for two tasks:

1. Deciding when a referral to a professional counselor is indicated.

2. Performing the role of counseling when circumstances warrant or when no other resource is available.

REFERRALS

Deciding whether or not to refer a tenant in trouble depends on two separate factors: whether the problem is too big for the administrator to handle, and the availability of a trained worker to whom the tenant can be referred. The latter consideration is all too frequently the determining one. Services seem to have become increasingly fragmented and specialized, and the bureaucratic process of actually getting an appointment with a helping professional is a formidable task. This aspect of the counseling role will be further discussed in the section on resources for referral below.

Deciding on the magnitude of the problem is no easy matter. Ideally, training for the administrator should include a course unit on the psychopathology of aging. Since this is rarely a realistic possibility, the administrator should be able to learn how to recognize some of the major signs of psychiatric illness in a tenant. The presence of any of them should occasion careful consideration and usually referral to a physician.

Depression   Depression is a frequent symptom among the aged, but it varies widely in severity. Not all depressed people are in need of psychiatric help. Many older people perceive very acutely that society does reject them, that people they love do die, and that their own vigor is not what it used to be. It is entirely possible for a person to talk about these negative changes in his life in a realistic way without being personally depressed. We have heard many older people acknowledge that "I was happiest when I was young" or "I'm pretty much just putting in my time now" *without* expressing the emotion of despair. The psychiatrist Humphrey Osmond is fond of describing his last contact with Carl Jung, the psychoanalyst, when Jung was in his eighties. Jung was a tall, vigorous man, and said in a booming voice, drink in one hand and clapping Dr. Osmond on the shoulder with the other hand, "You know, don't let anyone tell you it's any fun to be an old man!" The words sound depressed, but the man clearly was not. Grief can usually be distinguished from depression, although grief certainly can begin an extended depressive episode. In normal grief over the loss or sickness of a loved one, the individual usually is able to continue to perform his daily routine.

A person with the kind of depression that requires professional assistance is apt to appear sharply different from the person he was earlier. Many depressions occur in people who were previously particularly sociable, normally assertive, and optimistic people. A sudden change from this demeanor is an almost certain sign of need for referral. The deeper depression is frequently accompanied by a marked slowing down of body movements, speech, and accustomed speed of performing tasks. The person may begin to express thoughts about his unworthiness, sins he has committed, unrealistic fears about the death of others, and so on. The true depressive also usually has difficulty sleeping and loses his appetite, frequently with weight loss. He may suddenly lose interest in personal grooming or housekeeping. In these severe cases a physician should be consulted immediately. Depression is frequently associated with physical illness and at the same time is one of the symptoms most easily treated with psychiatric medication.

Suicidal Ideas   The surest sign of depression is talk of suicide. No overtly expressed suicidal thought should be ignored. The rate of suicide goes up drastically after the age of 60, especially among males. Any such talk should occasion a psychiatric referral. By no means are all suicides preventable. Both "successful" and unsuccessful suicides occur among people who have talked about it openly beforehand. An unfortunate number have talked about it so much that the people around them become desensitized to the point where they conclude that "He just likes to impress you with that talk; he'll never do anything about it." There is no security in such a conclusion. Only the physician can decide whether immediate hospitalization, outpatient psychotherapy, drug therapy, or no treatment is indicated. Since depression and suicide are so closely linked to physical illness, the medical referral is essential.

The administrator should not assume that a history of suicidal talk or even an earlier attempt is a contraindication to successful tenancy. Such moods are quite reversible. However, knowledge of this propensity should alert the administrator to pay particular attention to the day-to-day changes in the tenant.

Delusions   A true delusion involves a recurrent idea that cannot possibly be true: control of one's behavior by electronic devices, the existence of an elaborate plot against the individual, possession of God-like powers, grandiose ideas about personal wealth or influence. These are clearly pathological and demand immediate referral to a psychiatrist. Such ideas may or may not be accompanied by other signs of personal disorganization. It is entirely possible for such ideas to exist relatively autonomously. The tenant may simply be seclusive or "queer," but able to look after his basic needs and be no threat to anyone else. Such a person is infinitely better off in housing rather than in a mental hospital. Only if he shows signs, in addition, of being physically belligerent to others, suicidal, or unable to care for himself should transfer be considered, at the suggestion of the professional.

Hallucinations   The most usual form of hallucinations involves hearing voices, while "seeing things" is much less frequent. These are usually pathological signs demanding referral, although account should be taken of benign regional variations ("spooks"; "I speak with God in my prayers every day") and occasional misinterpretations of actual events (noises at night; "People look at me").

Ideas of Persecution   Severe persecutory (or "paranoid") ideas are easy to spot and should be handled as other major symptoms are. There are all degrees of paranoid thinking, however. Some people live entire lives with this orientation, collecting abuses and insults and nurturing the image of themselves as victims of the world's mistreatment, but never going beyond the bounds of the possible. Others may verge into the genuinely pathological area where they develop ideas about their telephone calls or mail being intercepted, their food being poisoned, their lives being the center of attention of others, and so on. If other pressures are mild, even this degree of pathology can co-exist with other healthier sectors of personality. It is very difficult to intercede in these cases. Attempts to discuss the problem or refer the person to a professional will frequently be worked into the tenant's persecutory system and may in fact destroy the balance in the direction of further disorganization. No kind of treatment is stupendously successful unless this symptom is accompanied by other major signs of disorganization. Therefore, to the extent that other tenants can tolerate such an individual, he might best be left alone. The administrator should be alert for any sign of aggressive behavior or failure to observe basic nutritional or hygienic principles.

Alcoholism   Alcoholism also becomes increasingly more frequent among older population groups, although many housing sponsors try hard to screen out such people. The "silent" alcoholic is mainly a threat to himself, through neglect of his own health. It will usually be his physical debilitation that signals the need for referral. On the other hand, the boisterous alcoholic will be apparent to everyone, and the manager will probably find himself defending to the other tenants such a person's continued presence in the housing. If the administrator gets pressure from tenants to remove such a person, he should clearly establish the extent to which the person's behavior actually gets in the way of his fellow tenants, and not react solely to the moral outrage of a few loud protestors.

The administrator should, of course, be certain that the alcoholic tenant has adequate medical care. He may, however, be the only person in a position to make a strong referral to anyone other than a physician. Therefore, he should provide himself with knowledge of other resources, such as the nearest Alcoholics Anonymous chapter or public clinic.

Other Behavior Problems   In our experience, stealing, sexual deviation, and criminal behavior are very rare in planned housing environments for older people. There are probably more stories than incidents. Many reported thefts are actually instances where a belonging has been misplaced or forgotten. Both tenants and staff tend to be oversensitive to real or imagined sexual transgressions, suffering from the cultural stereotype of revulsion at the idea of continued sexual activity among the aged. There are few instances of this miscellaneous collection of behavior deviations that demand immediate legal or psychiatric referral.

Loss of Memory   Most of what is called loss of memory is benign. Some such losses are pure fantasy. We learn to associate aging with memory loss and frequently attach a great deal of anxiety to the inevitable instances where a name will not come to mind, a thought is spoken to the same person twice, or a task is not remembered in time. This anxiety leads a number of tenants to fear that they are becoming "senile" and to convince the people around them that they are in worse shape than they really are.

Even where memory does begin to fail to a noticeable degree, both the older person himself and the environment may neutralize the loss by compensatory action. List making can be encouraged; the help of a spouse or a neighbor may be sought; gas jets are commonly provided with automatic shutoffs; and periodic apartment checks may be carried on for vulnerable individuals.

There is as yet relatively little to do for massive memory loss, which is a sign of brain damage. In these cases referral to a physician is less for the purpose of therapy than for an opinion regarding the future course of the illness, the possible risk to the person's life should he stay in a relatively independent living situation, and the advisability of a change in residence.

Wandering and Disorientation   These symptoms are major signs of organic brain disease and usually will prevent the tenant's remaining in the housing. Occasionally, the combination of medical treatment and the assistance of a competent spouse can prolong the person's stay as a tenant, but a person who is disoriented is apt to also be inadequately concerned about the hazards of traffic, stairways, fire, and self-care.

Deterioration in Personal Care   A decline in the care with which one's personal grooming or housekeeping is maintained is usually a sign of the onset of a major emotional or organic brain disease. Care must be taken to distinguish decline from carelessness that may have been a lifelong personality or cultural characteristic. Failure to groom in and of itself should be the occasion for the administrator to intercede in the hope of stimulating improvement. However, such failure may be only the most overt sign that signals the presence of some of the other malignant symptoms mentioned above. The burden is on the administrator to look carefully at any tenant who has seemed to deteriorate in this manner, and try to determine whether a referral should be made.

Discussion of each symptom has revealed that not even all of these major signs of mental disturbance require referral. There are in addition a wide variety of milder symptoms of psychoneuroses that may represent either lifelong symptoms or recently developed ones—spells of fear or anxiety, specific fears of such things as going outdoors, riding the elevator, or sleeping, exaggerated concern with physical symptoms (hypochondria), or irritability and contentiousness. Where these symptoms occur in the absence of more severe symptoms, they may be viewed as indications of disturbances that ideally should be treated by a professional but do not constitute psychiatric emergencies.

It is difficult to assess these milder neurotic disturbances to decide whether a referral is necessary or whether a friendly conversation is the best remedy. One of the best guides is how persistent the tenant is in bringing up the same problem over and over again. This dogged pressure to talk about the same thing is usually a sign that there is more to it than an administrator can deal with. Conversely, a tenant's withdrawal from contact with staff and other tenants, and his resistence to any opening conversation about the possibility of a problem may also suggest that a professional can be of potential assistance.

RESOURCES FOR REFERRAL

We have expressed some degree of pessimism about the possibility of locating adequate resources to help a tenant in trouble. For example, the National Institute of Mental Health has recently determined that only 4 percent of the services given by community mental centers are given to people aged 65 and over. However, part of the problem is the failure of the older person or the person making the referral to persist in the search for help.

Almost every service organization is subject to the same negative stereotypes about aging and older people that we as a society are burdened with. Therefore, obtaining service for an elderly client requires stronger advocacy than would be true for a younger client. This may mean that more phone calls are required in order to get the service and that great vigilance is required to maintain follow through. The manager will have to be ready to approach high-level administrators of helping facilities should the usual channels for obtaining service not work.

There are relatively few agencies that maintain a specialized service for older people. An occasional large agency may designate one or more of its staff to deal exclusively with older clients. This kind of service is so unusual that it will probably be well known to local referral sources. An inquiry to the local health and welfare council or family service agency may succeed in identifying such services. In the absence of specialized services, particularly likely resources follow.

Community Mental Health Centers   Almost every urban area now is served by one or more multiservice psychiatric agencies. In very large cities, geographic boundaries ("catchment areas") are rather strictly drawn, and it is important to identify the mental health center that serves the housing environment's own area. The center *must* accept every applicant for service; there may be difficulty in waiting time for a first appointment, but there should be no problem in the tenant's eventually being seen. The difficulty comes when the question of treatment arises. Clinics of all kinds are likely to write off too many difficulties as being "due to old age" and to perform nothing more than an evaluation. They are too often undiscriminating in turning down older clients for psychotherapy because they consider them incapable of changing. A personal call from an administrator to the clinic staff member assigned to the tenant may provide the counselor with information and a better rationale for thinking that the tenant can, in fact, change for the better.

Counseling is not the only type of service available through mental health centers. Large centers may operate a "day hospital" or have access to a "night hospital" for people whose problems require relatively intensive care short of full hospitalization. Pending national legislation gives some hope that special geriatric services may be substantially increased in the future in the mental health centers.

For the mental health center, as well as any other resource, lack of transportation may be a significant deterrent to utilization, and some help in access to the facility might be solicited by the housing manager.

General and Psychiatric Hospitals Most hospitals have an outpatient or diagnostic psychiatric service. Unlike the community mental health centers, these services may be very expensive, and it may require assistance from, or a primary referral by, a social worker to obtain service that can be paid for by public resources.

Public Welfare Offices Theoretically, psychiatrically oriented social casework and the possibility of referral to a psychiatrist are available from many state or municipal welfare offices. In actuality, many offices are too busy or lack the required skills to perform such functions.

Private Social Service Agencies Agencies such as The Family Service Association, Jewish Family Service, Catholic Social Services or Visiting Nurse Association will usually see an elderly client at least once to offer an opinion on what the next step should be. They may on occasion be able to furnish long-term counseling.

Senior Centers Most senior centers do not themselves have facilities for treatment, but of all local agencies, the center's director is most likely to have the widest knowledge as to where psychological services might be obtained. A few operate information and referral services for just such a purpose. The administrator should make a point of knowing personally the director of every senior center near his housing environment.

Private Nonprofit Institutions for the Aged   At present relatively few such institutions give direct service to people who do not reside in their own institution. However, the director of social service or the person who handles admissions to the institution is likely to be able to provide telephone information about local psychiatric resources. The coming years will see a major increase in these institutions' utilizing their resources to serve community residents of the area surrounding the institution. Such a program is now under way at the Philadelphia Geriatric Center under the direction of Dr. Leonard Gottesman.

State Mental Hospitals   Unfortunately, older people reside in state hospitals in disproportionate numbers. Therefore, their professional staffs at least have had some personal experience in dealing with older people. The social service department of a state hospital is a source of information about resources, but unless the hospital maintains its own out-patient service, treatment cannot ordinarily be obtained there.

Many of the above resources are inherently big-city operations. Rural areas are lucky if there is one mental health center for four or five far-ranging counties. State hospitals may be hundreds of miles from potential clients. Other organized services may be nonexistent. Therefore, less professionalized resources than those available in urban areas may be the only ones available.

The Private Physician   Every physician has had some exposure to psychiatric training, although as a group physicians are no more inclined than anyone else to be interested in treating the elderly. Medicare has raised the level of motivation of the physician to treat the elderly patient. However, it may be that the general practitioner is the only stop required for help with some personal problems. As has been mentioned before, physical and mental health are even more highly related in the elderly than in younger people. People with heart, diabetic, or arteriosclerotic problems are far likelier to have associated psychological symptoms than are those without such physical disorders. Physical treatment may thus lead to psychological improvement for some. For another segment, psychoactive drug therapy supervised through regular physician office visits may do the job. Yet another group may respond to the homemade psychotherapy incidental to the recitation of symptoms and the patient listening of the physician. One should remember, however, that psychiatry is the underdog among medical specialties, and some medical practitioners are actively antipsychological in their approach to patients. The administrator who refers a disturbed tenant to an nonpsychiatric physician would do well to keep in touch with anything the tenant may report about what happens during the consultation. If he reports unsympathetic contact with the physician, the administrator may have to think of an alternative referral.

Religious Counselors Large numbers of older people feel comfortable talking about personal matters only with a minister, priest, or rabbi. These may be the counselors of choice for such people even when there are more professionally trained people available. In many localities they may be virtually the only resource.

MAKING THE REFERRAL

Other things being equal, it is much better if any person seeks help himself. Psychologists have determined that a patient is much more likely to put his heart into trying to get better himself if he makes the important move of contacting a potential counselor himself. However, many older people are at a great disadvantage in taking such independent action. They find it difficult to perform any new task such as asking for help, since they have not grown up taking for granted that counseling is one of the ordinary services that people may need from time to time. Today's generation of older people is likely to view psychiatric treatment as a personal disgrace. Therefore, the administrator may have to take an active role in the process of obtaining treatment.

For some extremely pathological cases, the administrator may have to go directly to a professional person or agency and describe why he feels that help is necessary without the active participation of the tenant himself. Such unilateral referrals may be justifiable only in the case of a real emergency. Many agencies will not intercede at the request of a third party, although if a family member (spouse, child, or sibling) makes the contact they may be less reluctant.

More usually, the administrator will have to speak directly to the tenant about the problem. If possible, it is much better to ask the tenant to come into the office or to visit him in his own dwelling unit, where complete privacy is possible. It is crucial not to approach personal matters in the presence of other tenants, staff, or outsiders. Sometimes the tenant may initiate such a discussion when others are around, or during casual encounters in public places. Even at these times, the administrator should endeavor to get the tenant into his office, or at the very least, draw him to a private corner.

It seems unnecessary to caution the administrator to approach the tenant with both gentleness and directness. The Marine Sergeant may find it difficult to moderate his expectation of strength in the tenant. He must remind himself explicitly before talking to a tenant that his toughness or matter-of-factness may be threatening to an anxious person. The Bleeding Heart may be so concerned to cushion the blow that he hems and haws and leaves the tenant thoroughly confused about what he is driving at. For either type, or any managerial personality in between, effort should be made to create the impression that he is acting as the manager, not as a counselor. It is part of the job of the administrator to be concerned about the welfare of his tenants. This concern may be expressed by inquiring directly about the observed symptoms. The tenant should not be told that the administrator will solve his problem. At the stage of initiating a referral, the administrator must carefully present himself as a person who needs a little more information in order to help the tenant get to someone qualified to help him. Thus he must be careful not to question or probe the tenant's feelings beyond the area of the overt problem. The administrator may strongly suspect that a depression is closely related to a child's move to a distant city, but his conversation with the tenant should focus on the depression itself, not on the presumed cause—unless the tenant insists on broadening the discussion. In this case, the session becomes a counseling session; this will be discussed in more detail below.

Very concretely, a few words of pleasantry are never wasted in the beginning of such a conversation. A smile conveys a nonthreatening mood. However, a long prelude is unnecessary and may actually make it more difficult to get to the critical area. At some early point, the administrator can indicate that he has noticed the tenant's looking depressed, or has heard that she had some trouble getting her housework done. He would like to know whether the tenant sees this as a problem. The response will frequently be a simple "no"—

most people are apt to deny a problem at first. The administrator may ultimately have to disagree with the tenant if he persists in this denial. The tenant may steadfastly deny the existence of any problem, yet accept the final recommendation to seek help. Therefore, the administrator need not necessarily see his task as one of persuading the tenant during the initial discussion to agree that he has a problem.

The tenant may, of course, react very defensively and not only deny the problem but also refuse to take any action. The administrator must then decide whether to drop the matter, to turn directly to a third party such as a relative or professional, or to coerce the tenant into action. Once in a great while a direct choice between seeking help and leaving the housing site must be offered. This is, of course, a threat and should be used only where the tenant's mental state seems reasonably good. Some antisocial behavior problems may need to be handled this way.

Should a responsible family member be brought into the situation? It is very difficult to know when such action will help or when it may further discourage action by the tenant. There is a natural tendency to feel that ultimate responsibility rests with the relative, and for the administrator to want to turn the burden over to him. In general, we would suggest that this course of action be reserved for acute or extreme disabilities unless the administrator has evidence directly from the tenant that he would appreciate the relative's being called. If the administrator goes directly to the family member without the knowledge of the tenant, he runs the risk that the tenant may feel betrayed. There are many reasons why the tenant might feel more comfortable not to have a relative brought in. The tenant who is adamant in taking no action may be advised that the administrator has no alternative but to call a family member. He is thus done the courtesy of being advised beforehand, even though he may not like this procedure.

In other contexts, the tenant may wish the manager to speak to a relative, the surest sign being his direct request for him to do so. In other instances, it is certainly appropriate for the administrator to ask the tenant how he feels about the relative's being called. The administrator should be willing to abide by the tenant's wish, unless the circumstances are very compelling. It is rarely appropriate for him to call the relative without the tenant's knowledge after having asked the tenant's opinion on the matter and receiving a negative response.

The most usual response of the tenant will be to talk about his problem or to some extent admit that he could use help. The manager should be prepared at this point with information on the various possibilities for help. He should be most alert to pick up from the tenant's responses anything that might indicate the tenant's preference for one type of help or another. Personal prejudices and preferences may make all the difference. A person in psychological trouble is in no state to learn to overcome lifelong prejudices ("all shrinks are creeps") if there is an alternative referral possibility that will avoid the issue. The administrator must also try to judge during this discussion whether the tenant will actually take the responsibility himself from this point on. If not, the administrator may have to keep reminding or persuading the tenant to take the step. If self-initiated action is not forthcoming, the manager may decide that he must make the referral directly, with or without the help of a relative.

Whatever the resolution of the conference with the tenant, considerable anxiety is sure to have been aroused in the tenant. The manager will be sensitive in determining when to bring the session to a close. If the tenant is visibly upset, he probably will do best to prolong the contact through reassurance, possibly working the conversation back to more mundane matters. The tenant should not be allowed to walk out in tears or in anger. Having taken the responsibility of talking about personal matters, the administrator must assume the responsibility for ending the talk on a constructive note. A smile, a touch on the shoulder, or a handshake may be the equivalent of many words.

THE ADMINISTRATOR AS COUNSELOR

All of the foregoing discussion has been based on the idea that the administrator is not a professionally trained counselor and that for diagnosable mental disorders he should function primarily as a facilitator in the tenant's search for trained help.

Nevertheless, there are a number of circumstances that can make it necessary for the administrator to step further in the direction of giving help himself. In time of great anxiety, people simply spill over to the person in authority or the one nearest to him at the moment. The manager simply cannot turn away from a tenant who insists on talking about a marital problem, a fear, or a delusion. It is part of his job simply to listen, if nothing else, within the limits of his available time. Are there risks in just listening? There is such a thing as allowing a person to talk too much. Under the pressure of his anxiety he may reveal matters of which he is later ashamed. He may work himself into a crescendo of hostile or depressed feeling by being allowed to talk too long on too upsetting a topic.

Listening with the Third Ear is the title of a book by the psychoanalyst Theodor Reik. These words express very succinctly what the sensitive administrator must do in order to listen as a sympathetic human being. He should be ready to turn the conversation gently to seal up the wound where the tenant has gone too far in laying bare his soul. He should be humble about his own power to determine where the conversation goes, however. Under sufficient internal pressure the disturbed tenant *will* talk. The worst one can do is to recognize the signs of distress but come in with a brief "I'm too busy," or "Don't worry, you'll feel better tomorrow" comment. Even under great pressure of other things to do, the very least that should be done under these circumstances is to acknowledge the feeling that the tenant is expressing: "I know you must be pretty angry about that," or "This is a pretty bad day, isn't it," if these are really the feelings that are being expressed. This simple communication at least conveys to the tenant some sense of being worth the manager's trouble to respond. If the administrator genuinely cannot linger to continue the conversation, he should let the tenant know that he realizes that something more than usually bothersome is on his mind, and make some concrete suggestion about a time to go into it further. Once having said, "Can I see you about that later this afternoon?" it is, of course, extremely important not to forget or to put it off again. Even if the tenant does not wish to talk by the time the contact is resumed, he has obviously been reassured by the administrator's actions that he has a sympathetic person to turn to.

If the occasion seems even more urgent, it may be worth asking the tenant to wait in the office until the administrator can complete his immediately pressing business. The manager may also suggest that the tenant talk to another employee whose sensitivity is assured. If no other arrangement is possible, he may accompany the administrator on his errand and talk in transit or at least have the reassurance of his presence until a suitable conversation can be held.

Acknowledging feeling is really the cornerstone of all effective counseling. The administrator's primary concern with an anxious tenant should be to understand the pain, annoyance, resentfulness, sadness, or warmth that lies behind the words the tenant is speaking. Acknowledgment does not have to be verbal, as in the example above. It may be expressed as a nod, in meeting the eyes of the tenant, or in simply listening. In fact, the name of the feeling the tenant is experiencing frequently may not be clear to either person. The sign of acknowledgment may simply convey the manager's recognition that some strong feeling is being expressed, without taking the risk of identifying it by an incorrect name.

It is always a temptation for anyone to feel that advice is the best response to such a request for help. While this may certainly be true in some instances, the administrator should be aware that even overt requests for advice may be a pretext for the tenant to talk about something that bothers him. If there is factual information that will assist the tenant, this can be offered at a time that does not interrupt the flow of emotion. For example, if a tenant should say "I can't get over the feeling that I'm going to die tonight," this is probably not the moment to remind the tenant that his recent physical examination showed his health to be A-1. This might be a good statement with which to end the conversation, but the immediate response would do better to convey the administrator's wish to help, or his understanding of the problem: "I know that's hard to live with," or "A feeling like that is really hard to shake, isn't it?"

Advice, among other things, can often be wrong. A cardinal principle in counseling is that what a person does by himself, or conclusions he comes to on his own, are worth a lot more in building self-confidence and are more likely to be "right" than things urged on him by another. Perhaps even worse, the act of giving advice puts the giver's attention on himself, and he may "lose" the tenant psychologically. A person in trouble is quick to perceive when the counselor is more interested in his own message than in the tenant's problem.

Anything that tempts the counselor to talk more than listen should be resisted. Certainly, brief accounts of what the manager did in a similar situation are sometimes appropriate, but "This-is-how-I-handled-it" can easily supplant concern for the tenant's own problem. Even questions can be overdone. As listeners, we all experience the need to organize a faltering story being told by someone, to reconcile inconsistencies in the story, or to clear up our failure to understand. Stopping the flow of the tenant's talk with questions more often discourages the sharing of feeling, rather than aiding understanding. Clarification may occur spontaneously. Even if it does not, getting the story in organized form will usually prove to be less important than the feeling behind it.

The distressed tenant may seek reassurance from the administrator or press him to agree with some thought or action of the tenant. There is nothing wrong with doing so, if the reassurance or agreement is sincere. Frequently, however, such requests are more a manner of speaking, simply vehicles for allowing the tenant to mention the problem about which he needs reassurance. Therefore, a too-quick "Of course you did right not to lend your son-in-law money," or "I can guarantee that you won't die in your sleep tonight" will leave the tenant with no basis for continuing his talk, but with an "unfinished" and unconvinced feeling.

Above all, however, the administrator must remain a human being and relate to the tenant on that basis. Deep distress sometimes requires emergency reassurance, and the administrator should not feel embarrassed to offer it. Sometimes it is possible both to keep the subject of the conversation open and at the same time reassure the person: "Look, I know you well enough to know that you would not hurt her on purpose, but I also know that just telling you won't convince you." A statement like this provides an opening for the re-expression of guilt or doubt, if it still lurks.

Similarly, there are many occasions when a request for information is just that. The beginning counselor might respond to a question like, "When are the doctor's hours?" with "You're worried about your health?" or "I wonder why you ask that?" Slavish adherence to the counselor's "tricks" is just as bad as ignoring the tenant's feeling.

All experienced counselors learn to strike a happy medium between being themselves and acting as they have learned they should act when performing the counseling role. A soft-spoken manager cannot function effectively in the counselor's role if he tries to put on a loud, forceful, presumably "reassuring" manner, nor can an over-talkative, gregarious manager do well by forcing himself to be nondirective at every turn along the way. Small tricks of the counselor's trade can teach one to *moderate* his natural blind spots or insensitivities; they are not expected to supplant his real personality.

Sometimes the tenant may come to the administrator and speak of a problem but be unable to elaborate on it, or simply be inarticulate. Most older people in the current generation are not used to psychological thinking and may be unable to verbalize thoughts dealing with their inner states. This situation puts a greater burden of activity on the administrator. He may have to state and restate several times the basic thought or feeling the tenant originally expressed. He may feel that he must ask some questions (preferably relevant to the tenant's own original presentation). He may even come to the conclusion that some small talk to convey a simple one-human-being-to-another closeness is all that is needed. The inarticulate older person is sometimes helped by the other person's ease in talking to him. (But tone down any false heartiness!)

The tenant may come in without any request for help or statement of problem. Again, information transmission or small talk can in themselves be therapeutic for the lonely. It may be, however, that these occasions are preludes to the time when the tenant finally comes to reveal a barrel of trouble that he has heretofore been afraid to mention.

If the time comes when the administrator feels that the talk is getting too disturbing, or the problems beyond his competence to handle, what can he do? If possible he should try to bring the discussion to a close on a reassuring note. If the earlier discussion was focused on exploration of feelings, allowing the tenant to "get it off his chest," the manager might try at this point to give more active reassurance. The purpose is to offer whatever temporary relief of anxiety is possible, hoping that it will last until more effective help can be obtained. The manager will have to judge for himself whether the question of a referral should be discussed with the tenant on the spot. It would be better to give himself the chance to discuss the matter with a physician or someone trained in social work or counseling before bringing it up with the tenant. If he has no such resource, or if the tenant seems at that point to be in a mood where he might be especially open to such a suggestion, he might seize this opportunity to urge the tenant to see his physician.

A spell of crying can usually be waited out and is not necessarily a sign that the session should be ended or a referral made. More often than not, crying may be a sign that the counseling has "worked" for the moment and that the person is on his way to feeling better.

Suicidal talk should be the sign to pick up the phone immediately to alert the spouse, younger family, or physician. In extreme cases, someone should stay with the person until a meeting with a physician is arranged. Extreme paranoid or threatening aggressive talk is a sign that discussion with the tenant about getting help for his problem will be fruitless. A referral should be made as soon as possible.

The most general rule is to try to raise the tenant's mood as much as possible before parting from him.

SOME AIDS IN TALKING TO OLDER TENANTS

Everyone knows that hearing becomes more difficult as age increases. Some people go overboard in their enthusiasm to compensate for this deficit, and routinely shout at all older people. Sometimes a loud voice will help communication; more frequently it adds distortion and only annoys or distracts attention from what is being said. In fact, since shouting is something we do when we are angry, we may well convey this impression to the puzzled tenant. The most important thing a manager can do is to learn to discriminate among his tenants and remember to shout only to those who seem to comprehend no other way.

One reason shouting seems to aid in communication is that the shouter has to slow down his speech while shouting—it is impossible to shout in rapid-fire fashion! We mentioned the slower rate of dealing with new information that has been observed in older people. This principle is very important in ordinary conversation. Slow speech is more apt to communicate than simply loud speech. As thoughts become more complex or the ideas expressed more foreign, the speed with which they are expressed becomes more critical. Ordinary small talk or conversation about matters where the tenant feels completely at home are least likely to require change in one's speaking habits. It is critical to pace more slowly than normal speech talk about the tenant's health, instructions on how to fill out a Social Security form, or how to behave in a fire drill. Repetition of critical words or short simplified phrases is apt to reach the less comprehending. Announcements are best made both orally and as written notices posted on a bulletin board.

Many older people unconsciously learn to "amplify" their hearing by watching the speaker's lips. Thus, crisp articulation and looking directly at the tenant will help comprehension. Direct eye contact has other favorable effects. Attention is likely to be enhanced by engaging the eyes of the tenant during a conversation. Eye contact also signifies directness and respect for the tenant.

The position of the body itself during the interaction may signal positive or negative feelings to the tenant. Much has been written recently about how we unconsciously communicate wishes, aversions, love, respect, or hate through our "body language." For most of us in American society, touching and very close proximity to another person convey intimacy, lack of fear, willingness to expose ourselves to the feelings of others, and love. Conversely, we find it easier to talk at a greater distance with strangers, and feel uncomfortable if the stranger moves in too close, or if circumstances force close physical contact. The subway is notorious for evoking blank stares beyond the hairline of someone we are jammed up against.

There is some reason to believe that older people are very sensitive to the feelings communicated by the distance we assume and by our body talk. Some may move close to us to hear better, or to be able to engage us in eye contact. If we unconsciously move away, we signal our discomfort, which is interpreted as rejection. If we shout louder than we need to, considering the distance between us and the tenant, he may feel attacked. Even if we don't move away as the older person comes closer, we may avert our gaze, turn our body away from a direct face-to-face angle, or otherwise betray our anxiety.

Many have observed that older people reach out to touch another person. Sometimes this may be a compensation for failing sight or hearing. Feeling the person helps to compensate for the increased difficulty the older person may have in registering him through his eyes or ears. Even if the administrator's own personal style is not attuned to touching as a means of communication, anticipating that tenants may reach out to him will help him not to be put off by it. A friendly handshake, palm on the shoulder, or pat from the administrator is usually well received, provided one uses some discrimination in whom one touches. Caution in the use of touch is probably in order for particularly withdrawn, ascetic, humorless, or suspicious people.

In summary, the manager must definitely be able to perform the role of counselor and information referral specialist in emergency situations. Simply as a friend or as the responsible person in the organization, he will have repeated occasions to listen, offer advice, or give reassurance. Knowing when to do each of these is the essential task. We have learned from our research that while tenants do want the manager to involve himself in the life of the housing environment, many are also not keen on his intruding into their privacy. The safest rule is for the manager to reserve anything more than a friendly ear for occasions when the tenant presses his anxieties upon him, or when the problem is great enough to raise the question of a referral or a transfer.

chapter 13

On-site services—
some broad strokes

The definitive word on the conduct of the various services will have to be written by someone who has actually grappled with the many problems involved. However, our research and observations have resulted in some thoughts that might be helpful.

Many such programs can be carried out successfully by a tenants' group. Usually a particularly energetic and aggressive person is needed who will be able to phone, visit, or write to resources that can furnish entertainment. If the project is fortunate enough to recruit just one such person from among the tenants, a procedure can be established whereby steady sources of free films, volunteer performers, and service club programs are located. These can form the core of a continuing program from year to year, allowing for the introduction of new material each year.

There is ample work involved in such a program to keep a fair-sized committee busy. It helps to spread the jobs around so that the program chairman is someone other than the organization chairman. Publicity, fundraising, decoration, refreshment, and recruitment committees, with representatives spotted so as to involve all physical areas of the project, are desirable.

The administrator who can simply sit back and let such a tenant organization flourish is rare. Even the most self-sufficient tenant group can utilize some early assistance in convening a meeting, being provided the names of some key local contacts, reserving regular meeting space, and in becoming legitimate through official announcements, description in a tenants' handbook, and so on.

Every administrator should take the initiative periodically in communicating with the tenant activity leader, indicating his readiness to help, and if necessary, to rescue an operation that is threatening to fail. He may have to help find money, to suggest the appointment of a new tenant who shows promise of high involvement, or even to jump in and do a job himself if there is no tenant to do it. It is a fine line between this readiness to help and an authoritarian assumption of too much responsibility. Unfortunately, many people with the urge to help are insufficiently willing to let initiative be taken,

Fig. 1.   Tenants should be encouraged to take responsibility for activity programs. (Photo by Richard Mowrey.)

however falteringly, by the tenant. Resist the temptation to meddle! But, oppositely, a completely *laissez-faire* approach is inappropriate.

The administrator should do a major selling job to his board or sponsor for some minimal budget to support such tenant activity. A budget of even $100 per year may be viewed as seed money to motivate the search for other support.

Is a tenant-organized activity program superior to a professional program? Certainly not, if this is phrased as a categorical question. However, active tenant participation is an absolute necessity, and is possible to achieve even if there is a professionally organized program. Some public housing projects have carefully planned with local agencies the pooling of their resources to provide a full range of activities to serve tenants and, in some cases, both project tenants and older people living nearby. Anyone planning such programs should request recent information from HUD on where particularly successful activity programs have been carried out. The expertise of such sponsors as the housing authorities of Columbus, Ohio, Cleve-

Fig. 2.   On-site jobs help tenants practice work and social skills. (Photo by Sam Nocella.)

Fig. 3. It is desirable to have a paid activity worker in addition to tenant volunteers.

land, Chicago, or San Francisco is worth far more than any theoretical treatment. There is beginning to be a substantial amount of literature on senior centers which is most relevant to the activity program for a housing development.* Some fortunate 202 and 236 projects are able to afford activity directors, while most upper-income housing has one or more full-time workers.

The content of an ideal activity program is dependent on the individual needs of the tenants. Many projects have sizeable groups of tenants with common backgrounds that demand unique activities not suitable for other groups—a revival meeting, a baking contest, a Bonds for Israel rally, or a trip to a bocce court may hit the right spot in one location but not in another. Nevertheless, there is a basic core of activities that seem to be repeated and relatively successful in many locations.

Film Programs A certain number of films are available free from

* Information is available from the National Council on Aging, 1828 L St., N.W., Washington, D.C. 20005

state, municipal, or school libraries. A fee may be charged for mailing, or the fee may be avoided sometimes by personal pickup. Many large companies and nonprofit corporations have films for free showing. Catalogues may be obtained at most public libraries. Occasionally a source may be located to lend commercial or TV rerun films. A dependable film projector and screen are two of the basic expenditures necessary for a successful activity program.

Local Entertainments A number of organizations will provide shows for institutions. Schools, scout troops, service clubs, and churches are likely prospects, as well as individual contacts who may be able to provide a pianist, a magician, or a lecturer.

Discussion Groups The discussion group does not catch on everywhere, but there is a strong need, particularly among some life-long urban residents or better-educated tenants, to be stimulated to continue thinking and "sound off" as one thinks. Some local school systems are able to furnish discussion leaders as part of their adult education activities. More frequently a volunteer must be recruited, although a tenant may sometimes function in this role.

Parties Once a month or once a season seems to be the norm for frequently of organized parties, where the feature is eating. Special seasons like Halloween, Christmas, or Passover may occasion parties with extensive decoration, entertainment, and food preparation. Other more modest parties may be utilized as "bait" to encourage attendance at a preceding business meeting. Meaningful activities for many may be encouraged by sharing cooking duties.

Off-Site Visits Providing bus transportation is expensive, and except for the events occurring in the few housing sites for really affluent people, usually requires both a subsidy and the strong hand of external direction. However, even if done only once or twice a year, such trips not only have intrinsic interest, but as occasions to anticipate, they demarcate time and thus keep alive the very necessary orientation toward the future. While wide-ranging local contacts are indispensable for finding free tickets to ball games, the theater, or the local historical shrine, tenants can and should be trained to do the legwork in making such arrangements.

Games Time, place, and equipment are what make many games work—personnel are frequently superfluous. Basic equipment at

every housing site should include checkers, chess sets, cards, tables
for them (both indoors and outdoors), a horseshoe pit, even a shuf-
fleboard. It helps to have a room labeled "card room" or "game
room," although one can certainly live without this refinement.
Bingo wins hands down as a perennial drawing card and lends itself
well to total tenant control, including managing the payoff. Local
variations, such as the fortune wheel, also attract interest. The
physically and financially elite are likely consumers of more
strenous pursuits like golf, baseball, tennis, or swimming.

Dancing A dance can be a great success or a great bust. There
probably are fewer who will dance than participate in some of the
other activities, but it is an excellent spectator sport if a minimum
number of "performing" couples can be recruited. It would be difficult to hope for a successful dance if there are fewer than 20 or 30
men to draw from—on the theory that 10 to 20 percent is a good
recruitment rate! But it can help to bring in "ringers"—older people
from the community or staff, volunteers, or relatives to help get
things started.

Religious Services For many reasons, it is desirable wherever
possible to foster religious participation in local institutions, rather
than on the site. Permanent religious space is not permitted in
federally aided buildings. More important, local churches and synagogues enrich tenants' lives more if attendance at their church-based
activities is encouraged, rather than allowing the tenant the too-easy
option of attending only an on-site observance in the same community room where a dozen other activities are held.

Arts, Crafts, Hobbies Painting and sewing are two hobbies that
have some hope of attracting enough interest to warrant recruitment
of volunteer leaders and equipment. Other types of solitary creative
activity involve more expensive equipment and are likely to find only
occasional "takers"—sculpture, ceramics, weaving, machine shops.
A great difficulty with this generation of older people is that such
activities (sewing excepted) are foreign to their background. Their
lives have been too full of work and too spare financially to allow
the development of such basically middle-class interests. This situation will no doubt change, as our present leisure-activity oriented
middle-aged group ages.

Music   Existing musical talent should be utilized as solo performers or accompanists. A few fortunate establishments have both enough people who are used to singing (rural and small-town church attenders, for instance) and the services of someone with a talent for direction to produce a functioning choir.

House Newspaper   A tenant publication is a sure sign of vitality in a housing environment, and it should be pushed by the administrator to whatever degree is required to make it appear regularly. Nothing is so demoralizing as a paper that appears sporadically with news that is out of date, or that carries announcements of events that have long since taken place. In some resource-rich establishments, tenants may be encouraged to produce literary publications, write or revise orientation booklets for new tenants, do art work for the publications, or do the typing or printing.

The space for such activities has been discussed elsewhere. However, the question about participation is most important. Many visitors, on first walking into housing for the elderly, are depressed by the look of many people sitting in public places doing nothing; at the sight of unused activity space; or at the thought of so many people alone in their apartments. Their impression is correct: even with the most active programming, very few events attract a majority of tenants, and regularly occurring activities are lucky to have eight or ten perennial participants. These are facts of life. On the other hand, few stop to wonder what percentage of the residents of all ages in a community participate in the flower show, the PTA, the local drama group, or the adult education classes. We don't have figures to guide us, but our feeling is that the percentages of tenants recruited for programs from a housing project for the elderly may not be substantially lower than similar rates among younger people for activities offered in their communities. Therefore, anyone who feels discouraged that "the same five people always show up for sewing" is simply expecting too much. One may decide to discontinue an activity because personnel time is too expensive, or not to start a craft class because of the large financial investment it requires, but the sole criterion should not be the activity's ability to fill a room. The volunteer director or the skilled staff worker may need considerable reassurance that he is *not* failing simply because less than 5 percent of the tenants ever participate in any of these

Fig. 4. An arts and crafts program is a specialty service that will enrich the lives of all tenants, not just the few creative people who produce the work. (Photo by Richard Mowrey.)

specialty activities. Every project ought to have a few such low-participation but enriching activities. The impact of exhibiting a few people's handiwork goes far beyond the fruitful hours of work of those who produced it, just as society's willingness to support a few creative people enriches many who never recognize the process explicitly.

Recent policy of HUD and of thought leaders in gerontology has favored the idea of serving more than just tenants in on-site service programs. This is not a new idea. Dr. Carp's study of Victoria Plaza in San Antonio tells of the effort to serve both community and housing project in a senior center. There were many difficulties involved in such a venture, as she has vividly described in *A Future for the Aged*. Tenants felt as if Victoria Plaza was their turf, while community residents were highly sensitive to this attitude and were sometimes discouraged from participation.

Fig. 5. On-site senior centers and lunch programs should make active effort to recruit participants living in the community. (Photo by Sam Nocella.)

Lessons learned from experiences like these make clear how important community participation is in order to create an atmosphere where all belong. The logic of the situation is strongly against a project's running a program only for itself. Tenants become stagnant if they interact only with insiders. Many more activities can be supported if people who are strongly involved in the outer community can evoke the community's interest in supporting the activities. Social psychologists have shown that a minimum number of participants is necessary to make certain activities survive. Frequently the pool of eligibles in a housing environment is nowhere near great enough to provide this minimum number. Finally, in any program that uses tax money for partial support, it is simply not morally acceptable to build an ingrown program. Therefore pressure on sponsors to serve more than their own tenants is bound to increase.

How can the effort to serve both tenants and the wider community be planned to maximize its chance for success? The most important consideration is the conviction of the administrator (and ultimately the sponsor or authority) that it is good to have such mixing. If he cannot honestly feel that serving the wider community is proper, he is bound to communicate this attitude to his activity director, his tenants, and the community residents. Ideally he should hire an activity director with the explicit understanding that a joint program is desirable. If he comes into an established program, or must deal with community volunteer or tenant leaders, he must be firm in his insistence that tenants and local residents are equally important participants.

Selling tenants on the idea is certainly not easy, particularly when there is competition for important positions. While it would not be desirable to appear patronizing in official announcements, tenants' welfare instincts can informally be appealed to by reminding them of their fortunate status as tenants, and asking that they share what they can. The desirability of maintaining contact with the community can be justified to some tenant leaders as enlightened self-interest, calling their attention to the potential gains involved in governmental funding and the interest of important community agencies or individuals gained by virtue of this extension of the housing service.

Unquestionably the acceptability of outsiders will be enhanced if their background characteristics are consonant with those of tenants. Another fine line must be drawn here: what recruiting practices are exclusionary and therefore unacceptable in the context of an open society? We do not know how many site locations can be completely consonant with the characteristics of the tenants in a project. Some notable examples of extremely dissonant placements can be called to mind: the location of a project in a high-crime area, or in a new young-family area with no access to local resources. In the former case, the elderly local residents are likely to be in great need of special attention and similar to tenants at least in economic status. In the latter case, the relatively few elderly people living in young households may be quite different from tenants, possibly being of higher socioeconomic background, or perhaps living with younger family members because they are less independent. In both of these instances a viable community-tenant mixture will be more difficult to obtain. Successful integration will be easier in instances where the housing tenants are lifelong residents of the area, or where their dominant national or ethnic background matches that of the community. The greater problem will be to accommodate the individual community residents who are "different" from tenants. Very few reports have been made of either successful or unsuccessful attempts to conduct such programs. Until this information is disseminated, it will be difficult to establish adequate guidelines for those who want to make a wide-range activity program succeed.

MEDICAL PROGRAMS

Traditionally a number of public-housing projects have been able to provide medical programs with the help of community organizations. As yet, there is no HUD money available to support such programs, and the housing authority is in the position of begging for the service. Having thus relatively little choice in the matter, it is not surprising that many such programs are inadequate and unstable, dependent each year upon the decision of people outside the housing environment as to whether it can live another year or not.

There are also relatively few such services in the 202 program. We do not yet know how the 236 program has worked in this respect. The 231, on the other hand, has frequently provided major health services—another indication, perhaps, that with sufficient income to exercise an option, older people will choose the environment with health services. The 202s have been financially limited in the extent of medical service that they could furnish. Our own research has afforded the opportunity of observing a number of variations in type and extent of medical service. Some of these will be described, but consultation in depth on the specifics of such programs must come from housing and health care leaders who have actually had experience along these lines. We shall begin with the most modest programs.

The Physician on Call   The minimum that every project should provide is the names of *several* physicians who will agree to accept telephone calls from tenants or staff and in an emergency guarantee their willingness to make house calls to the site. The posting of their names, addresses, and telephone numbers in public places, and their publication in the tenant information booklet at the least provide free advertising for the physician and should be a sufficient inducement to make him commit himself to house calls. It would be

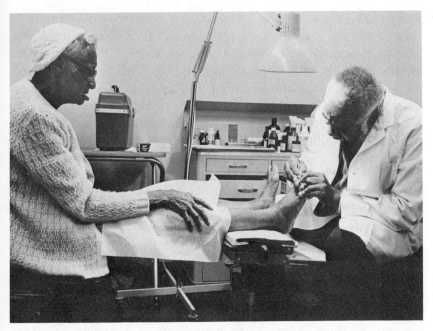

Fig. 6. Podiatric services are among the most frequently requested medical services. When they are done on the site, they can serve some tenants who might have difficulty going to an office. (Photo by Richard Mowrey.)

even better to provide every tenant with a card listing these facts to post or keep near his phone. These must, of course, be quickly updated as changes occur. Management must monitor these arrangements. Tenants should be encouraged to let the administration know about the quality of service obtained from the physicians who are so listed. An occasional phone call from a board member or sponsor official can frequently bring back on course a physician whose guarantees are loosely observed. At worst, a physician who does not come when needed should be immediately deleted from the list. The administrator should also be quick to pass around the word informally (probably not in writing) about any physician whose reputation among tenants is particularly good. In order to avoid any charge of favoritism, the administrator might arbitrarily contact *all* physicians within a given geographic area and put the names of all who agree to make house calls on the list.

Private Physician's Office   A relatively inexpensive investment in floor space and equipment can provide an office where a local physician can engage in outpatient practice among the tenants. Obviously a certain minimum patient load is required to make it worth his while, and, a certain minimum frequency of office hours is required to make it really serve the needs of the tenants. Guidelines are difficult to provide. One of the Philadelphia Geriatric Center's apartment buildings with 250 tenants in less-than-average good health requires about four hours per day of physician time. A 100-unit or smaller building for generally healthy tenants could probably not support a daily physician visit. At least one and preferably two weekly office hours are probably necessary to make the service act as a security-inducing agent for the tenant.

Finding a physician who will provide the service is no easy matter. In most instances (unless the on-site service is free to the tenant or included in his total housing cost) half or more of the tenants will continue to use their own physicians. The doctor can always fill his time easily, and perhaps at greater profit, by using his own more convenient office. Some extra inducement is probably necessary unless the physician is new in the area or has some unusual reason to wish to recruit more patients. Some fortunate sponsors may be able to offer a retainer or guaranteed minimum, or possibly an additional fee to the physician. Much more desirable would be the active recruitment by the sponsor of a physician who has a personal desire to work in geriatric medicine. Such a person may frequently be identified through the sponsoring organization or through a board member (one good reason for having a physician on the board). People willing to work with the elderly are frequently people with a social conscience, people who have been particularly attached to parents and grandparents (frequently feeling guilty in some way about their own relationships with deceased relatives), and people with some anxiety about their own aging. None of these reasons for interest are disqualifying—there are good and bad workers with each of these motivations. In the case of physicians as well as any other occupational group, we are fortunate that people with interest do exist, and we should utilize every means possible to locate them. Every area should be able to provide in response to active recruitment by management, board, or sponsor, a physician willing at least to put up with the inconvenience of traveling twice a week for office hours in return for his regular Medicare fee and the positive self-fulfillment of doing something for older people.

Nursing Services The effectiveness of functioning of any nursing service presumes the availability of a physcan somewhere in the background. A fairly frequent service combination involves a nurse's being in attendance more hours than a physician, with her work, of course, being supervised by the latter. The exact scope of the independent work that can be performed by the nurse at times when the physician is absent would have to be worked out very carefully. However, it is clear that there are many services that can be performed by the nurse that do not require the doctor's presence, and that would both give needed treatment and, especially, convey a sense of security to the tenant population. For some less competent or temporarily disabled tenants, regular medication may best be administered by a nurse directly rather than being left in the tenant's hands. Some treatments require a registered nurse. By far the most important gain from having a staff nurse is the knowledge by tenants that someone is on the premises to give emergency treatment and has the experience and judgment required to make the best referral or take the most effective action in a time of crisis.

A full-time nurse is certainly an expense that many projects cannot afford, even granting that such a person can be found. Our York House has one full-time nurse for its 250 tenants, plus a resident nurse who is on call at other times and on occasions when the full-time nurse needs help. For many projects a half-time nurse, or even a one-hour-per-day visit by a nurse would be sufficient. Again, it is difficult to employ nurses under these conditions. One possibility might be for three or more housing projects to share the time of a single nurse. The sponsor of a private housing project might consider advertising for a registered nurse, in the younger end of the age range eligible to be a tenant, who would be willing either to work or to serve on call in return for some adjustment in rent. In this case the sponsor would have to make sure that the arrangement could be reviewed annually or on the occasion of any change in health of the nurse tenant. There could, to be sure, be problems in a tenant's giving intimate services to fellow tenants. However, there have been a number of very successful arrangements like this, and it is easy to recommend heartily.

Fig. 7. An on-site nurse is the best single investment in medical services. (Photo by Richard Mowrey.)

The other major nursing service is delivered by local organizations like the Visiting Nurse Association or a visiting nurse from a municipal health department. These nurses work, of course, under the supervision of physicians, and are likely to have fairly rigidly specified limits to the kinds of services they can perform. Their services are frequently reserved for people with no other resource for service, and for bedfast, housebound, or other major-disability patients—people who would be unlikely to reside in most senior housing projects. However, every manager with no other prospect of on-site medical service should personally investigate local possibilities of this type. We have known some projects that have persuaded local visiting nurse organizations to set up a special service based in their housing environment. One rationale for such an innovation was that the concentration of 100 or more older people constituted adequate justification for the new location of their services. In addition, such an arrangement is also an ideal focus for extending the housing's services into the community, thus breaking down the undesirable barrier between housing and community. The organization might be offered office space for a local base, or dispensary space to which both community residents and tenants could come.

The home health aide is a relatively recently established paraprofessional specialist. She receives short-term training in nursing techniques that do not require the full nursing degree. She works under the supervision of a registered nurse (and ultimately a physician) and travels to the domiciles of people needing health care at home, or personal services secondary to a health condition. While the number of tenants in housing for the elderly who might need this kind of care is probably small, the administrator should visit whatever local agencies provide such services and become completely familiar with how he can obtain this care should a tenant need it.

The On-Site Medical Clinic   The discussion above has emphasized individuals (frequently working part-time) performing specific functions. Much more ideal is an outpatient clinic with a regular physician, reasonably complete nursing service, and with established channels for referral to speciality diagnostic services, medical and surgical consultants, and hospitals. Such a clinic ideally requires an office for physician or nurse, a treatment room, and a waiting room. In this format the look of the complex is like that of any physician's office in the community. It is *not* perceived as depressing by the tenants and does not contribute to a "sick atmosphere." The waiting room functions as a social center and has some group therapeutic value. This arrangement is immensely preferable to making the tenants wait in the lobby or on chairs in the hall beside the office door.

The clinic must offer both diagnosis and treatment. We have seen several plans fail completely because the decision was made to operate solely as a diagnostic service, or to emphasize health maintenance without offering on-site treatment. It seems debatable whether this is even economically preferable to giving full treatment on site. Certainly it is insupportable psychologically. Tenants quickly learn that they get turned away when ordinary symptoms are reported; older people are no better than the rest of us in overcoming their inertia about engaging in health maintenance behavior in the absence of symptoms.

Once in a while this kind of complete clinic can be provided and financed by local hospitals or municipal units. Notable examples of such operations have been written up by the Cleveland Metropolitan Housing Authority about its Springbrook Apartments and by the New York City Housing Authority about its Queensbridge project. Hopefully there will be more flexibly available federal funding in the future to allow such projects to multiply. For the present, however, it is extremely difficult to find resources to support such operations, and even the very best of them do not seem to last very long. They are expensive, they seem like a luxury to a voluntary hospital, and they are very subject to the vagaries of local medical and governmental politics.

Thus, it is primarily the affluent housing environments that can offer the full medical clinic. We have described various aspects of our York House service. To recapitulate these briefly, the 250 tenants have available to them a half-time physician with offices on the site, physicians on call 24 hours, a full-time nurse, a resident on-call nurse, a full complement of specialty consultants, and the partial service of a pharmacist and free medication. Thus, all services other than acute hospital treatment are provided. There are many considerations that will determine the cost of such an operation. Medicare payments alone certainly cannot begin to pay for the comprehensiveness and the security-building coverage given by a full clinic. As of 1974, about 3 percent of the $310 monthly cost for a single tenant (or $9) was accounted for by the medical package detailed above in York House North. Certainly anyone contemplating a similar service should research much more deeply how other such operations work out financially before assuming that this experience can be duplicated or bettered in other locations.

The Infirmary for Short-Term Illness   The idea of maintaining a small infirmary where intercurrent illnesses can be treated briefly, and tenants then sent back to their own apartments, seems like a natural idea for a large service-oriented housing environment. Treatment here should be cheaper than hospital treatment, more adequate than treatment given in the dwelling unit, and the trauma to the patient far less than transfer to a hospital. Alas, this good idea seems almost impossible to actualize in most housing environments. A "bed" in the hospital sense immediately calls into operation the immense machinery of the medical and bureaucratic establishment, invoking new license classifications, standards for certification, and conditions of governmental regulation, to say nothing of totally different funding channels. In short, it is impossible to maintain such an infirmary except as a fully licensed medical or long-term care institution. There are a few housing environments with interlocking intermediate care, nursing home, or hospital facilities where a true infirmary arrangement is possible, operating in conjunction with these other large subunits. Otherwise, however, the cost of a free-standing small infirmary in an environment that is primarily housing for the well elderly is prohibitive.

The Special-Care Area One major variation that will probably be adopted more in the future is the setting aside of an area of the housing project where less capable tenants can live permanently and receive more services than the average tenant.

A pioneer in this form was York House South, the second of the Philadelphia Geriatric Center's two apartment buildings. The model can be best illustrated by a detailed description of how special care operates here. One floor, containing 32 apartments designed in identical fashion to those throughout the building, is set aside for either York House tenants or residents of the community who are ill enough to require either (*a*) daily medical or nursing care, or (*b*) personal services such as aid in dressing, grooming, eating, and ambulation, but still are independent enough to be unsuitable for nursing home care. On this floor there is 24-hour nursing care, daily rounds by the physician, personal service by aides and housekeepers, and meal service in the apartment *if* both tenant and physician deem it advisable. A major effort is made to preserve the apartment, rather than the institutional look. The "nurses station" is an office without the usual large glass windows, and there is no medical equipment in evidence. Regular beds are used, hallways are decorated apartment-style, and all tenants who are able to go to meals in the common dining room and engage in the normal activities of the housing environment.

It should be noted, nonetheless, that this is clearly a medical operation. It could not function without its full complement of medical staff and without its proximate relationship to the rest of the nursing and hospital facilities of the Philadelphia Geriatric Center. It is also expensive. In 1974, a single tenant's monthly charge (inclusive of everything except special private nursing care or acute hospital expense) was $575. This kind of arrangement, while now a resource available only to the affluent, may easily be adapted to other situations if sources of funding can be opened up.

In contrast to the full-time clinic, however, the special-care area does contribute strongly to changing the total milieu in the direction of the "sick" environment. A substantial minority of tenants would prefer not to have such a service in the same building where they live. Some are also very sensitive to the fact that this floor populates the dining room with "sick"-looking people and causes nurses in uniform to be visible in other areas of the building. In our research we looked very hard at the possible effects of having this special care area in our second building. We found that the newness of York House South (and its being slightly more expensive) had a strong effect in raising its status relative to the older York House North. The presence of the health facility in York House South did not lower the perceived status of the building, nor were there any differences in well-being between the noncare area tenants of York House South and those of York House North. When questioned in depth about their attitude to the special-care facility, tenants frequently could say in the same sentence that they didn't like its being located in their building, but that it was still a good thing, since they themselves might need it some day. For this population, at least, the net balance was obviously in favor of having such a place to go to if one's health declined. Still, it is probably true that the presence of the special-care area screens out a certain number of people who are oversensitive to the "sick" atmosphere from ever applying for admission. We have determined that the applicants to York House South are older and less independent than those applying to some other housing. Therefore, as mentioned in the last chapter, the sponsor would have to be willing to deal permanently with a less independent tenant population if he decided to include a special-care area in his building.

The "Congregate-Housing" idea The central aspect of the congregate-housing plan authorized in the 1970 Housing Act was the idea that there was a great need for services in addition to mere housing—services short of medical care, which if provided, would forestall transfer to an institution. While the act was never fully implemented, the idea will no doubt become incorporated into future housing schemes. One important part of the definition of congregate housing is the provision of "personal services"—assistance in the tasks necessary to daily living, such as shopping, cooking, eating, dressing, grooming, and housekeeping. These tasks are sharply distinguished from nursing care and are presumed to be appropriately performed by relatively untrained housekeepers or personal aides. People impaired enough to need nursing care are explicitly excluded from the congregate-care facility. This conception thus implies that there is a continuum that runs thus:

Full Independence———Personal Care———Nursing Care

One cannot speak confidently at this point either in support of or against the relevance of this continuum for the planning of services in the housing environment. However, on the basis of our experience, it seems to us that people may need help in dealing with some personal tasks long before they need help with others. Our whole discussion of services has emphasized that many services are designed to compensate for the increasing difficulty that older people have in getting *connected* with resources available outside their housing environments. Thus, transportation is an essential link to shopping, cultural activity, social interaction, and medical care. Locating some of these resources on the site may prove a link for some people equivalent to the link that transportation provides for others. Thus meals, activities, and a medical clinic on the site allow fairly well-functioning people easier access to basic necessities. These people may then maintain their own dwelling units without difficulty.

It seems to us that a distinctly lesser state of competence is exhibited by the person who needs help *within his own apartment or dwelling unit* as contrasted with help that is provided within the common spaces of the housing environment. Research has shown us that food preparation, eating, grooming, and housekeeping are skills that are maintained by older people up until the time when gross physical or mental infirmity intrudes. Therefore, it is difficult to imagine these highly personal, in-dwelling-unit services being required by anyone who does not also require some medical services that go beyond the usual doctor's-office care. Our version of the continuum of care would look thus:

Full Independence———On-Site Services———Personal and Nursing Services———Full Medical Services

We suggest that the housing sponsor contemplating use of the congregate housing program think primarily in terms of the services provided for the more independent, that is, an activity program, an outpatient clinic, transportation, and possibly congregate meals. If he is prepared to go into the less independent end of the continuum, the special-care area with both nursing facilities and personal care capability should be added.

However, we shall need to watch very carefully the experience of sponsors who use the congregate-housing program. There may be only enough partially impaired people in some housing environments to warrant the addition of staff to perform these personal services for that minority. The majority of relatively independent tenants would need nothing more than the usual facilities for medical care available to all tenants. It would be important in this instance to be able to maintain a flexible level of personal-care staff to be able to meet the needs of the less competent, without having an oversupply that might tempt one to push such help on those who do not really require it.

One critical issue raised by these fine lines of distinction about what constitutes personal care is whether kitchens are to be supplied or not. If one accepts the personal-care idea at its extreme, it leads to a decision to build dwelling units without kitchens for the least competent. Again, is it conceivable that anyone not able to cook for herself will also not require close medical or nursing attention? Our conviction is that the presence of a kitchen contributes to the image of independence and may allow the continued exercise of talents; its absence will in an irrevocable way erode these talents. In the case of single men with no inclination to change roles in later life, one can make a case for the omission of a kitchen. However, it is a decision requiring the utmost caution: is the financial saving achieved consistent with the total overall goal of congregate housing, which is to prolong independence?

A more comprehensive treatment of the complicated issues of meal services will have to be provided by others. For sponsors and public-housing authorities, new mechanisms opened up under the Older Americans Act of 1973 make economic considerations no longer rule out meal programs for some housing projects. In the past it has been very difficult for on-site meals to be provided without a sub-sidy. A perhaps over-simplified summary of past experience leads us to state that the only way meals can be provided without a subsidy is to make mandatory the taking of all or a majority of meals in the common dining room. This, of course, drives the cost of the housing package up to a point where another segment of the elderly popu-lation is priced out of the possibility of living there. The nutrition program included in Title VII of the Older Americans Act will enable many sponsors to offer less expensive meals and also to be able to offer more options to tenants. While these nutrition pro-grams are by no means limited to housing for the elderly, these are natural locations from which to serve both tenants and community residents. Some of the possible variations in type of meal service follow.

Full Central-Dining-Room Service   For the most part only luxury retirement centers can provide all three meals, since there is no satis-factory way that this can be done utilizing a single eight-hour work shift. The cost of providing the third meal thus goes up dispropor-tionately, with correspondingly higher charges being necessary. Breakfast is not a difficult meal to prepare, and a number of housing operations serve a noon and an evening meal. A light lunch is easy to prepare in a relatively short time after staff reports on duty, leaving the longer time for preparing and serving the larger evening meal, although a compromise in the direction of early din-ner may still have to be made.

Midday Dining-Room Meal Service   One of the usual types of service is lunch or a noon-time dinner, on the theory that one hot planned meal per day can assure minimum nutritional requirements, while still staying within reasonable cost bounds. Serving the entire tenant group requires a full dining room where multipurpose use is somewhat limited, even if only one meal is served there. Some

Fig. 8. A hot-lunch program is feasible for a low-cost housing program. Tenant help should be encouraged, with pay if possible. (Photo by Richard Mowrey.)

housing environments choose to provide both breakfast and a midday dinner, leaving tenants to prepare their own light suppers.

Midday-Snack Lunches   Even more frequent is the small lunch that does not require a full kitchen to prepare. A community room is generally used, in connection with a party-type kitchen where soup can be heated, fruit and juice kept cool, and sandwiches and salad prepared. On this scale it is possible to make the lunches optional and inexpensive. Volunteer or modestly paid tenant help is ideal for this kind of program. We have not seen many such programs completely managed by tenants. Usually a volunteer, a paid supervisor or cook, or an outside agency provides the overall direction, including the recruitment of tenant help. Food preparation, some shopping, cooking, table setting, and cleanup can provide meaningful activity for tenants. A number of activity programs run by local agencies or city recreation departments include such a hot lunch program. Surplus foods may further reduce the cost of the program, and poverty funds may be available to pay tenants to do some of the work.

Snack Bar and Grill A grill requires relatively expensive equipment and the services of someone who can work under the strain of short-order cooking. A project cannot count on always having such a person among its tenants. Unlike the soup-sandwich-salad-drink operation, a certain level of business is necessary to reach the break-even point and maintain the flow of fresh meat. We have seen several such enterprises fail after cutting back services, because of low demand, and finding that the cutting back itself was the final blow. The grill probably should be a professional operation reserved for a large project.

The Coffee Bar A warm, comfortable, intimate corner decorated for relaxation is an ideal locale for an endless coffee pot. A tenants' organization can usually manage a coffee bar, including other of-

Fig. 9. An open coffee pot brightens the day for some people. A comfortable arrangement of coffee-bar furniture can add to the satisfaction.

ferings such as tea, doughnuts, toast, cookies, and so on. They are more likely to be offered a community room, or a corner of some other common space, than an ideally decorated coffee bar, but even so, the opportunity to sip with a friend enlarges the social life of the environment. Our impression is that there is less contention if a standard charge is made per cup of coffee than if a voluntary contribution is sought.

More and more housing sites are utilizing catering services for their regular meal services. Expert consultation should be sought in order to compare the costs of catered as compared to staff-produced meals, and to make decisions regarding the amount of kitchen equipment required for each.

The physical characteristics of the dining room have been discussed previously. As for seating, there are strong adherents of the assigned-seat approach and equally vociferous defendants of the open-seating restaurant-style approach. Assigning seats clearly is easiest for management and acceptable to a majority of tenants, provided there is complete flexibility about making seating changes at the request of tenants. If open seating is allowed, territories will quickly be established and a substantial proportion of tenants will come to "own" seats as definitely as under the assigned-seat plan. The ultimate decision may well hinge on the administrator's assessment of the tradition of his tenant population. The more competent tenant with a middle-class life style may be happier under conditions of free choice, while the less healthy or those more used to unquestioning acquiescence to authority may experience less strain by not having to deal with constant choices.

Food-service personnel require training and continued reinforcement regarding their work with older people. Especially where tenants are whites from relatively privileged backgrounds and waitresses are younger blacks, constant alertness to the feelings of staff as they serve tenants is required. They may feel outraged at the demandingness of a few tenants, yet be able to deal constructively with the outrageous demand if given a chance to talk about it in periodic meetings with the administrator or supervisor.

The special diet is a fact of life that the project offering meals must face. Again, training for the waitress is necessary to impress upon her the importance of compulsive attention to such orders.

It is more expensive to offer a choice of meals rather than a single platter, but highly worthwhile in maintaining morale. It is possible to provide a changing daily special, but maintain a battery of alternate easy-to-prepare platters that are always available. In our York House, it is usually possible to order a fruit and cottage cheese platter, tuna salad, a cold fish platter, or a sliced cheese platter as alternative lunch choices, or chicken as a dinner alternative to the daily special.

It also helps to provide a mechanism for tenant input into menu planning. Some tenant organizations have a food committee that meets periodically with the administrator. It goes without saying that it is far better to have no such committee unless its suggestions can sometimes be taken. If food is discussed with staff in the context of a general tenant meeting, the discussion may never end. Thus, it is better either to deal with a separate food committee or to set an arbitrary limit on the time allotted to this subject. Needless to say, much of the content of any such session is pure griping, but most administrators can take it, and it may help the tenants.

Whether everyone is served at one sitting, at two separate sittings, or at any time during a designated interval, is largely a matter of economics, and should be settled with expert consultation long before building plans are complete. The savings gained from the lower construction cost of a smaller dining room may be eaten up by the lesser efficiency of the staggered or multiple seating schedule. Our preference is for scheduled seating times, based primarily on the idea that the high social point of the day is the half hour before and the half hour after the meal, when people are all waiting together for the dining room to open or are leisurely leaving the area.

Communication is also easier when most people can be assumed to be present for announcements made in the dining room. A public address system, either built-in or a portable cordless one, is essential.

The minute participation in the meal program is made voluntary, the volume of use will decrease below a break-even point. Some projects have adopted different compromises in order to allow some choice within the framework of compulsory meals. A standard rental fee including all meals may be charged, but people allowed to apply for refunds (usually less than the actual prorated per-person meal cost) if they wish not to take meals at all for a specified period,—one month or three months. Other sites include in their monthly charge payment for a minimum number of meals per month, allowing people to buy additional meals on a per-meal basis if they wish. One enterprising site both kept its financial balance in the black and at the same time maintained a policy of voluntary tenant meal participation by encouraging outside individuals to eat with tenants and renting their kitchen and dining facilities to outside groups for special occasions.

The lesser meal programs generally are utilized relatively sparsely, much to the consternation of the administration or meal sponsor. Among several of our research sites offering voluntary lunch programs, about 23 percent of tenants availed themselves of the lunch once a week or more (as of several years before this book was written). Even where meals are low in cost, most relatively competent tenants appear to prefer to cook their own meals at their own convenience. While active solicitation may be necessary to get the socially retiring tenant to try such a program, it is probably not reasonable to expect anywhere near a majority of tenants to patronize a lunch program except under the compulsion of the flat monthly fee.

HOUSEKEEPING SERVICES

Housekeeping is a low-demand service, as measured by the stated wishes of the large number of people we have interviewed, whether they be tenants in housing for the elderly, prospective tenants, or people residing in the community. Among this relatively competent group of people, assistance in performing chores is construed as a luxury item. Those with limited incomes do not even consider this service a possibility. We do not have information on whether people of limited independence would be more likely to want daily or weekly apartment cleaning services than do the more competent.

The congregate-housing idea assumes that assistance with house cleaning will be a part of the personal care given. Thus one way to organize such a service is to make it available from a class of employee who might be called a "personal-care aide." These people would have to be given some early training and continuing supervision in meeting the necessary physical and psychological demands of the job. House cleaning would be included, although a fine line would have to be drawn to encourage the aide to develop a role conception of himself as a personal-care specialist without encouraging him to professionalize this role so much that he rejected the more menial tasks of cleaning and cooking.

There would seem to be some advantages to setting up maid services so that they are elective, rather than compulsory. If a project is planned so that housekeeping services are available to everyone and included in a single monthly fee, no tenant is going to decline to accept the service. It seems clear that doing one's own household work offers much that is ego-building to many elderly people; therefore we suggest that the administrator not make it so easy for the tenant to relinquish this role.

It is difficult enough in urban areas to maintain a steady staff of housekeeping personnel, and probably even more difficult to keep adequately staffed when the need for housekeeping time ebbs and flows as it would if it is elective for the tenants. When building a new project, if such a service is to be offered, management should ask applicants to commit themselves one way or the other, and work out a way to contract for a specified period of service in advance, paying for it as a part of the monthly rental. Management can over-charge enough to maintain a reserve available to maintain staff during periods when the demand for services drops temporarily.

Ideally, different options should be available, ranging from full service through daily light housekeeping to once-a-week service. It might be possible for an administrator to work out a subcontracting arrangement with a commercial service so that work could be done on call. These services are normally quite expensive, with rates being calculated on the basis of the normal household's high level of use and clutter. Care should be taken to negotiate a rate that takes ac-count of the much easier task of cleaning the average elderly person's unit.

TRANSPORTATION

Some housing projects have chosen a site without transportation facilities and then pressured their municipality or local bus line to establish special service, to extend an existing line, or to change a route to serve their tenants better. More often the housing itself has had to provide transportation. There is a great variety of custom-made transportation schemes, all of them either expensive or with substantial weaknesses. Expensive though it is, however, some kind of transportation is an essential link between the housing and the wider community where some of the basic facilities are lacking in close proximity to the housing. The time will probably soon come

Fig. 10. Community organizations may be better equipped than a housing sponsor to furnish dependable transportation services. (Photo by Richard Mowrey.)

when a transportation plan may be required as a part of the application package for federal assistance.

A few particularly well-organized sponsors or community groups are able to keep a squad of volunteer drivers on a regular schedule of pickups at the housing site, delivery to a multifunction shopping center, assistance with ambulation, finding goods in the stores, carrying packages, and delivery of tenants back to the site. Volunteer transportation programs frequently have trouble because of the difficulty in assuring regularity of service. The times when service may be most needed are the times when volunteers are unavailable: evenings, holidays, bad weather days. Maintaining one's own transportation service is very expensive. The minimum cost includes cost of the vehicle, an operator, and maintenance. Some organizations furnish individualized services on order, usually performing them only for particularly needy people or for especially critical purposes, such as doctor appointments.

One other possibility is to hire individuals who drive their own cars to commit themselves to making specified trips each week. Students will often welcome this kind of job, although public utility regulations and insurance restrictions may constitute barriers in some localities. Anyone performing such driving tasks will have to be instructed carefully in how to help older people into the car, assist them in loading bundles, and so on.

As transportation is recognized more and more to be a crucial

Fig. 11. The driver must be well trained to assist older people as they get on and off and to be psychologically supportive as he does his work. (Photo by Richard Mowrey.)

element in keeping older people in the mainstream of competent living, communities will give more attention to the provision of transportation services to all elderly. Some housing sites are served by community-based agencies whose clients may or may not be residents of planned housing environments. Large cities usually have some existing service that will provide transportation assistance, whether through a public or private agency. Where there are no such services, a survey of potential tenant need, showing percentages of tenants who do not leave their buildings, and percentages who would perform any of several activities if transportation were available, may constitute a convincing piece of evidence to present to a health and welfare council as evidence that such a service should be instituted. In situations where a housing environment is really isolated it may be necessary to maintain a bus and driver, or to hire a service that will make a daily trip to a shopping center. More usually, a station wagon or small jitney driven by a maintenance man several times per week, as well as being utilized for maintenance operations, will be adequate. The administrator should know whether there are local agencies with organized transportation facilities that might be made available to his tenants.

Activity, medical, meal, housekeeping, and transportation services are thus the major types of service that housing environments will require. No prescription will fit all locations. We have tried to describe as many variations as possible, but undoubtedly each administrator will have to design a unique package for his own use.

chapter 14

Conclusion

At this point it is difficult not to be pessimistic about the short-range future of housing for the elderly in this country. Experience has proven that successful programs for the elderly must be conceived with the special needs of older people in mind, and that above all they must be assured special funds to insure that adequate investment is made in this negatively stereotyped group. On the other hand, the magnitude of the demand for adequate housing will increase greatly as the sheer number of older people increases over the next 50 years. Thus, we would be foolish to allow our planning efforts to subside in the face of what is clearly a temporary failure of national policy in this area.

The entire thrust of this book has been to emphasize that design and management are partners in fashioning an environment for living that is consistent with the past experiences and present capabilities of the older person. Further, while by habit one tends to speak of "the aged," the effort has been made to portray the diversity of this group and to delineate the necessity of tailoring environmental and administrative planning to provide maximum options for the individual. Only in this way can individual well-being be enhanced.

The initiation of a project should immediately involve not only the sponsor (private developer, non-profit organization, local housing authority) but also the architect, someone who will ultimately be involved in administration, and wherever possible, some prospective tenants. The housing consultant will frequently be the agent capable of determining the quality of this team effort. There will by no means always be such a consultant, however, nor will he always be able to function as a consultant on the human quality of the environment in addition to his concern with the financial and bureaucratic aspects of the planning. Therefore, the ultimate burden is on the sponsor to insure the input of adequate concern for the social and psychological milieu.

Much of the discussion has utilized instances of nonprofit or public-housing sponsorship as examples. Commercially developed and managed housing for the elderly has been examined in much less depth because knowledge about it is sparse. It is clear that for privately developed housing for the elderly to succeed in the broad mission of providing a true home for its tenants, enlightened management will be required. Training such people in the human side of management is a major goal of the National Center for Housing Management. There is no reason why the private sector should not be able to function effectively in this area. However, the far greater need will always be for subsidized units to serve the elderly with limited incomes. Innovative leadership in trying out new kinds of environments requires the continued effort of nonprofit and public sponsors.

The administrator must be able to function in an extremely varied number of roles, from maintenance man and purchasing agent to psychotherapist. It is difficult to understand how 15 years of senior housing production were allowed to elapse before any organized program for training administrators came into being. Such training cannot help but benefit tenants, by way of increasing the self-image of the administrators themselves.

The future will see the further development of housing-based supportive services and experimentation with mixing tenants and community residents in different service situations. Undoubtedly, considerably more variety in housing assistance will develop, based on methods that will give older people more choice about where and how they live, and at the same time, better access to services that have heretofore been clustered in housing or institutions. Creative ideas about remodeling older housing stock, and ways of delivering services in scattered housing locations, are badly needed.

None of the goals discussed in this presentation can be met without a consistent and aggressive federal housing policy that encourages the simultaneous development of housing by the public, commercial, and nonprofit sectors. It is difficult to see how high standards for location, site selection, architectural design, admission policy, service planning, management, and research can be maintained without strong federal direction. One of the unknown factors for the immediate future is the extent to which national, as opposed to local, standards will prevail. Not enough is known about the capability of municipalities, counties, or even states to function effectively either in maintaining standards or assuring an adequate flow of funds into housing programs for the elderly. Ideally, experience with an increased level of local control should make it possible both to take advantage of the incentives that accrue from the personal investment inherent in local self-determination, and to learn which segments of planning and management are best done at a national level. Whatever the allocation of responsibility to federal and local levels, continual pressure from citizen and professional advocates for the elderly will be necessary to insure that the elderly get their proper share. Hopefully the sharing of the thoughts contained in this book will help this pressure to be exerted more effectively by planners, sponsors, architects, and administrators.

The following organizations with an interest in housing and aging may be able to provide information on the subject of housing for the elderly:

Administration on Aging, U.S. Department of Health, Education and Welfare, Washington, D.C. 20201

American Association of Homes for the Aged, 374 National Press Building, 14th & F Streets, N.W., Washington, D.C. 20004

American Association of Retired Persons, 1909 K Street, N.W., Washington, D.C. 20006

American Institute of Architects, 1785 Massachusetts Avenue, N.W., Washington, D.C. 20036

Gerontological Society, One Dupont Circle, N.W., Washington, D.C. 20036

National Center for Housing Management, 1133 Fifteenth Street, N.W., Washington, D.C. 20005

National Association of Housing and Redevelopment Officials, 2600 Virginia Avenue, N.W., Washington, D.C. 20037

National Council on Aging, 1828 L Street, N.W., Washington, D.C. 20036

National Council of Senior Citizens, 1627 K Street, N.W., Washington, D.C. 20006

Senate Special Committee on Aging, New Senate Office Building, Washington, D.C. 20510

U.S. Department of Housing and Urban Development, Washington, D.C. 20410

The Urban Institute, 2100 M Street, N.W., Washington, D.C. 20037

References

A. Aging

Atchley, R. C. *Social forces in later life: An introduction to social gerontology.* Belmont, California: Wadsworth, 1972.

Eisdorfer, C. & Lawton, M. P. (Ed.) *The psychology of adult development and aging.* Washington: American Psychological Association, 1973.

Riley, M. W. & Foner, A. *Aging and Society.* New York: Russell Sage Foundation, 1968.

Shanas, E., Townsend, P., Wedderburn, D., Friis, H., Milhoj, P., & Stehouwer, J. *Old people in three industrial societies.* New York: Atherton, 1968.

B. Books on Housing for the Elderly

Beyer, G. G. & Nierstrasz, F. H. J. *Housing the aged in western countries.* New York: Elsevier, 1967.

Byerts, T. O. (Ed.) *Housing and environments for the elderly.* Washington: Gerontological Society, 1974.

Carp, F. M. *A future for the aged.* Austin: University of Texas Press, 1966.

Musson, N. & Heusenkveld, H. *Buildings for the elderly.* New York; Reinhold, 1963.

Newman, O. *Defensible space.* New York: Macmillan, 1972.

Rosow, I. *Social integration of the aged.* Glencoe, Illinois: Free Press, 1967.

Senate Special Committee on Aging. *Housing for the elderly: A status report.* Washington, D.C.: Government Printing Office, 1973.

Weiss, J. D. *Better buildings for the aged.* New York: Hopkinson and Blake, 1969.

Westmeyer, T. R. *Management of public housing for the elderly.* New York: Graduate School of Public Administration, New York University, 1963.

C. Publications of the United States Department of Housing and Urban Development

Lawton, M. Powell & Byerts, Thomas O. (Ed.) *Community planning for the elderly.*

Minimum Property Standards (Elderly Housing). General Revision No. E-3, HUD PG 46.

Management of housing for the elderly. HUD Publication HMG7460.3. Washington: Department of Housing and Urban Development, December, 1972.

YORK HOUSE
YORK HOUSE SOUTH

DATE _____

MEDICAL FORM

MALE
NAME OF APPLICANT _____ AGE _____ FEMALE

ADDRESS _____

A. MEDICAL HISTORY

1. PRESENT COMPLAINTS AND HISTORY OF PRESENT ILLNESS

2. DRUGS CURRENTLY PRESCRIBED _____

_____ DRUG ALLERGIES _____

_____

3. DIET (CIRCLE ONE) REGULAR SPECIAL – DESCRIBE _____

4. MEDICAL CARE PAST 12 MOS. (CIRCLE ONE)

   A) DAILY B) WEEKLY C) MONTHLY D) _____ TIMES/YR

5. HOSPITALIZATIONS (DATES, NAME OF HOSPITAL, DIAGNOSIS)

6. PAST MEDICAL HISTORY (STATE YEAR IF APPLICABLE; SPECIFY IF POSSIBLE)

ADDICTION	CONSTIPATION	PARALYSIS
ALLERGY	CORONARY OCCLUSION	PEPTIC ULCER
ANEMIA	DIABETES	PLEURISY
ANGINA	DIARRHEA	PNEUMONIA
ARTHRITIS	EPILEPSY	STROKE
ASTHMA	FRACTURES	TUBERCULOSIS
CATARACT	GALL BLADDER	TYPHOID
CHRONIC BRONCHITIS	G. I. BLEEDING	URINARY CALCULUS
HEMIPLEGIA	GLAUCOMA	URINARY INFECTION
HEMORRHOIDS	GOITER	VARICOSE VEINS
HERNIA	GOUT	VENEREAL DISEASE
HYPERTENSION	HEART FAILURE	WEAKNESS OF EXTREMITIES
JAUNDICE	MALARIA	OTHER

7. RECENT REPORTS OF X-RAY EXAMINATION (GIVE DATES)

8. RECENT REPORTS—LABORATORY TESTS, ETC. (GIVE DATES)

B. CAPACITIES

	CHECK APPROPRIATE CATEGORY		
	INDEPENDENT	NEEDS HELP OCCASIONALLY	NEEDS MUCH HELP
DRESSING AND GROOMING			
COOKING AND HOUSEKEEPING			
MONEY MANAGEMENT			
BATHING			
TOILETING			

HAS HE ANY SENSORY LIMITATION (SPECIFY)   VISION _____

HEARING _____ OTHER _____

HAS HE EVER HAD TREATMENT FOR A PSYCHIATRIC CONDITION? (SPECIFY DATE, DIAGNOSIS, DRUGS AND TREATMENT RECEIVED, IF KNOWN)

C. PSYCHOSOCIAL CHARACTERISTICS
(CHECK 1, 2, OR 3 FOR EACH CHARACTERISTIC)

CHARACTERISTIC	1	2	3
A. EXPRESSION	UNCOMMUNICATIVE	TALKS NORMAL AMOUNT	OVERTALKATIVE
B. EMOTIONAL STATE	TENDS TO BE DEPRESSED	NORMAL EMOTIONAL STATE	SOMEWHAT ELATED
C. MEMORY	FREQUENT MEMORY FAILURE	OCCASIONALLY FORGETFUL	UNIMPAIRED MEMORY
D. SOCIABILITY	WITHDRAWN	NORMALLY SOCIABLE	OVERLY GREGARIOUS
E. ANXIETY	A WORRIER	WORRIES APPROPRIATELY	DENIES ALL WORRY
F. SATISFACTION	DISSATISFIED, DEMANDING	MAKES APPROPRIATE REQUESTS	WON'T COMPLAIN OR REQUEST ANYTHING
G. ACTIVITY	PREFERS TO BE IDLE	NORMALLY ACTIVE FOR AGE	CONTENT ONLY WHEN BUSY

D. COMMENTS

DATE _____   _____ M.D.
SIGNATURE OF ATTENDING PHYSICIAN

SAMPLE

COMMUNITY SURVEY: HOUSING PREFERENCES*

1. If you were thinking of moving from your present housing, which type of housing would you perfer? (Please check the appropriate box)

   A house

   An apartment with bedroom, bathroom, kitchen, and living room in which I could live independently.

   An apartment, but with the opportunity to take my meals in a dining room with the other residents.

   Hotel style with my own bedroom and bath with all services (such as meals and cleaning) provided for me.

   Other _____

   a) Is this the *same* or *different* from your present housing? (circle)
   b) How long have you lived at your present address? ____ yrs. ____ mos.

2. Where would you prefer that your housing be? (Please check as many answers as you wish.)

   a. ☐ In downtown city
      ☐ In _____ neighborhood
      ☐ In _____ suburb
      ☐ Outside of city but in county
      ☐ Other _____

   b. ☐ Near a shopping center
      ☐ Near churches
      ☐ Near a hospital or other medical facility
      ☐ Near parks and recreation facilities
      ☐ Near public transportation
      ☐ Other _____

   c. ☐ Near people my own age
      ☐ Near people of all ages
      ☐ Near my friends

---

* *Source:* Derived from Pastalan, L. *Retirement housing study,* Madison: The Methodist Hospital of Madison, Wisconsin, July 1972.

3. What services would you like provided within the actual building where you live? (You may check more than one answer.)
    - ☐ Shopping   ☐ Barber and beauty shop
      (drugs and grocery)   ☐ Recreation and hobby rooms
    - ☐ Restaurant   ☐ Gardening plots, greenhouse
    - ☐ Library
    - ☐ Chapel
    - ☐ Other _____

4. Would you like medical services provided?
    - ☐ Yes   ☐ No

    If yes, what medical services would you like?
    - ☐ Nurse on call or scheduled 1/week
    - ☐ Doctor on call or scheduled 1/mo.
    - ☐ Nurse on duty and available at all times
    - ☐ Physical therapy or Exercise Program
    - ☐ Clinic which provides daily medicine
    - ☐ Small hospital bed area for residents who become ill
    - ☐ Other _____

5. What features are important to you in selecting a new neighborhood?
    - ☐ Closer to shopping   ☐ Closer to friends or relatives
    - ☐ Quieter   ☐ Less crime
    - ☐ Less traffic   ☐ Other

6. What features would you consider in selecting another home now?
    - ☐ Small kitchen   ☐ central laundry
    - ☐ Fewer bedrooms   ☐ newer, less maintenance and
    - ☐ All on one floor   repair
    - ☐ Building with elevator   ☐ other
    - ☐ patio or balcony

7. If services such as health care, meals and cleaning assistance could be provided to you in this home, would you prefer to remain here rather than move?
    - ☐ Yes   ☐No

8. Are you planning on moving:
    Within the next year   ☐ Yes   ☐ No
    Within the next one to three years   ☐ Yes   ☐ No
    Within the next three to five years   ☐ Yes   ☐ No

9. If you plan on moving within the next five years and if housing
    is   developed   at _____ site,
    _____ site, _____ site,
    would you consider moving in? _____ site:
    1. ☐ Very likely   4. ☐ Probably no
    2. ☐ Possibly yes   5. ☐ Very unlikely
    3. ☐ Perhaps
    _____ site:
    1. ☐ Very likely   4. ☐ Probably no
    2. ☐ Possibly yes   5. ☐ Very unlikely
    3. ☐ Perhaps
    _____ site:
    1. ☐ Very likely   4. ☐ Probably no
    2. ☐ Possibly yes   5. ☐ Very unlikely
    3. ☐ Perhaps
10. What events that might occur in the future would cause you to
    consider moving? (List in order of response).
    _____
    _____
    _____

11. What type of housing do you live in now?
    ☐ I own my own home
    ☐ I live in a rented house
    ☐ I live in an apartment
    ☐ I rent a room
12. How many people live with you in the same unit?
    ☐ Myself only
    ☐ One other (specify spouse, child, sibling, non-related)
    ☐ Two others (specify)
    ☐ More than two (specify)
13. How much money per month do you currently spend on
    housing?
    _____ dollars per month,
    on utilities? _____
14. What type of transportation do you use most often?
    ☐ Car   ☐ Bus
    ☐ Taxi   ☐ Walk
    ☐ Other _____

15. What, if any, physical or health problems do you have that limit your activities or require the regular assistance of another person?

16. What is your age?
    - ☐ 60 to 65 years
    - ☐ 66 to 70 years
    - ☐ male ☐ female
    - ☐ 71 to 75 years
    - ☐ 76 to 80 years
    - ☐ over 80 years

17. Do you feel there is a need for housing for retired people in this community?
    - ☐ No need
    - ☐ Some need
    - ☐ Great need
    - ☐ Very great need
    - ☐ I have no opinion

18. Are there any other services for retired people that you feel are particularly needed in this community?

19. Please use this space for any additional remarks you wish to make.

Index

Grocery stores, 87
Grooming, 148-149
Gulledge, Eugene, 40

Halfway houses, 53
Hallucinations, 271
Hallways, 138, 156-158, 183-186,
   215-216
Hamovitch, Maurice, 73
Handrails, 124, 156, 211, 214
Havighurst, Robert, 11, 20
Hazards, natural, 99
Health, 4-6, 8, 47, 104-107,
   229-230, 238, 241-243, 263-
   266
Henry, William, 25
Highland Heights, 79
High-rise buildings, 132, 140-
   143, 177, 188, 209
Home health aides, 303
Homemaker service, 63
Homeownership, 45
Hospitals, day, 275
 general, 87, 275
 night, 275
 psychiatric, 275
Housekeeping, 149-152, 214, 307
 services, 40, 111, 314-315
Housing Act, 1949, 41, 42
 1950, 42
 1959, 35
 1964, 42
 1965, 36, 43
 1968, 39, 42
 1970, 306
 1974, 38, 39
Housing allowance, 29-30, 50
Housing and Urban Development,
   U.S. Department of (HUD),
   29, 30, 38, 53, 76, 92, 177,
   322, 323
Housing authority, 29, 30, 78,
   136-137, 222, 223, 251, 253-
   256, 262-263
Howell, Sandra, 197
HUD Challenge, 255
HUD News, 255

Income, tenants, 36, 262-263
Independence, 104, 112, 229-

   232, 263-264
Infirmary, 110, 127, 304
Inner-city areas, 45-46, 48, 75
Institutions, 4, 63, 101, 264,
   276
Instrumental activities of
   daily living, 14
Integration, age, 34, 50, 97,
   101, 114-116
 racial, 93, 100, 116-118
Intelligence, 6-9
Interest abatement program, 42
Involvement of administrator,
   233-234
Isolation, 12, 20-22, 75

Jewish elderly, 78, 80
Jewish Family Service, 275
Journal of Housing, 255
Jung, Carl, 269

Kahana, Eva, 58
Kitchens, 149-152, 308
Kuhn, Margaret, 91

Laundry rooms, 198, 216
Leases, 248
Liesure World, 43
Libraries, 87, 175
Life satisfaction, 237-238
Lighting, 124, 132-133, 148,
   150, 155, 183, 211-212, 214
Lobby, 131-132, 135-136, 165,
   192-195, 215, 236-237
Locked entrances, 248
Longitudinal studies of aging,
   8
Lowenthal, Marjorie Fiske, 21
Low-rise buildings, 133, 140-
   143, 177, 209-210

Maintenance repairs, 45, 258,
   262, 267
Manager, *see* Administrator
Marine Sergeant attitude, 104,
   229-238, 278
Massachusetts Institute of
   Technology, 197
Meal services, 37, 107-109,
   113, 309-314